EUROPE
IN THE AGE OF
LOUIS XIV

D1334946

£1.05 net
£1 1s net
IN UK ONLY

EUROPE
IN THE AGE OF
LOUIS XIV

RAGNHILD HATTON

with 213 illustrations, 14 in colour

THAMES AND HUDSON · LONDON

1 *Frontispiece*
Louis XIV, courtiers, grooms and
peasants in the grounds of
the Palace of Versailles, *c.* 1689

2 Louis XIV in the costume of
'Roi Soleil' in the ballet
La Nuit, 1653

Printed in Great Britain by Jarrold and Sons Ltd, Norwich

500 32016 0   *clothbound*
500 33016 6   *paperbound*

CONTENTS

PREFACE

In the period covered by the reign of Louis XIV of France, Europe developed a cosmopolitan civilization. The more historians learn about the second half of the seventeenth century and the first quarter of the eighteenth, the more clearly does this fact emerge. The phrase 'the scientific revolution of the seventeenth century' is one which has been current for some time, and in the history of art we have always accepted that trends and fashions know frontiers as little as do philosophical ideas. But in the last few years historians have had to coin new labels (or revive old ones), such as 'the commercial revolution' and 'the financial revolution' to characterize the results of their researches into other aspects of European development at this time; while for the intellectual climate of Europe as a whole the term *Frühaufklärung*, that is, the 'Early Enlightenment', or, as the accepted but less meaningful translation has it, the 'Pre-Enlightenment', is gaining ground. There is much evidence, though as yet no general treatment, of an unprecedented mobility of the European population, in the social sense as well as in the physical one, in the period.

This growing cosmopolitanism is one of the main themes of this book, but our awareness of it must not be allowed to obscure the paramount influence which the national preoccupations of the individual states of Europe had on those who lived and died as the subjects of its kings and princes, its republics and commonwealths. Next to natural catastrophes and unexpected regional fluctuations in climate, the decisions of those who held political power affected the governed most strongly. The problems which faced the European states, in the domestic as in the foreign fields, are legitimate and, in my opinion, essential aspects of any study of the history of European civilization: indeed, the solutions attempted directly affected, for better or worse, that civilization. In their turn, since policies adopted often led to war, or could not prevent war when so intended, those who held political power became increasingly preoccupied with what William III called 'the indivisibility of the peace': how could a balance of power be preserved, how could war be prevented or at least restrained from escalation into ruinous long-lasting campaigns?

◀ 3 Peter I's ratification of the Russo-Swedish peace treaty of Nystad, 1721. Note the delicate flower-embroidery on the binding and the fine gilt box, with the Russian arms, for the seal

Princes and statesmen studied and annotated 'the true interests of states' which, if harmonized, were assumed to preserve peace, and at the Quadruple Alliance of 1718 the duty of states to submit their differences to congresses before resorting to war was explicitly stated for the first time in modern history. In this search for a panacea for war they were no more successful than later generations: their own miscalculations and inability to foresee the reactions of others trapped them as much as did historical 'accident'. But in their very search they, as well as those who did not as yet subscribe to the idea of a tribunal of Europe, bore witness to the fact that such an idea had taken root as part of the civilization of the age.

Louis XIV was one of those rulers who learnt in a long reign, and sometimes from his own mistakes, that such a tribunal did exist. The country he represented was a powerful one and for this, as well as for the duration and the culture of his reign, his name has imprinted itself on the period for contemporaries (a French traveller in far-away Russia was proudly shown a medal of 'your King') and posterity alike. For this reason I have been content to use the conventional label for my essay, though the dates within which I have confined it, 1648–1721, do not fit with exactitude the formal reign of Louis (1643–1715) nor the effective reign (1661–1715). Nor have I been content to take my examples from France alone since I have been concerned, in so far as my linguistic and historical knowledge permits, with Europe as a whole: with France but also with Russia and Sweden, with the Maritime Powers but also with the Austrian and Spanish Habsburgs.

My debt to friends and scholars in many lands is great. Where I have made direct use of their researches a footnote will give the source of my information and the Bibliography will further indicate my indebtedness in respect of some recent works. The scope of this series does, however, preclude full annotation and recognition of what I owe to others beyond this general expression of gratitude for the learning of past and present generations of historians. The essay draws also on my own researches, but, again, annotation has been possible only for direct quotations from archive material or printed sources. Finally it is a particular pleasure to acknowledge the stimulus and help I have received from the general editor of this series and those who have read the book in manuscript: Stanley Baron of Thames and Hudson, Professor Andrew Lossky, Dr Isabel de Madariaga and Graham Gibbs, MA.

I POPULATION AND MOBILITY

Our knowledge about the population of Europe in the age of Louis XIV rests on material which only for certain periods and for certain localities permits statistical treatment. The registers of baptisms and funerals are perfectly reliable for some inquiries but unsuitable for others. We know for instance exactly how many Danes died of that terrible epidemic which, from the camp of the Polish allies in the war against Sweden, swept Sleswig and southern Jutland between 1659 and 1662,[1] but attempts to use baptismal records to assess the incidence of illegitimate births in a given community may be bedevilled by our inability to discover how many infants born out of wedlock were – for fear of the moral disapproval of the clergy or the social stigma attached to illegitimacy – registered in the name of a conniving relative. From church registers and tax-lists of various kinds combined, modern demographers can, however, say with certainty that the European population as a whole declined in our period though that of some individual countries increased, usually by conquest of new territory – the figures accepted being a decline from perhaps 118 million in 1648 to perhaps 102 million in 1713.

The reasons for the overall loss of population are to be found in the many epidemics, above all the plague, which ravaged Europe at intervals; and in the famines which hit agricultural areas when the harvest failed, due more often to cold and dry springs than to rainy summers. In such circumstances many died, if not from direct starvation then from illnesses against which malnutrition had weakened their resistance. For a French locality (Beauvais) the death-rate among the poorer peasants can be shown to have doubled and even trebled in times of famine, while the birth-rate sank to nought as malnutrition rendered the women temporarily sterile.[2]

Recurrent bad harvests (most widespread in 1660–63, 1675–79, 1693–94 and 1708–09) encouraged movement from the countryside to the towns where alternative employment as well as charity were more readily available. But it was the poorer town-dwellers who in their turn proved likely victims of plague and other epidemics;

they were less well nourished and hence less able to fight contagion, they had lower standards of hygiene and were without the economic resources to organize a speedy move from the area of worst danger. The plague of 1656 killed 130,000 in Naples, that of 1665 in London 100,000; Danzig suffered heavy losses in recurrent plague years in the 1650s, as did Amsterdam and Frankfurt in the mid-1660s; Stockholm lost one-third of its population in the plague of 1710 to 1711; Vienna was hard hit in the first decade of the eighteenth century in spite of the closing of the frontier with the Ottoman empire from 1710 to 1714; Marseilles lost half its inhabitants in the plague year 1720 to 1721. Other killing epidemics were typhus, measles and various forms of malarial fevers usually referred to as agues, and – at times – smallpox, though it proved less fatal than in earlier periods.

The movements of armies sometimes brought these epidemics in their train (as well as slower killers such as syphilis), though improvements in hygiene and stricter discipline – for example, the prohibition against eating raw fruit that dysentery might be prevented – lessened, as intended, the loss of soldiers' lives and, incidentally, civilian casualties. During sieges, however, civilians suffered as much, if not more, than the soldiers from the privations which were part and parcel of this form of warfare. Devastation of the countryside in war for strategic reasons – such as the destruction of the Palatinate by the French in 1689, the 'scorched-earth' tactics of Peter the Great in Poland-Lithuania in 1707–08 and of the Swedes in the Ukraine in the winter of 1709 – often brought more than misery to the civilians affected: robbed of their homes and goods they tended to fall prey to any epidemic going. Another hazard to civilian food supplies and thus to health were the cattle-plagues (*rinderpest*) endemic in eastern Europe, which spread when masses of cattle were collected for armies on the

4 Flight from the Rome plague of 1657 with (*left*) burial of the dead

5 Protective clothing suggested for physicians treating plague victims

6 Map showing spread of the cattle-plague, 1709–13

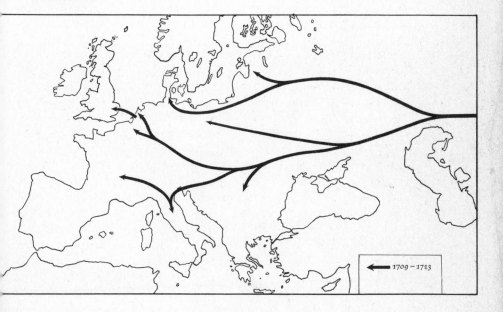

1709 – 1713

move. There was one serious outbreak in the 1650s and another in 1710–11 which can be followed from the Habsburg dominions to Germany proper and the Low Countries, and thence to France and also across the Channel to England. There it wrought less havoc than on the Continent, thanks to the speedy slaughtering of sick beasts and the burying of carcasses suggested by one of Queen Anne's physicians.[3]

The loss of life in the many wars of the period would seem to be statistically less significant in respect of loss of population (with the exception of Poland-Lithuania in the 1650–80 period) though some pitched battles, such as Malplaquet and Poltava, were bloody indeed. In countries where material for comparative investigation exists, such losses – spread over the whole country or even over more than one country in the case of hired troops – were made good sooner than the damage inflicted by a sweeping epidemic. In the case of the Jutland deaths mentioned earlier the population did not regain its pre-epidemic figure till a whole century had passed.

A contributory factor to the decline in population may have been a change in the marriage pattern, beginning in the early part of the seventeenth century, which diverged sharply both from previous European custom and from the practice of the indigenous races of other continents – that of relatively late marriages. Various hypotheses have been advanced to explain this new pattern. One concerns the

7, 8 Birth of a Spanish Bourbon prince in 1707 (left) and childhood portrait, 1659, by Velázquez, of a Spanish Habsburg prince (above)

9 Funeral procession of a Swedish king, Charles XII, 1719

known retardment in the age of female puberty. From classical
times onwards the average age at which menstruation commenced
had remained at fourteen; now, for reasons not fully understood,
girls began to menstruate considerably later. Another is connected
with the need, particularly in the urban environment, for a young
man to establish himself in his craft or profession after longer years
of apprenticeship or study than hitherto: he could therefore not
afford the responsibilities of marriage, home and family till well into
his twenties. The change in the definition of legal majority from
fourteen years in the sixteenth century to sixteen in some countries,
and eighteen in others in the seventeenth, would seem to be a consequence of these biological and social changes. Only in cases where
much was at stake, as in the struggle between crown and high nobility
during royal minorities, were boys whom contemporaries still
thought of as minors declared of age lest the power of the over-
mighty subject wax too strong. Louis XIV of France and Charles
XII of Sweden entered on their majorities at fourteen and fifteen
respectively for reasons of state, and those who successfully urged
the step harked back to the 'ancient days' for justification.

13

Once marriages had been entered into, three already established trends continued to operate. One was the likelihood that, of the children born of any one union, several would die in infancy. Statistically expressed, only half of all infants born survived their first year, though the incidence of loss differed with area, social class and the health of the parents. For those that survived, the average life expectancy has been estimated as between forty-eight and fifty-six if the family was wealthy and thirty to forty if the family was poor. But such averages may obscure the fact that children remained particularly vulnerable even in families that did not suffer the hardship of poverty. Epidemics carried away those who were not strong – King Charles XI of Sweden lost four sons in the 1680s by a wife who was not robust, while of the five children born to Louis XIV and Maria Teresa all but the Dauphin died in infancy – and victors in the struggle for survival were usually healthy enough to be vouchsafed a longer life than the statistical figures of average life expectancy would suggest. Secondly, it was highly probable that the marriage entered into would be broken by the death of one of the partners, the wife (if both were relatively young) being more apt to die first, often from breakdown in health associated with frequent miscarriages and childbirths. Finally, it was very likely that the surviving spouse

11 *The Van Goyen Family*. Note in this painting by Jan Steen (intended to com-memorate at least one and possibly two of the women portrayed) the *memento mori* attribute of the death's head on the mantelpiece and the meticulously observed details of daily life in the household of a prosperous artist

would remarry, the widow nearly as readily as the widower in an age when women at varying levels of society had possessions or income, or could contribute to the family's keep by work even if their only paid employment was that of a wet nurse, robbing their own infants of existence.

POLITICAL ARITHMETIC

Governments were aware of decline in population either in their own or neighbouring countries, or feared that decline would overtake them unless they encouraged growth in this most precious of the nation's resources. Demographic information, comprised within the seventeenth-century term 'political arithmetic' (i.e. the use of mathematics for social and economic purposes), was therefore valued, though our own age has judged that little use was made of the mathematics of probability worked out by Christiaan Huygens or the

15

10 Marriage procession of the Dutch artist, D. Teniers, 1651

compilation of the quite reliable table of life expectancy by Edmund Halley. The reason for this was the prime concern of the governments of the day with practical measures: to reward those families in which numerous children survived by tax relief or by money prizes, to encourage others to emulate them in both the breeding and the care of children, to alleviate the adverse effects of bad harvests by transport or purchase of corn and grain from unaffected areas, to encourage the welfare and prosperity of their subjects by provision of work. The cameralists of the second half of the seventeenth century did not tire of preaching that the real riches of any country depended on the number of its healthy and working inhabitants. This was the theme of Wilhelm von Schröder's *Fürstliche Schatz und Rent-Cammer*, published in 1686, often reprinted and read far beyond the Austrian Habsburg state for the benefit of whose ruler it had been written; this was the recurrent exhortation in the many pamphlets and memoranda written by the political arithmeticians in France – men like Seigneur de Belesbat and Pierre de Boisguilbert. The Northern Netherlands, with their teeming population devoted to hard work, were as much envied as their taxation methods, judged eminently sensible, were admired; the 'Dutch tax', with its percentage calculation, allowed the governments of the seven provinces which made up the United Provinces to obtain their fair share in rising values, a model to which others aspired but found themselves incapable of introducing or maintaining against the opposition of vested interests.

The density of population varied in different states with geographical and climatic conditions and the state of economic development. The Italian peninsula was the only area with a density assessed by modern historians as higher than that of the Low Countries: 44 inhabitants per square kilometre to the 40 of the Northern and Southern Netherlands regarded as one unit. France came next with 34, then England with 30, the Germanies with 28, the Iberian peninsula with 17, Denmark-Norway and Poland-Lithuania with 14 and Sweden-Finland with 13. Russia, with a population estimated at 10 million at least, would have come even lower down the scale in view of the vastness of her territory; but this figure, as those for other states and areas in the period we are examining, could be abruptly modified whenever conquests in war increased the number of inhabitants. Russia's acquisition of Sweden's East Baltic provinces after 1709 added significantly to her resources in manpower as well as to her commercial opportunities and strategic advantages; Austria's conquest of the larger part of Greater Hungary brought her population up to more than $7\frac{1}{2}$ million, a figure equalled by Great Britain after the Union of England and Scotland. In Britain's case the increase was contributed to also by some natural growth for England and Wales and by foreign immigration. Twenty thousand Huguenot French went to England around 1685, and 4,000 Catholic weavers from Normandy arrived at the end of the seventeenth century to avail themselves of better economic opportunities. Swiss Catholic immigration into France was similarly a feature of the post-1648 period – into Alsace and Franche-Comté in particular.[4] Conversely, other states lost inhabitants through defeat in war, through large-scale emigration, or by economic stagnation. The Polish-Lithuanian Commonwealth lost territory and population to Brandenburg and Russia between 1650 and 1680, though she reconquered what she had lost to Turkey by 1699. The Swedish empire which, at its largest extent, had contained some 3 million people was by 1719–21 reduced, through the loss of all its Baltic and most of its German provinces, to 2 million. Spain suffered a serious drop, from at least 9 million to 7 million, because of the drain of people to her overseas territories, the standstill in the economy and the high prices of food at home, and possibly also because she was a battlefield after 1702. France, though 200,000 Huguenots – contrary to expectation and government desire – left the country before and after the Revocation of the Edict of Nantes in 1685, still showed a small increase and had an estimated population of 19 million towards the end of Louis XIV's reign.

In the case of France this figure undoubtedly implied power and resources, but size of population by itself had no political meaning. On the Italian peninsula, as within the borders of the Holy Roman Empire of the German Nation, the Italian and German-speaking populations were split into autonomous and often rival states. Italy's 13 million counted for relatively little compared with the 2 million Dutchmen of the United Provinces, and even the larger German states were weak in relation to the Austro-Hungarian dominions, the ruler of which was traditionally German Emperor. Political weakness also resulted where the central government was feeble, as in the *Rzeczpospolita Polska* towards the end of the century, though here there was always the hope, with concomitant fear by neighbours, that political reform would permit the elected king to utilize the potential power of a country that counted possibly 11 millions, even after the losses of territory. In all the states of Europe, most certainly west of the Elbe, the towns, for which more reliable records are preserved than for the countryside, grew. Not only did periodic famines, as already mentioned, exert a pull towards the town. Many people gravitated from rural areas to the towns, and particularly to the capital towns, for the economic opportunities which were offered by growing trade and by rapid increase in the bureaucratic machinery; while wars, which made vast areas of Europe battlefields after 1680, also encouraged movement to towns for greater security. Paris and London are known to have had over 400,000 inhabitants within their city boundaries by the third quarter of the seventeenth century; before the end of that century London had overtaken Paris and reached the 500,000 mark and Vienna, Madrid, Naples, Stockholm and Amsterdam also increased considerably in size.

MOBILITY OF POPULATION

Reference has already been made to the 4,000 Normandy weavers who moved to England in search of better livelihoods, and to the Huguenots, some 200,000 in all, who left France when intensification of intolerance leading to the Revocation robbed them of religious liberty. Recent research suggests an accidental aspect to the Revocation (Louis having been told by his Catholic advisers that so many Huguenots had come back to the Church of their own free will that the Edict had become anachronistic[5]) and has also established that the effect on French economic life of the exodus that ensued was not as disastrous as was hitherto believed. By systematic examination of

13 A galley with slaves rowing

the crafts and guilds, Scoville has shown that those that did decline
had already started to do so before 1685 or suffered for reasons
unconnected with the Revocation, while Lüthy has demonstrated
how lively and mutually beneficial were the contacts between
Huguenot bankers settled in Geneva after 1685 and the government
of Louis XIV: without the co-operation of these (and other, e.g.
Dutch) financiers the wars of France in the latter part of the reign
could not have been sustained.[6] The Revocation had, however,
adverse political effects, which will be discussed later, for Louis XIV,
and the access of strength through thrifty and skilled immigrants –
often with capital and financial expertise – to countries that later
fought France (e.g., England and Brandenburg-Prussia) must not be
forgotten.[7]

Other movements of population, not freely undertaken, were on a
smaller scale. Civilians were at times taken into captivity and sold as
slaves. The Russian transportation of many Swedes or Swedish
Baltic subjects during the Great Northern War to the Ottoman
empire, where they were sold to Turks and Tartars, is one case in
point. Another is the sale by the Emperor of Hungarian Protestants
to serve as galley-slaves in the Venetian fleet; while the Danish King's
disposing of Swedish prisoners of war to the same republic might
(though strongly criticized by contemporaries) be regarded as a
return to older concepts of the right of the conqueror to use his

19

12 Allegorical Protestant representation of French Huguenots leaving France to
seek religious liberty abroad. Flights started in the 1670s and continued in the 1680s

14, 15, 16
Swedish sawmill, 1674 (above);
Polish salt mine, 1649s (top);
and Dutch weaver, 1694 (right)

booty as he saw fit. Not all surviving Swedish prisoners of war in
Russia returned home at the end of hostilities in 1721. A colony of
them was forgotten in a remote district in the Ukraine; when their
descendants were discovered in the nineteenth century they had
maintained a Swedish language of sorts and still observed some
Swedish customs. An element of coercion is also present in the movement of political non-Huguenot religious refugees. English and
Scottish Jacobites found refuge in France, Spain, Sweden and Russia;
William III and the Dutch helped to settle Savoyard Protestants in
Switzerland when their Duke, encouraged by Louis XIV (who
feared that they might serve as a rallying point for allied-financed
invasions of France), turned against them. But, broadly speaking,
transfer of self, family, goods and capital was voluntary and indivi-
dually motivated. Opportunities for making a better living by
exploiting skills wanted abroad meant that foundry-workers and

mining engineers from the Southern Netherlands, France and Germany moved to Sweden in the 1680s, while improved metallurgic techniques developed in Sweden made their exponents welcome in both France and Germany in the early eighteenth century. Weavers from England and the Netherlands were tempted with high offers from other countries where their superior knowledge was necessary to start domestic production of the finer kinds of cloth, and though some of those successfully enticed later returned home (as was the case with the Dutchmen whom Colbert persuaded to come to southern France) they 'left the mysteries of their trade behind them'.[8] Skilled bureaucrats were always in demand and moved from one German state to another as chances for promotion and the prospect of greater influence offered; since the German language was used in part of the Danish administration (that concerned with the two rich duchies of Sleswig and Holstein) they found careers open to talents also in Copenhagen. Linguists were often drawn into the position of confidential secretaries of rulers or into the diplomatic service. Two examples are the Huguenot Jean de Robethon, who served William

17 Chamber in a copper mine, 1683

21

E. Van Hoie fecit

Sould By Samuel Speed Neere ye Inner Temple Gate In Fleetestreete Aº 1668.

18 Agricultural instruction:
the title-page to J. Worlidge's
book of 1668

19 Norwegian cork sculpture
of a skipper or navigator,
early eighteenth century

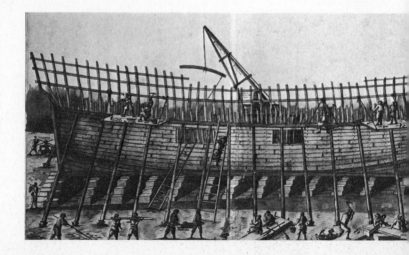

22

III and George I as secretary, and the Swiss-born Sir Luke Schaub who became a diplomat in the reign of the latter. Dutch and Danish shipwrights were recruited by Peter the Great; so were Scottish naval officers and German military men, of whom a considerable number settled in Russia. The advanced agricultural techniques of the Netherlanders made them attractive immigrants, especially for countries such as Brandenburg where, it was said, nature was steeped in sand and mankind in misery. Successive Electors of Brandenburg took active steps to secure as many as possible of them, and Dutch experience in the construction of dikes and canals was also widely utilized. Indeed, with the rivalry between states – a rivalry which will be analyzed in due course – for domestic economic development and for the improvement of trade in Europe and overseas, there was general willingness to welcome anyone who claimed specific knowledge that might give an edge in the competition, whether that knowledge was one of a given process of manufacture, the cutting of canals, dredging and improving harbours, making rivers navigable, or who offered ready cash or loans that seemed tempting in return for monopolies or other privileges. The suggestion by a consortium of Jacobite privateers operating from Madagascar that they should become subjects of Sweden was seriously considered by Charles XII and (after 1718) by his successors, since it was hoped thus to lay the foundation of regular Swedish trade in those areas of the world of which the privateers claimed experience.[9] Bergeyck and his compatriots diligently sought loopholes in international treaties in their attempts to convince Madrid of the right of the Spanish Netherlands to establish a local company for trade with the East Indies.[10]

20 Far left, building of a Spanish frigate, late seventeenth century

21 Left, merchants of the 1670s

23

Some of the entrepreneurs who offered their services to kings and princes in these and other matters had not originally intended to settle for good outside their native land or state, but in most cases this was the result if their undertaking prospered. In countries which needed foreign capital to exploit mineral and other resources, such as Sweden and Russia, this is particularly noticeable. In the courts of the German princes the 'Court-Jew', the ruler's man of business, who raised loans thanks to his international contacts, also tended to strike roots and marry locally, sometimes into the ranks of the nobility. So did Dutch bankers who moved to London, and many of the Huguenot merchants and bankers who had scattered to the financial centres of Protestant Europe after 1685.

But quite apart from those who settled permanently in a new country and whose families (particularly with ennoblement) became absorbed into the very fabric of its society, there were other groups who lived abroad to earn their living without wishing to become naturalized subjects and who usually intended to move back, or at least retire, to their native land. This was typical in mercantile circles of English, Scottish and Dutch traders and, to a lesser extent, also of French and German ones. Colonies of merchants abroad often enjoyed privileges in respect of taxation which would be forfeit if they 'became subjects'. Opportunities to enter such trading communities usually came through family connections; but in the commercial Mecca of the Dutch Republic so many young foreigners, particularly Scots and English, wished to be apprenticed to Amsterdam and Rotterdam merchants and ship-chandlers that a regular agency – run by an Englishman – existed to see them settled against a fee.[11] One of those apprenticed by this agent in 1659 was a John Drummond, who in due course set up in business on his own, married a native of this new country and indeed lived long enough in Amsterdam for Dutchmen to look upon him as one of themselves. Yet he never meant to settle; sentiment impelled him, as many others, to work for the day when he would have accumulated enough capital to live like a *rentier* at home. He confessed to James Brydges, the English paymaster-general with whom he corresponded after he had, half-reluctantly, moved from trading to banking during the War of the Spanish Succession, that his aim remained, since he had always regarded himself as 'the Queen's subject', to move to England as soon as he could do so with a little style.[12]

Marriages contracted in the United Provinces by foreigners who kept their own nationality led to no international complication, but the fate of English and Dutch merchants who were numerous in the ports of France became an issue of negotiations after 1685 if they had married Frenchwomen of the Huguenot religion. Even if the men had not become naturalized, their wives and children became subject to the rigours of the Catholic persecution. Considerable diplomatic pressure was necessary before such families were permitted to leave France.[13] The husbands usually contrived to settle their affairs in France before repatriating themselves. One consequence of the Revocation was thus that the foreigner in French trade became more of a rarity – a development which, though not consciously initiated, was welcomed by the advocates of mercantilism in France. In Spain and Portugal, French, Dutch, English and Scots merchants and factors were numerous: indeed, the domestic trade of Spain was so much in the hands of non-Spaniards that a recent investigation has shown that the heavy losses, assumed to be wholly Spanish, imposed by the Anglo-Dutch capture of the Spanish treasure fleet in Vigo Bay in 1702, were in reality largely borne by the English and Dutch creditors of Spanish firms. These had bought goods for dispatch to Spanish America from the Maritime Powers, and a large part of the bullion captured by William III's ships was in fact that earmarked for payment of such goods.[14]

Whereas the mercantile community, whether on the Baltic, Atlantic or Mediterranean coasts, tended to retain a distinct and separate character, an enclave on foreign soil, other strangers were by the very diversity of their employment more readily absorbed (for the duration of their visit or for life) into the native circles to which their artistic gifts or their learning had procured them invitations. This was the case with architects, painters and musicians called to courts and noble households, with professors at various universities, with learned men who were entrusted, like Pufendorf in Sweden and Brandenburg, and Leibniz in Hanover, with the writing of histories to glorify the royal houses they served and to perform a variety of duties. Pufendorf at one stage acted as secretary and librarian to Queen Ulrika Eleonora the elder of Sweden, and Leibniz's first charge at Hanover was to disperse the tedium of state affairs for his prince by conversing with him, after the day's work was done, on 'matters of interest, especially mathematical'.[15] Foreign tutors, dancing-masters, actors and singers usually led a more peripatetic life, but even among these we know of some who stayed for a

22, 23 Two peripatetic German scholars: Samuel Pufendorf and G. W. Leibniz

considerable time or who settled permanently and founded families that merged into their adoptive land.

Further examples of 'immigrants' can be found among those who changed their country because their master or mistress did. Royal brides brought their attendants and physicians across frontiers as they had done from time immemorial. What is more surprising, but possibly typical of the mobility of our period, is the number of monarchs and princes who secured thrones outside the country of their birth and with whom travelled advisers and men of business as well as relatives, servants and favourites: to England with William III and George I from the United Provinces and Hanover respectively, with the Elector of Saxony when he was chosen King of Poland, with the Duke of Anjou when the will of Carlos II made him Philip V of Spain, with the Electoral Prince of Hesse-Cassel when he – by marriage to Charles XII's sister Ulrika Eleonora – became one of the candidates for the Swedish crown. Rulers driven into exile similarly occasioned the upheaval of individuals and their families. There was a Jacobite court at Saint-Germain between 1688 and 1713; and when the Austrian Habsburg whom Catalonia and Valencia had recognized as Carlos III had to leave Barcelona in 1711, he took with him to Vienna a Spanish Council which exercised considerable influence on his policies as the Emperor Charles VI.

The movement of individual families from one country to another did not always promote a European outlook. Where religious or ethnical groups arrived or congregated in relatively large numbers there was often exclusiveness on the one hand and suspicion of the foreigner on the other. But by and large individual families who settled, while keeping contacts with relatives in their country of origin or those dispersed in other parts of Europe, contributed to a certain cosmopolitan outlook in the period before absorption of their families took place. So did the artists and architects and the men of letters who stayed for any length of time. But the European cosmopolitanism of our period was fashioned even more by the growth of a network of European connections on a hitherto unprecedented scale. An astonishing number of young people spent formative years outside their own country, usually to prepare themselves for a career with better prospects at home, and they tended to keep up contacts made abroad long after their return. It could be argued that this development was initiated by the big peace congresses which met for long years at Osnabrück and Münster while the negotiations for the Peace of 1648 were hammered out: with the belligerents and their mediators hardly a ruler was unrepresented apart from those of the east – Poland and Russia. Each mission included experienced and skilled negotiators who were regular administrators, royal advisers or even career diplomats, but there were also the minor secretaries and cavaliers, relatives or protégés of the important men, who came to learn the ways of the world and acquire polish and languages. Bonds of interest and friendship were established, and when the children of these men were sent out in the world in their turn, they came with useful introductions to circles close to the centre of government. Whole dynasties, specializing, so to speak, in informed knowledge of European affairs, developed under the impetus of governments' increasing need for trained officials – the younger d'Avaux, who had served with his uncle in the Westphalian negotiations, became one of the most skilled diplomats of Louis XIV and, at the Congress of Nijmegen of 1678–79, formed yet another circle of useful acquaintances. Bengt Oxenstierna, Chancellor of Sweden from 1680 till his death in 1702, kept the line to Vienna, inaugurated at Münster, open for the rest of his career, while also establishing (partly through the military service of his son in the army of William III) a special relationship with the Maritime

27

Powers. Personal knowledge of adversary or ally was not only extremely useful in delicate and important negotiations but helped to create a European outlook and a bond of fellow-feeling among men who struggled with tough and, at times, intractable problems. The diplomat was not usually the man who dipped his pen in the hyperbole of propaganda: ideological attacks would ruin his usefulness when the situation – as it was bound to do – changed and would prejudice the chances of his own sons or relatives making full use of their opportunities during the grand tour of preparation for service in the administration or in political life, which became the rule rather than the exception after 1648. It was not uncommon for a young man to be away for two or three years, to travel at first in the company of a tutor who supervised studies, but, with growing maturity and command of languages, to take greater responsibility himself and seize what chances offered: a trip down the Danube in the company of the English mediator at the Karlowitz peace negotiations with the Turks, a visit to a German court obviously growing in importance, talks with experts in international law at Dutch universities, discussions with fashionable cameralists in Vienna. There were relaxations, of course: sightseeing and carnivals, art galleries and opera, attendance at court functions of many kinds, sitting for one's portrait and being given commissions to buy paintings, china and wine, and even to secure the services of landscape gardeners or artist-craftsmen for the parental home where buildings and improvements were, as likely as not, in progress. But essentially

Turkish passport, 1670

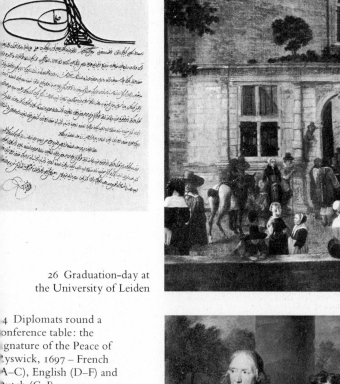

26 Graduation-day at
the University of Leiden

24 Diplomats round a
conference table: the
signature of the Peace of
Ryswick, 1697 – French
(A–C), English (D–F) and
Dutch (G–I)
plenipotentiaries, and (K)
the Swedish mediator

27 Young man
(possibly James
Edward Stuart)
with his tutor,
painted in 1685
by Largillière

29

the purpose was serious study by observation and discourse, and the making of useful contacts. The writing of reports on various aspects of the economy, political institutions, personalities with influence at court, etc., formed part of the exercise and served, at times, as a means of bringing the young man to the notice of rulers and ministers. The protégés of Sir Joseph Williamson made their mark in London by just such reports; young Torcy's potentialities were judged from the letters his father encouraged him to write to Louis XIV while on a mission of politeness to Copenhagen and Stockholm which, on the surface, involved no more than the handing over of royal presents;[16] young Bothmer was similarly tested on behalf of the Hanoverian court, but was sorely tried by the crowds which gathered at the sight of the large boxes (so large that he had to hire a special cart to accommodate them) in which the presents were packed: it was rumoured that they contained wild animals or female Turkish slaves.[17] Memoirs which have survived, for example those of Fabrice the younger of Hanover and Nils Reuterholm of Sweden, afford us an excellent insight into the way this semi-official training of future administrators and diplomats took place. Attached to these young men of important or well-to-do families who received a European education, others, of much humbler origin, participated in the benefits of travel and sojourns. The tutors who accompanied them were frequently men not much older than their charges who had received a university education at home and now, by assiduous contact with men of learning or business abroad, laid the foundation for their future careers as academic teachers or officials. In some Protestant countries there was what might be described as a ladder of social mobility whereby the poor but bright lad was helped to study for the church and in his turn – possibly because he himself had experienced lack of religious vocation – took care that his son, via such tutorships, should fit himself for the bureaucratic life with its more varied opportunities. In Catholic countries the poor and bright lad was similarly helped to enter the church; but where he had no vocation celibacy denied him the sublimation of arranging careers more to his own bent for his sons; hence, possibly, the virulent atheist and 'communist' memoirs of the French peasant-lad who found himself serving as a *curé* without faith.[18]

An even closer European *esprit de corps* than that of the diplomat and administrator tended to develop among military and naval officers. Service abroad for shorter or longer periods was encouraged, even

28 James II arriving at Saint-Germain in 1688. From his court in exile, and that of his son James III (James Edward Stuart, the 'Old Pretender'), Jacobitism became a significant factor in European diplomacy – French, Swedish, Russian and Spanish – until 1719

at times when the native country was involved in war, in order that experience should be gained under famous captains. Political alliances often influenced where a young officer applied for a commission or for the status of 'volunteer', but family connections counted even more. If your father had happy memories of a military or diplomatic appointment in France you were more likely to join Louis XIV's army; if he had found the Dutch more congenial, a regiment in William III's forces was usually chosen. Marlborough and Prince Eugène were great draws and there was lively competition to serve under either of them. The need of Peter the Great's army for foreign officers in the early years of the Great Northern War proved a magnet particularly for German officers and artillery experts; and French officers joined Charles XII's army after 1713 because the Swedes were in need of experienced fortification officers and also because of the attraction which the generalship of the Swedish King had for officers, like Folard, fascinated by the theoretical side of the art of war.[19]

With the officers, as with the young civilian travellers, went their servants, and it should not be forgotten that this group or calling benefited in various ways from their opportunity to live abroad for a period of time. A knowledge of languages was the most obvious gain. Even the class most rooted to the soil, that of the peasants (often migratory within their own states), went 'travelling' all over Europe in the nearly continuous warfare of the period: against Turks and Tartars, for or against Louis XIV, involved in that long struggle for the partition of the Swedish empire known as the Great Northern War when Danes and Russians, Saxons and Poles, Prussians and Hanoverians attacked Charles XII. The campaigns were particularly far-ranging. The Swedish army, largely national, but with some foreign regiments (e.g. German hired dragoons and French battalions which, according to the custom of the time, had exchanged Saxon for Swedish service after the battle of Fraustadt), crossed and recrossed Poland-Lithuania, stayed in Saxony for a year, penetrated into the Ukraine, and remnants of it lived for several years in Turkey before the return to the Empire in 1714. Russian troops found themselves, in the post-1714 stages of the war, stationed as far west as Mecklenburg and Denmark. Auxiliary troops, Danish and German from many states and even a Russian regiment (transferred from Saxon to Imperial service), participated in the Allied campaigns in the Low Countries or on the Rhine during the War of the Spanish Succession, while English regiments were sent to the Iberian peninsula or to the German fields of operation. Often they found Irish or Scottish Catholics in the ranks opposing them.

Sailors had always roamed the seas and the Dutch merchant navy in particular could not have been manned without recruitment from other countries, particularly Norway. The Russian navy developed by Peter the Great used, particularly in its early stages, foreign officers and these were recruited (often with ships) from the Maritime Powers. The commercial revolution brought more nations into shipping which touched the ports of all the European oceans and seas, as well as those of the West Indies, North America, Africa, the East Indies and China.

Less 'corps'-orientated than those who intended to make their career either in the civilian or military services were the travels and studies of those with a more individual bent: the promising artist who was sent abroad to study, usually financed by a royal or noble patron; the young mining engineer or scientist who sought the practical and theoretical experts in his field (the famous Oxford mathematician Dr Wallis and Leibniz at Hanover attracted visitors as well as correspondents); the royal gardeners or masters of horse on briefer missions to obtain rare plants or thoroughbreds. Sometimes individuals were offered the opportunity to study abroad by a foreign government. One case is that of a young Swede, Samuel Åkerhielm, who spent three years at the University of Oxford at the expense of Queen Anne; but this was in the nature of a 'gratification' to gain favour with the young man's father, a chancery official, and with the hope of laying a foundation for good will when he in his turn embarked on a chancery career.[20] In something of the same spirit Louis XIV agreed to attach foreign officers to the staff of the marshals of France, and William III consented to promote beyond merit military men from abroad with politically influential relatives.

For whatever reasons travels abroad or longer stays were undertaken, contacts formed by personal encounters remained long-lived, often lifelong. Learned men corresponded with each other and with royal or princely persons of similar interests. The Electress Sophia of Hanover, for example, had a wide circle of such correspondents and took care to question visitors to Herrenhausen about famous or talked-of persons she had not as yet had the opportunity to meet.[21] Scientifically inclined scholars, such as Count Marsigli of Bologna, valued memories of occasions when they had spoken before one of the committees of the Royal Society,[22] and many sent copies of their manuscripts and books, for the library of the Society. The treatise on vaccination against smallpox by the Greek doctor Timoni, working in Turkey, reached London in this manner.[23]

29 English East Indiamen off Deptford, 1675

English scholars secured plants and fossils from Lapland from their Swedish opposite numbers, and three-cornered correspondence between Paris, London and Stockholm on various problems (e.g. whether drowned persons could be resuscitated and the temperature at which various liquids froze) was quite common, as was discussion by letter between two and more continental scholars.[24]

Those of a practical bent sent their designs to friends and patrons abroad, whether they concerned improved plumbing, splendid castles and beautiful decorations or ingenious secret weapons for armies and navies. Those more philosophically inclined, but yet motivated by a desire for practical achievement, exchanged blueprints (or bestowed them on rulers and ministers whom they knew only by reputation) for economic and administrative reforms or for the unification of the divided churches and the total abolition of war.

It may be regarded as a mark of a more diversified European cosmopolitanism that such memorials and the kind of correspondence mentioned above were no longer confined to the traditional *lingua franca* of learned men. Latin was still much used by theologians, and books on natural science or philosophy written by men whose mother-tongue was neither French nor German were frequently printed in Latin. But these two languages, French and German, became those mainly used in correspondence across frontiers, as in conversation during personal contact, and in the pamphlet, periodical and newspaper literature intended for a European market. Spanish and Portuguese were becoming relatively rare accomplishments outside the Iberian peninsula and the Americas, though Italian kept some of its ancient hold in the world of art and architecture. Knowledge of English tended to be restricted on the Continent to those who had spent considerable time in England for the sake of their studies or as diplomats, agents or refugees of various kinds. Some educated men (and a few women) felt it desirable to master four modern languages, Italian and English as well as German and French, in addition to Latin; but with the three last no one felt outside the European community of civilized conversation. If fate brought one to regions so isolated as to offer no opportunity for talk in any of them, then the traveller regarded himself unlucky indeed, like the Swedish officer who in 1702 from deep in rural Lithuania complained to his brother: 'I find myself without conversation, as if robbed of speech.'[25]

II CLASS AND CALLING

The frequency with which men and women settled in foreign countries, and the high incidence of men who in their youth pursued studies abroad in preparation for earning their living at home, must not be allowed to obscure the fact that the majority of Europeans lived their lives within the frontiers of the state in which they were born and often within a confined region of it. Some, of course, travelled regularly inside their own country, and even crossed into neighbouring ones, by the very nature of their work: employed by those licensed to operate postal services, connected with transport by road, river or canal, peripatetic as peddlars or itinerant entertainers. But most stayed put once their years of apprenticeship were over or their education completed: the craftsman in his shop, the manufacturer at his works, the clergyman in his parish and the bureaucrat and courtier moving no further than the court moved.

The largest section of the population of any one country, that of the peasantry, was the least mobile of all, particularly in central and eastern Europe. Here, in lands dependent on large-scale agricultural production, serfdom had taken root and has been shown to have spread rather than contracted in our period, since falling grain prices provided the estate owners with an impetus both to extend the system and to exploit it. We now know that Hungary's conquest by the Habsburgs led to the extension of serfdom into areas hitherto relatively free from it,[1] that serfdom became more general in central and southern Russia, and that it strengthened its hold in the Polish-Lithuanian Commonwealth, in Germany east of the Elbe, and even in some areas of Germany west of that river. The fall in grain prices was due to less demand, in its turn conditioned by the drop in population and, even more, by the fact that large-scale cultivation of maize in Italy and buckwheat in the sandy unfertile soils of central and southern Europe generally made these areas less dependent on imports. The vigorous Dutch trade in Baltic grain was a thing of the past.[2] Cultivation of the potato also contributed to the lessening demand for grain, and the fact that England changed from being an importer of grain to an exporter in our period must likewise be taken into account. In the west of Europe serfdom was dying out, though one-tenth of French peasants could still be classed as serfs and serfdom was not abolished on the royal Portuguese estates till 1702. The Dutch province of Overijssel partook of the feudal character of the North German territories. In Scandinavia serfdom had disappeared centuries ago, but increasing severity of bondage to the estate on which male peasants were born spread in Denmark, encouraged by the need of the state for soldiers, the desire of the nobility for a captive labour-force and the example of ducal Holstein where serfdom existed. In the Swedish empire Charles XI found himself prevented from freeing the serfs in his Baltic and German provinces, as he wished to do from religious conviction of the evil of the system – in the former case because the Baltic landowners, including those resident in Sweden proper, strenuously opposed him, and in the latter because the 1648 peace settlement laid down that the Swedish crown could not change the form of government in those parts of the Empire ceded to it. Swedish absolutism, introduced in Charles XI's reign, did not extend to the Estates of Pomerania, Bremen and Verden and could not force its will upon them.

30, 31 French peasant by his fields in the Paris region (far left); and Swedish peasants in their Sunday best, Mora, Dalecarlia, c. 1700

32, 33, 34 Left, peasants at table painted by a professional (L. Le Nain), 1642; above, Livonian peasant in everyday garb; below, peasants dancing, painted by an amateur (Queen Ulrika Eleonora the elder), 1682

Generally speaking, the conditions of the peasantry were best in the neighbourhood of large towns where intensive husbandry took place. The agricultural revolution, it is now accepted, took place much earlier than previously assumed, and in the Low Countries, the Ile de France and in the neighbourhood of most capital cities, clover and root crops were grown which helped to feed cattle over the winter; organic fertilizer was used; market gardening of fruit and vegetables was extensive; barley and hops were cultivated for brewing; landlords, large and small, whether temporal or ecclesiastic, worked intelligently to improve the land. Hartlieb's *Discours of Husbandrie used in Brabant and Flanders*, published in 1652, helped to spread the gospel of intensive cultivation to English landlords keen to profit from the agricultural revolution, and for the next half-century there was a ready market for publications which extolled new methods, among them Yarranton, *The Great Improvement of Lands by Clover*; Worlidge, *Systema Agriculturae*; Houghton, *Collections of Letters for the Improvement of Husbandry and Trade*. Tenant farmers at times learnt by example, first of all in East Anglia and Norfolk. But further away from the regular demand of towns, agriculture tended to concentrate on few crops, and specialist researches on individual regions, e.g. Provence,[3] have established that it was reluctance to change time-honoured methods which prevented increase of crops even where this was desperately needed to feed the local population. These methods were surprisingly similar in the backward regions all over the Continent: ploughs were wooden, fields were open and often cultivated on the strip plan so that each peasant family had its share of good and less good soil; depending on the quality of the soil and differences in climate, fields needed to lie fallow every other year or every third year. In wooded parts in France, in Sweden-Finland and elsewhere, good crops could be grown in the ashes of woodland burnt to the ground on purpose, though such short-sighted methods were not always encouraged by the authorities.

It is impossible to generalize about the life of those who lived from tilling the land except to stress that, as a class, they were particularly vulnerable to the deterioration in climate which, it is generally agreed, was a feature of the period. There were well-to-do freeholders in all countries where serfdom had not won the day, and the position of tenant farmers, whether they paid in money or in a share of the crop (which varied between one-fifth and one-half of the produce), was determined by local conditions and the vagaries of wind and weather. Even the smallholder or the landless labourer was not always miserable and undernourished, as we can deduce from accounts giving details of daily rations on individual estates. The paintings of peasants at work, in their homes at mealtimes or engaged in their pastimes, whether by professionals like Le Nain or amateurs like Queen Ulrika of Sweden, reflect health and enjoyment. But undoubtedly the tillers of the soil as a class were particularly exposed to hardships, and evidence of pauperization, especially in time of war,[4] is indisputable. The position of peasants in Spain, where the *Mesta* rights of the sheep-owners reduced the amount of land available for cultivation and where the irrigation skills of the Moriscos were largely lost, was possibly the worst among those out of bondage.

Many peasants found additional sources of income. They fished if they lived in coastal districts, and the whole family engaged in crafts of various kinds if suitable markets or fairs were within reach. In any but the poorest sections of peasant communities, near-self-sufficiency in artefacts and clothing was the rule: spinning and weaving, the fashioning of tallow candles, wooden utensils and tools, were everyday skills. It was partly because of a lack of demand for domestic goods – each village having its own blacksmith and miller, cooper and tanner, shoemaker, tailor and cabinet-cum-coffin maker – that manufacture for the domestic markets played so minute a role compared to that intended for export or for the armed services. What domestic markets existed were to be found in the towns, but here again production tended to be local, with craftsmen for most goods and services organized in guilds. Only for some luxury articles, such as silks and damasks, gobelins and embroidered tapestries, china and glass, can we talk of manufacture proper, and frequently such manufacture was started to prevent the drain of money abroad. Colbert, for example, initiated the first production of mirrors outside Venice since vast quantities were needed for decorative purposes in Louis XIV's building schemes. Building operations, whether of royal and princely palaces, churches or even of new towns such as the Tsar's Cronstadt and Petersburg (to say nothing of the amount of rebuilding due to fires that swept towns nearly as periodically as the plague), absorbed more domestic labour than did manufacture proper. The cutting and transport of stone and timber, the actual building – even though many an architect with his new machines and four men did the work of forty[5] – above all the decoration and furnishing employed vast numbers of men. So did the laying out of the grounds and the statuary, topiary and floral decorations connected with landscape-gardening. Full-grown trees had at times to be transplanted (as for the Versailles gardens and those at Blenheim) long distances. In some countries the work of clearing wooded terrain or levelling hills was part of the necessary preparation for the splendid palaces and monuments built for the glory of the family, the ruler or the nation. Such building sometimes cost lives: thousands died from the fevers which spread during work on Versailles and on Petersburg. But what we might think of as conspicious consumption in housing, dress and the number of servants needed to run noble and royal households and their gardens was held to be good for the nation in that it provided work for many of those thought of as the 'common people'. Large numbers of men and women were also employed at the cutting of canals, the most famous of them the Languedoc canal begun in 1666 and opened in 1684: projects which, however big a labour-force was assembled, still needed years for completion. Less concentrated work was done on roads. Those who shared the duty of upkeep of a given stretch of road were often reluctant to pave it or improve it for the benefit of a government which desired good roads for the army, the post and the royal progresses. Leopold I of Austria, for example, undertook some forty-three long journeys inside his own dominions in a reign of forty-eight years; but his subjects disliked the roads' being improved by initiative from above, since hard roads meant more wear on the wheels of their own carts and on the horseshoes of their own horses.[6] In other countries we have evidence of resistance to roads for fear of competition to local trade.[7]

35 Sledge of a Russian noblewoman, 1670s

36 A loaded cart outside New College, Oxford

37 The coach of Augustus of
[Sax]ony (where he was hereditary
[Elect]or) entering Poland (where he
was elected King)

[38] A sedan chair being carried
into a Vienna palace

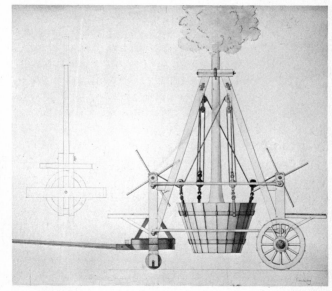

39 Tessin's machine for transporting orange trees

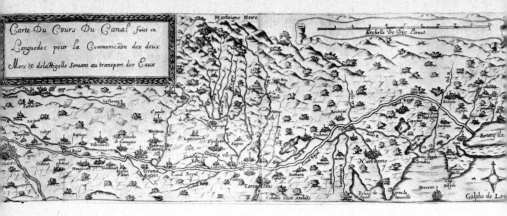

Rivers and canals were in any case more important than roads for transport of goods intended for export or for the armed forces. In the northern and eastern countries snow and frost made roads more serviceable in the winter when horses could drag sledges faster than carriages and carts on the same roads at other times. Frozen lakes provided welcome short-cuts for travellers as well as for carters. But even so, and particularly in Russia with its many rivers connected by canals and portages, water-transport was the cheaper and therefore the usual mode of moving goods. The building of ships, barges for inland and a large variety of craft for coastal, European and overseas trade and fishing was thus an important industry everywhere, quite apart from the building of galleys and sailed men-of-war. What the merchant ships carried at home and abroad differed with the resources of the country. The lighter Russian goods, such as tallow and furs, could bear the cost of the long voyage from Archangel; but grain and naval stores of many kinds, masts and planks and hemp and pitch and tar from the Russian and Polish-Lithuanian river basins, were shipped from Narva, Reval and Riga in the Swedish Baltic provinces and from the Courland and East and West Prussian harbours, supreme among them Danzig. Grain export was, as already mentioned, of less general importance than in earlier years (though for some countries, e.g. Sweden and Norway, imports were essential), but the significance of naval stores in this period can hardly be exaggerated. Quite apart from the merchant shipping of every nation depending on them, the warships of the great western powers could not be fitted out without the tar and pitch, while hemp and timber and masts were needed to keep the fleets in good repair. Louis XIV's galley-fleet was largely

42

40 Map of the
Languedoc canal

41 Danzig harbour
scene, 1680s

Das Grüne Thor.

42 Bird's-eye view
map of Bergen,
Norway, *c.* 1740,
showing the town as
rebuilt immediately
after the big fire of
1702. For its period of
prosperity, 1680 to
1720, see p. 44

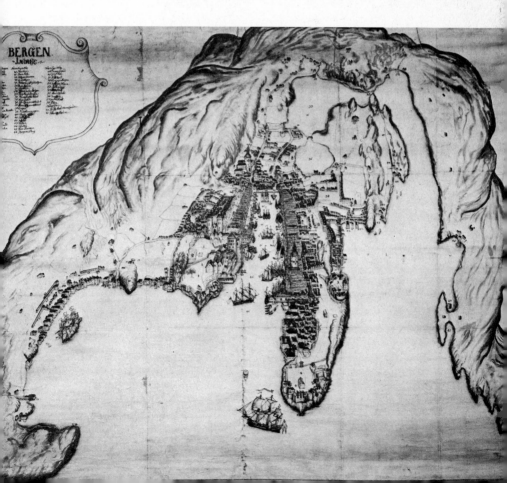

BERGEN

built from French materials,[8] but the big seagoing fleets of France, Spain, the Dutch Republic and England were dependent on Scandinavian and Baltic supplies. There was near-panic in Whitehall at a critical moment during the Nine Years War when Sweden and Denmark-Norway seemed reluctant to let the Anglo-Dutch merchantmen, laden with naval stores, leave the Sound. Only the timely sacrifice of the Maritime Powers' prohibition of neutral trade with France averted what William III referred to as 'a disaster'.[9]

The many wars in which an Anglo-Dutch coalition faced Louis XIV created opportunities in particular for the shipping of the Scandinavian nations, thanks in part to diplomatic co-operation between the traditional enemies, Denmark-Norway and Sweden-Finland. Their merchant fleets rapidly increased, less by fictitious transfer from belligerent owners than by purchase of ships and by rapid building which shared costs, risks and profits among many partners. The case-study of Bergen on the west coast of Norway, which had a remarkable shipping growth between 1688 and 1709 (when Denmark-Norway once more actively joined the anti-Swedish coalition and Bergen ships became liable to capture by Swedish privateers), has demonstrated the way in which people of relatively small fortune participated in the boom.[10] And the numbers in which, during the Nine Years War and the War of the Spanish Succession, northern ships entered the Mediterranean trade was startling enough to alarm Anglo-Dutch circles. Before these late wars, Drummond wrote to Harley in 1704, they never ventured into the Mediterranean proper – now they were becoming serious rivals.[11] Tsar Peter ardently wished to participate directly in European trade. His desire for 'a window on the Baltic' explains, in large measure, his attack on Sweden in 1700; and his treaty with Mecklenburg in 1715 would, he hoped, provide him with a commercial ally (some would say client-state) so far west as to permit the cutting of a canal at Kiel to bypass the Sound.[12] Production of Russian iron had begun, stimulated by the needs of the Great Northern War, and here also Tsar Peter planned to outdistance Sweden in the future. But at the time Sweden still held her near-monopoly of best quality iron and steel. Her ore was purer than most, she had timber enough for charcoal, and government policy regulated production both to conserve the forests and to keep prices high. While her copper export had petered out after the Thirty Years War, due to competition from other parts of the world, her iron exports were flourishing. Indeed, when

43 A sugar plantation in the West Indies, busy in a period when European consumption of sugar increased rapidly and when many refineries were built in Europe itself

44 The privateering captain from Dunkirk, Jean Bart, smoking the tobacco which Europe imported in large quantities from overseas

George I – out of concern for his Hanoverian policy – persuaded the English Parliament in 1717 to prohibit all imports from Sweden, English merchants and manufacturers found themselves obliged to buy what they needed via Dutch middlemen at increased prices.[13]

The goods which the north of Europe desperately needed from outside were few. Salt was the one essential, fetched from France and Spain; spices, sugar, tobacco, and saltpetre for gunpowder were near-essentials. The rest of the cargoes brought back were semi-luxuries – brandy, wine and dried fruits from France and the Mediterranean countries; fine cloth from England and the Dutch Republic; and luxuries in the form of clocks and furniture, lace and rich materials, paintings, sculpture and *objets d'art* of many kinds from all over Europe. It was inescapable, therefore, that the trade with northern Europe was one which, particularly for the Maritime Powers, produced an adverse trade-balance. Even when due account has been taken of luxury goods smuggled into the north,[14] the unavoidable expenditure on naval stores meant that the west of Europe needed to recuperate their losses in bullion elsewhere. This is one of the

45

reasons behind the 'commercial revolution',[15] an intensification of trade particularly from England but also from the rest of western Europe to overseas countries. All kinds of manufactured goods were exported either directly or indirectly (as in the case of South America, where English and Dutch vessels sailed under Spanish and Portuguese colours or provided the cargoes even if the ships were genuinely Iberian-owned) and fierce competition began for the slave trade from Africa to the West Indies and to the Americas. The bullion which came to Europe in return supplemented the income from the staples of colonial possessions, tobacco, fish and sugar, and helped to offset the losses which had to be accepted from the Baltic trade.

Loss of bullion was also a feature of trade with the East Indies and the Far East. Europe had, if not a need, at least a great appetite for goods from these areas. The caravans from China and India had from time immemorial had outlets in both southern and northern Europe. Venetian galleys had been the main carriers of spices, silk and jewellery fetched from Egypt and the Levant in general; but another route had ended in the Baltic harbours. The dream of reopening such a route never faded. Embassies were sent from Sweden and Denmark to China, and part of Sweden's commercial 'theory of empire' was based on the prospect of trade not only with China but with Turkey and Persia along the rivers of the Don and Vistula basins. Peter the Great had similar hopes of trade with the west in eastern as well as Russian goods. The western maritime powers had, however, succeeded in establishing direct seaborne trade with the Levant, the Indian Ocean and the Far East and proved too secure to be dislodged by the northern powers. There was some specialization among the successful nations (the French were powerful in the Turkey and Levant trade, the Dutch in the East Indies and in Japan, the English in India and, increasingly, in China where porcelain and tea were bought) though they all competed for the largest share of the many desirable goods to be found east of the Cape of Good Hope. We know a great deal about this trade and of the life of those who manned the ships from reports and accounts that have survived. Most graphic perhaps is the journal written and illustrated by Edward Barlow, who, after service in the navy, sailed east as a seaman in 1670 and went back time and again because he had 'a mind to travel and to see strange things in other countries'.[16] Portuguese ships also sailed the Cape route to the Far East, but in the case of Spain there was an alternative route, used from 1565 onwards (when

45 English clock in silver case, made by Edward Webbe, 1676

46 Christoffer Polhem (1661–1751), who started an industrialized manufacture of watches in Sweden before 1720

the sailor-monk Andrés de Urdaneta managed the east-west passage), whereby ships from Spanish America crossed the Pacific to fetch goods in China; on their return some of their cargoes were carried across the isthmus and re-exported to Europe via the Atlantic route. Scholars have long been aware of this trade, but it has recently been highlighted by the raising, off Florida, of cargo from a convoy of Spanish ships sunk in the terrible storm of 1715: among the items recovered are freshly minted coins from Peru, jewellery and toys from Spanish America and Chinese porcelain packed for export.[17]

Common to all traders to the east was the necessity to carry bullion to pay for their goods. There was hardly anything the east wanted from Europe, and – as far as China was concerned – the clocks and watches, which were the only items coveted, traders and officials expected to receive as gifts.[18] The drain of bullion to the east was much resented. In England opposition to it led, by 1720, to the prohibition of the import of Indian muslins and cottons; but generally speaking it was felt to be unavoidable and gave yet another spur to the competition for trade (whether legal or not) with South America where bullion could most easily be earned. The recovery now in progress of masses of Spanish coins from a seventeenth-century Dutch ship foundered off the Australian coast[19] may be seen as exemplifying the adverse trade-balance between east and west.

47

Divers in leather suits were sometimes employed when valuable cargo had gone to the bottom of seas shallow enough to offer prospects of success. Copper shaped into squares, coins of any kind, or cannon from ships sunk were considered worth the attempt; and we have several reports of success. But most of the goods lost at sea were either sunk far from land or were too heavy to make salvage possible. Insurance of goods became more regular to minimize the risks implicit in the commercial revolution.

In some ways the 'commercial revolution' overlapped with the 'financial revolution',[20] though the latter was essentially caused more directly by governments' needs to raise money for war and to cope with their long-term debts. Men connected with government finance became very rich in most European countries (the exceptions were those in which the government exercised a close control, e.g. Sweden and Russia), whether they were financiers by profession or government servants who more or less legitimately used government money in the intervals (which could be stretched) between specific sums reaching them and being handed to the rightful creditor. Paymasters-general of the forces were in particularly favourable positions in this respect and fortunes were made (among others, by James Brydges and Robert Walpole) through their having previous, but still secret, knowledge as to when auxiliary troops were to be paid and offering, at a considerable discount, to pay commanders from their own pockets in the certainty of a fine profit. The Dutch *ontvanger-generaal* van Ellemeet became fantastically rich, by perfectly legitimate methods, during the War of the Spanish Succession;[21] Robert Walpole and Brydges were thought to have been less scrupulous. Many army officers and officials increased their income by means of betting large sums on dates when a fortress would fall or a treaty be signed, making sure, from information surreptitiously gained, that the element of risk was very low indeed.[22] The financial revolution proper was not concerned with the fortunes made by individuals, though governments became intent on solving financial problems partly because of the galling sight of individuals growing rich while the state sank further into debt. The solutions involved the funding of debts, the sale of annuities and other ways of financing government expenditure, and these spilt over into the problem of tax reform. Here we are concerned mainly with the growing number of men who made their living by lending governments money against interest, and this included not only financiers but *rentiers* and people who invested larger or smaller sums in annuities to afford them an income in retirement or to provide for their widows and children.

The professions, as we would call them, the more or less gentlemanly pursuits, also tended to increase after 1648. The diplomatic service expanded as intercourse between Catholic and Protestant states resumed; new universities were founded; apothecaries, physicians and surgeons were much in demand as their gains in knowledge became popularized; notaries and lawyers found more clients as a result of the growth in commercial and financial transactions; above all, the number of men employed directly by the state multiplied. This sometimes happened, as in France, because offices were sold for cash and because office-holders could be taxed; but more specifically, in France and elsewhere, it happened because the government needed inspectors to verify that ordnance for armies and navies was correctly cast, that uniforms, arms and ammunition were standard, that quality in goods for export was maintained; because it needed customs-officers to restrain smuggling; and because it needed administrators to handle army, navy, diplomacy, trade, finance, taxation and accountancy.

SOCIAL MOBILITY AND DAILY LIFE

European society was hierarchical. Everyone was supposed to know his or her place, and rebukes, if not downright fines, were meted out to those who, for example, dressed above their rank. The sovereign ruler* had the right of ennoblement, and the aristocracy and nobility reckoned their right of precedence and similar privileges according to the class of their title (princes and dukes were ahead of counts who in their turn ranked above barons and *Freiherren* and the lesser nobility) and the date of their noble lineage. Some of the magnates – those of Spain and Bohemia, for instance – were rich enough to keep a princely court; and the spread, from Spain, of the *fideikommiss* method of entail saved their estates from partition. Apart from this numerically small and powerful class of aristocracy and nobility (which might be taken to include among its lesser part also the English gentry), some French seventeenth-century commentators distinguished five further orders of society: the clergy, the office-holders, the merchants, the artisans and the peasants.[23] Such a division is not exhaustive – the armed forces are not included, nor are the professions, neither being thought of as 'productive' in terms of

49

* It should be noted that inside the Holy Roman Empire only the Emperor had the right to give high noble titles: he would do so at the petition of individual princes if he saw fit.

income for the state. The division between Jew and Gentile in western Europe was becoming less sharp. Here the Jews had generally emerged from the ghetto existence which was still their lot in the eastern European countries. They played significant parts in the financial life of Spain, Italy and the Netherlands and, increasingly, in Germany. They were free to settle in England from Cromwell's time onwards, though not yet admitted as citizens to the Scandinavian states. Persecutions were less frequent even in eastern Europe: there were no significant pogroms in our period after those in the Ukraine during the violent Bogdan Khmelnitsky rising of the 1650s.

In reality there was considerable social mobility in our period, probably more than in the post-1721 years of the *Ancien Régime* with its more settled conditions. The way in which the bright peasant-lads were at times helped to higher schooling and university has been touched on above; the poorer townsman's clever child was similarly encouraged if he impressed his teachers. Gifted youngsters who entered domestic service could often improve their lot, though their talents were not usually spotted early enough to admit them to formal education. Ambitious town-dwellers managed with relative ease to educate their children better than they themselves had fared; in Paris, for example, among the 3,000 students at the Jesuit college 'Louis le Grand', a minority *élite* was composed of boarders, while the great majority were day-boys from a mixed social background.[24]

שמי חולך למרחקים : כאחר מכני העגקים :
אבל הרואה אותי : יאמר בן נגס רמותי :

47 Jacob Riis, Jewish dwarf jester at Charles VI's court, Vienna. Sephardic Jews had by this time usually adopted western clothes. Azhkenazi Jews on the whole still retained traditional costume, though 'Court Jews' engaged in finance and administration tended to conform to the fashions of the day

50

Hungarian noblemen. Note the 'hrygian' cap (right-hand figure): ough of elegant material, it differs little shape from the 'peasant' cap of many ountries

49 Russian aristocrat, Prince Menshikov, who rose from being a cook's apprentice

The most frequented ladder to advancement was the educational one, and the seal was set on meritocracy when the trained administrator and official was ennobled. In some countries the *letrado* nobility and the *noblesse de robe* remained, in theory anyhow, inferior to that of the older originally feudal nobility, though we should remember that Saint-Simon's ducal contempt for the origins of the ennobled Colbert and Pontchartrain families may have been intended to silence his consciousness of a grandmother who was rich but socially humble. In other countries bureaucratic promotion could lead to the highest ranks, though such titles came usually to administrators who had become 'cabinet ministers' in practice if not in name: Count Piper in Sweden and Count Flemming in Saxony are instances. Outstanding service in the armed forces, or in the realm of finance also led to ennoblement and often to land donations, either as a reward for services rendered or as security for loans which, with repayment outstanding, in time became virtually indistinguishable from donations: here Prince Menshikov of Russia and the Duke of

51

Chandos in England are good examples of the first kind, while German and Scandinavian history offers innumerable cases of the latter. Another ladder was provided by money *per se*. A successful merchant of humble origin rose in the world by the purchase of land in some countries, by the buying of office (even office which carried with it the possibility of ennoblement) in others, and – everywhere – by his sons and daughters, because of their fortunes, making splendid matches. The heiress or fortuned widow offered yet another avenue to money and position, though in most cases she had relatives who watched sharply lest she should receive in return a fortune-hunter with no redeeming prospects.

Society as a whole became more polite in our period. Even at the lowest level individual plates began to replace the communal bowl and dish; individual glasses, instead of the large vessel that went round for supping, became commonplace; table napkins and soup-ladles appeared, and etiquette books were printed in great numbers. Tsar Peter had one printed for use in Russia so that his subjects should be able to conform to the customs he had witnessed abroad, and with his own hand penned the western modes of address and signature which he wished his nobles to employ. Nearer the top of the social pyramid, education was more appreciated than before even for those destined for the army and the court. In his day, grumbled one of the older Frenchmen, it had been enough to ride, dance, play the lute and know a bit of mathematics: 'Du latin, de mon temps, du latin! Un gentilhomme en eût été déshonoré!'[25] Manners became more polished and the conventions of the *précieuses* (who were easy to ridicule and were magnificently teased by Molière in his *Les Précieuses ridicules* of 1659 and *L'École des femmes* of 1662) did contribute to conversation among men and women in high society if not on learned subjects at least on literary ones. No writer could as yet live from the direct sale of the products of his pen, but plays, poems and distinguished prose earned patronage, noble and royal. Men and women practised amateur writing. Ladies excelled in letters, sometimes in the highly emotional exaggerated style which – in the case of Queen Anne and the Duchess of Marlborough, and Queen Christina and the Countess Ebba Sparre – have made those unacquainted with the genre attribute lesbian tendencies to them on the evidence of the letters alone. Gentlemen specialized in memoirs, usually written in their old age and not intended for publication. They often justified themselves with the interest expressed by children and grandchildren, but the natural urge of the older person to transmit to paper the happenings of his own life and his interpretation of the age in which he had lived was usually also operative. Where memoirs have survived, it is clear that they were frequently based on diaries and journals (some of which have also been found and printed), and at times they include or refer to official or semi-official correspondence or documents. One proof of the dominant position of the French language is that men with no direct contact with France – like Fabrice, whose career took him all over Germany, to Turkey, to England and to Sweden (but never to France), and the Swedish von Löwen, whose service had been with the Allied armies and with Charles XII (but never with Louis XIV) – wrote their memoirs in French.[26] That the art of writing, if not that of literature, was common lower down the social pyramid is amply proved by business letters and account books of beautiful calligraphy and exquisite tidiness. But of those whose education had ended early or had been non-existent, we know, for example, from the fact that private soldiers dictated letters home or had them composed by those who made a little profit from such services, that writing was beyond them, though we need not assume that they were completely illiterate.

Schooling for the less well-to-do tended to be most diffused in the Protestant countries. The demand in the Lutheran ones for a knowledge of and examination in the catechism before confirmation encouraged reading, though some no doubt managed by memorizing from what had been read aloud. Conversely, poorer Catholics had greater contact with sculpture, painting, music and Baroque art in general in their church life; the Protestants had to make do with hymns alone if their creed was Puritan or Nonconformist, though music to the glory of God was acceptable in the Lutheran churches and also in the Church of England after 1660. The central position of the hymns and oratorios in Protestant countries derives from this difference: they had feast days and holidays originating in ancient saints' days as well as church festivals, but the religious processions, with their element of 'show' mixed with devotion, of the Catholic lands were missing. To some extent this was compensated for by the popularity of theatre and opera and concerts all over Europe. But for the less educated masses what was accessible, apart from church culture, were the puppet shows of the fair and *kermesse*, and those primitive 'films' which consisted of stories being told against the background of changing illustrations to old legends, such as those of

53

Dr Faustus and Don Juan. We should be careful, however, not to underestimate the way in which purveyors of entertainment then, as now, included items which might be considered semi-educational: an inn in Germany had a life-like wax model of Gustavus Adolphus which rose from his seat when the door of the room was opened. It drew travellers from afar, as we can see from notes in almanacs and journals.[27]

The daily life of all classes had much in common. The day was regulated by church bells or secular clock-tower bells in town and country; and the discipline of the church, especially on Sundays, was maintained by government decree. Hard work was the lot, or the delight, of most people and even those generally considered today as mere drones at fashionable courts may have been hard at work maintaining the family position by cultivating opportunities for rich marriages, suitable posts and perquisites for themselves or younger relatives. Authenticated accounts of food provided for inmates of charity houses in Amsterdam and labourers on noble estates in Sweden show that their menus were basically those of the better-off classes*. The well-to-do had, of course, more variety in their diet, and the very rich, by inclination or the need to show off, often had sumptuous fare. Generally speaking, the rural population,

54

* In the first case the staple items were soup, beans, dried fish, blood-sausage; with marmalade, rice, meat and prunes for feast-days; in the latter the staples were beer, bacon, bread, lentils, sour milk and herring – again with occasional festive fare. The liberal army rations can also be taken as a guide to normal diet; a typical one consisted of meat or fish, bread, lentils, beer and a ration of brandy, plus money for tobacco.

50, 51 Italian family group at *al fresco* feast (far left), and Dutch fishmarket 1660s (left)

52, 53, 54 Top, banquet of the Regensburg Diet, 1717; left, Charles XII entertains Augustus of Saxony at Altranstädt, 7/17 December 1706; above, behind the scenes: work in the kitchen.

55

where it lived above the pauper level, had a tradition of frugality in everyday life and excess – usually for prestige reasons – at big occasions such as weddings and funerals. That this was typical (at least in some countries) also of urban society is proved by edicts against needlessly elaborate funerals which were deemed to detract from the religious ceremony.

Skating and sledging, fishing, sailing and rowing were pastimes all classes had in common, depending on the part of Europe inhabited. Wrestling and archery were popular sports; dancing and singing were universal, as were games including dominoes and playing cards. Billiards, tennis and fencing were confined to gentlefolk. The sport of horse-racing was as yet limited to England and travellers commented on its colourful jockeys and its valuable silver prizes. Hunting and shooting usually depended on social status and in some countries the game laws were strict enough to constitute a real class barrier. English landowning peasants (the yeomen), for example, were frequently not allowed to shoot over their own land. Rich and poor enjoyed tobacco (even after its beneficial medicinal effect had come to be doubted[28]) and might be equally addicted to gambling and drink; but it was at the courts that gentlemen ran the greatest risk of having to eat and drink too much in order not to offend their hosts, and of losing more money at cards than they could afford lest they be despised as unwilling to venture. The smaller the court the more given to conspicuous consumption it frequently was. Temple complained bitterly of the way in which it was *de rigueur* to drink oneself under the table at the Bishop of Münster's court; Fabrice poked sly fun at the Sachsen-Weissenfels duke who aped what he assumed to be the glories of the fashionable capitals with his zoo, his elaborate ceremonials and his train of dwarfs.[29]

55 Louis XIV, dressed as
a Roman Emperor, and
attendants at a
carousel of 1662

56, 57 Below, game of tennis;
right, the end of a hunt

58 Cheating at cards: note the
mirror held by the figure on the
left and the accusing finger of the
spectator

59 The menagerie of Prince
Eugène of Savoy

Fashion exercised attraction among high and low and in many different aspects of life. The fashionable preacher was adored and had vast congregations; the spa of the moment (though also that at which an important political figure was taking the cure) became a busy one; coffee-houses had to take in the popular newspapers or they lost custom; hair-styles and dresses were imitated; fashionable furniture and jewellery were bought; men were flattered to receive as gifts wines that they had not hitherto been accustomed to drink if they were told that 'sack' or 'burgundy' was now all the rage; flowers brought long distances to thrive in Europe – such as the chrysanthemum from Japan and the pelargonium from the Cape Colony – gave pleasure not only in themselves but because they were exotic plants to put beside earlier importations, e.g. the tulip, to show that one could afford what was new and expensive. Slavery to fashion was, of course, often criticized or ridiculed. The Duchess of Marlborough stressed the fire-risk (from candles) to the pleated lace headdresses, shaped as fans, that she wore to be in the fashion. 'There,' she wrote to a friend, 'I have burnt my best head writing to you.'[30] Some waxed censorious of the new-fangled whims of others. The men looked like women with long skirts to their coats, reported one lady from St James's, and the pale colours they chose were 'prodigiously effeminate.'[31]

61 Fashionable if inflammable head-dress, 1708

62 Princess dressed in fashion, 1696

60 Fashionable preacher, 1659

63 The King and Queen's Bath at Bath, 1672

◀ 64 Mother-of-pearl figure set in slate showing Frederick III of Denmark in finery of the mid-1660s

65, 66 French fashion plate for winter clothing from *Mercure Galant*, 1678, and French fashion plate for summer dress in pirated Dutch edition of *Mercure Galant*, 1678

◀ 67 Satire on the wearing of wigs

Beneath such superficialities, human fate was the common lot of all, as were the human drives, the passions and appetites of mind and body. The statistics of infant mortality show how common the loss of children must have been; the grief this brought we know from other sources. 'I never knew it could hurt so much to lose a child,' wrote Charles XI to a friend – deeply religious though he was, he found it hard to reconcile himself to God's will. King Pedro of Portugal experienced such grief when his daughter died of smallpox at the age of eight that he shut himself in his room for thirty-six days. Marlborough never recovered from the death of his son and heir at the age of seventeen and Prince Eugène mourned the loss of a nephew, his last surviving close relative.[32] Brydges had strange, dreadful nightmares which he wrote down after he had lost several children; he realized that they had a connection with his bereavement and they make, in the light of modern psychological interpretation, shattering reading.[33] Louis XIV tried hard to combat his grief, when he lost a son, a grandson and a beloved granddaughter-in-law as well as a great-grandson within a short time, by the reflection that he must have merited such punishment from God. Plagues and wars were often taken as collective punishment for a nation's misdeeds, or this was at least preached from the pulpits of the clergy. The hazards of everyday life were the same for all. Men were prone to accidents while riding, the common mode of conveyance, whether their horse stumbled or they themselves made an error of judgment. Carts and carriages overturned and the occupants were lucky if they escaped with bruises, which were common enough even without spills when journeys were long. Ships got wrecked and passengers were grateful to escape with their lives, though the better-off later mourned the loss of prized possessions or irreplaceable letters and manuscripts. In civilian life epidemics had no respect for persons, and in war officers were more likely to lose their lives than privates. Rich and poor were – as a rule – equally concerned to provide for their families and improve their status.

The more well-to-do obviously had greater resources to mend broken health and to stave off death. Bleeding and purging were commonplace remedies, used on poor and rich alike; but only the rich could afford medicines with expensive ingredients – such as the one administered to the new-born Prince of Wales the night James II sat up till dawn fearing his son would die[34] – or cures such as that given the Swedish officer Edvard Gyldenstolpe in Germany

68 Memorial for a pewtermaker, Johan Lang, 1710

69 Memorial for the Duke and Duchess of Marlborough and the two sons whose loss they had mourned ▶

after he had been hit in the arm by a bullet: a live dog was split open for every treatment and the wounded limb was plunged into the dog's still pulsing entrails. Gyldenstolpe's biographer wonders whether this might constitute a primitive kind of blood-transfusion.[35] It may well have been; blood-transfusions were successfully attempted in the second half of the seventeenth century. In any case the young man recovered, and soldiered on till he fell in battle in 1709. The Duchess of Marlborough, at Bath, was able to send for a box of vipers from Montpellier to make a broth for the Duke in order 'to mend the blood' after his stroke of 1716. Expense was no problem and the 'Mumpillio vipers' were reckoned the best.[36]

The rich had extravagant amusements – joustings and carousels, elaborate masques and balls and receptions – which, at the courts of the great powers, could cost them a great deal of money in clothes.

61

At Whitehall, though anyone decently attired as a gentleman (and willing to slip a footman a coin) could gain access to the more ordinary functions, the dresses and suits for the birthdays of the King and Queen were nicely judged as compliments to their Majesties according to their novelty and cost. Ladies of noble rank grieved if, from temporary pecuniary embarrassment, they could not afford to be present. The rich did not always disdain the cruder pleasures of the 'common people': the bull and bear-baiting, the cock-fighting (inseparable from betting) and the sport of 'gooseriding', tearing – at a full gallop – the greased neck off a live goose hung in a kind of gallows.[37] In Spain bull-fighting on horseback was largely a sport of gentlemen though all classes gloried in the spectacle.

The life of the well-to-do offered more in the field of culture if they were so inclined. They could buy books and musical instruments, they could hire orchestras to play for them. The men (and a few women) could travel – at least once – to see the wonders of architecture and art, and listen to singing where it was thought most sublime: in Naples and other Italian courts where the *castrati* were bliss to the ear if not to the eye. If they had collectors' tastes, they could indulge them. There were art-dealers in all major towns (and paintings were even sold in the market-places in the Dutch Republic, where people whom the moneyed collectors regarded as 'of the common sort' bought pictures for their houses and carpets for their tables), and an elaborate European network existed whereby paintings and rare books could be bought for commission. Authenticity was less easily ascertained in respect of paintings than books, and a portrait of Charles V for which Senserf, a Rotterdam banker, tried to play Brydges, Marlborough and Eugène off against each other, was (though the would-be seller had no intention of cheating) in reality one of Philip II.[38] Those who were rich enough could embark on the construction of stately homes, and even palaces, to house their libraries and their china cabinets and to display their paintings. They

71 A 'Bull Feast' in Portugal. Note balconies used as boxes (see p. 126)

72 Scene from
Bartholomew Fair,
1721. Note (left) the
peepshow entitled
'The Siege of Gibraltar'

◄ 70 Art gallery
in Amsterdam

could afford to landscape their gardens according to their taste, which tended to be modelled either on the example of Versailles or on the paintings from Italy of the French-born Claude Lorraine. It is amazing how true to Lorraine, who himself was not always true to life, individual gardens were made, with bridges and temples positioned as on his canvases. Those who rebelled against imitation of either studied the native landscape and improved on it; in England the vogue for the 'Chinese garden' or the 'natural park', with its careful planting of trees and artificial lakes, made itself felt towards the end of the period. In Sweden the concern for the view over inlets of the sea and islands was at times victorious over the plans of even eminent architects.

Great differences clearly existed in the opportunities for fulfilment of ambitions and interests, but we have little information which would permit us to assess the feeling of contentment with class – if this label be permitted for segments of the hierarchical pyramid – and calling. Famine or intolerable burdens of taxation provoked revolts (those of France and Russia being the best documented of our period[39]) in claustrophobic peasant communities; but we know less of the contented ones or of the attitudes of the same regions in better times. The calling itself, whether it was to church, monastery or college, the restricted confines of a craftsman's guild or a profession which emphasized solidarity, the *esprit de corps* of a regiment or a bureaucratic board, usually offered a social purpose which helped to reconcile the individual to personal grief, whether his position inside his chosen field was high or low in respect of rank. Many well-to-do people found a vocation in charitable work or exercised their ingenuity in wrestling with the problem of 'the poor', the unemployed and the unemployable. Nuns specialized in caring for the sick.

The competitive individual was often drawn to certain callings, notably in the realm of commerce, finance and politics, and enjoyed the excitement of the battle, as the careerist gloried in the successive stages of success. Contemporaries liked to explain people's characteristics according to their physical and psychological types: the 'humours' and 'gases' of the body were thought to account for hot and dry temperaments, for the melancholy and the bellicose.[40] But there is much evidence to suggest that whatever one's type, something personal and individual still decided one's degree of contentment and happiness, from the emotional anchorage and joy of marriage and children (even if that marriage was more likely to

73 Landscape by Claude Lorraine, 1672, *Aeneas at Delos*, which is known to have influenced landscape gardening ▶

have been arranged than not) to the intellectual satisfaction derived from speculation, whether on a practical or philosophical plane. One did not exclude the other – or any of the variants in between, such as the blessings of contemplation, the compensation for duties fulfilled or ideals pursued – but it cannot be denied that the highest manifestations of intellectual and artistic culture were open only to those with trained minds. Even when such minds expressed their views of human felicity and happiness they couched them in terms which made it impossible for the non-educated, though he might intuitively share the sentiments expressed, to follow the processes of thought and the definitions behind the concepts. A good example of this is Leibniz's words in *Principles of Nature and Grace*:

It is true that supreme felicity (by whatever beatific vision or knowledge of God it may be accompanied) can never be complete, because God, being infinite, cannot be entirely known. Thus our happiness will never consist (and it is right that it should not consist) in complete enjoyment, which would leave nothing more to be desired and would make our *esprit* stupid; but it must consist in a perpetual progress to new pleasures and new perfections.

III DOMESTIC ISSUES

The years of crisis on an international scale during the Thirty Years War had meant general postponement in tackling domestic problems. These had at best been patched up while energies were absorbed by the need to wage war, and when historians talk of 'the general crisis of the seventeenth century' they have in mind both the problems and the strong differences, leading at times to violence, about the solutions. For the Holy Roman Empire of the German Nation the 1648 settlement had brought one decision: Germany was to have not one ruler but many, for in the struggle between the Austrian Habsburgs for a unitary *Monarchie* comprising 'the Germanies', and the princes, Protestant and Catholic alike, who resisted such an aim, victory had gone to the princes. By 1648 an elector, duke, landgrave or margrave (or whatever title the individual prince held) possessed a French and Swedish guarantee of his *Landeshoheit*, so that power over his own territory was as near sovereignty as made little difference in practice, though it was only via the Emperor that he could procure the title of count or baron for a deserving subject: he himself could ennoble but only within the range of *von* or *von-und-zu*.[1] The ruler could decide the religion of his own state and work out its form of government with his own subjects, that is, with the Estates of Clergy, Nobility and Burghers who traditionally had a share in the levying of taxes. The compromise reached differed from region to region, but it is noticeable that the form of government tended in the larger states towards absolutism, which contemporaries usually labelled 'sovereign monarchy' to distinguish it from a 'limited monarchy', in which the Estates remained powerful. Countries with an oligarchic structure, such as the Venetian and Dutch republics, or commonwealths where the king was either elected (as in the Polish-Lithuanian one) or where the head of the executive had some other title (such as that of Protector in the English Commonwealth before 1660) were even more sharply distinguished from the absolute monarchies. Absolute monarchy is too frequently equated nowadays with tyrannical or arbitrary government. Europeans of the seventeenth century might fear that absolutism would

67

◀ 74 Matter, Form and Power: title-page to Hobbes's *Leviathan*, 1651 become tyrannical, but they classed only two countries as possessing rulers who governed without the restraint of the law, namely the Sultan of the Ottoman empire and the Tsar of Muscovy. These two, from what was known of happenings that far east, claimed the right to dispose over a subject's life and property according to personal whim and not according to the processes of the law.

Discussion on the form of government and on the relative merits and danger of monarchies (sovereign or limited) and republics and commonwealth was rife all over Europe. Political theorists agreed that all forms of government went back to a contract between ruler and subjects; what divided them was the amount of central power necessary to prevent anarchy on the one hand and to curb the 'over-mighty subject' on the other. 'Better one king than many' was a common saying among those who had suffered from the class interest of the nobility in times of royal minorities. The need for a king to be the father of his people and reconcile the conflicting interests of his children was stressed; the picture of the state as needing a head to govern the limbs was another simile applied. It is not accidental that those countries which had experienced several minorities within living memory, like France and Sweden, should be drawn towards absolutism. In France the high nobility had looked to the Holy Roman Empire of the German Nation as their model: regional division of the huge territory of the French, with strictly limited and preferably honorific power only for the king, seemed more sensible (as well as more prestigious and profitable for themselves) than the centralized power Henry IV had imposed and Louis XIII and Richelieu partially restored once Louis's minority was over. The revolt of the nobility, the Fronde, broke out mainly because the Queen-Mother and Mazarin tried to maintain the power of the crown on behalf of Louis XIV, five years old at the death of his father in 1643. The opposition of Paris and the lawyers, forming a Fronde of the Third Estate with constitutional ideas of a monarchy limited by powerful Diets of Estates, co-operated for some time with that of the nobility. But discrepancies between their objectives as well as bourgeois fear of feudal anarchy helped to make sovereign absolutism acceptable. At the earliest possible age, fourteen, Louis XIV was declared to have entered his majority in order that the symbol of a ruler who 'enjoyed his own' might help reunify a country unwilling to submit to the 'foreign plotter', Mazarin. From now on problems could be – and were – vigorously tackled: the war with Spain, the

75, 76 Medals celebrating Louis XIV's accessibility to his subjects, 1661 (left), and the restoration of military discipline in his reign, 1665

bad coinage which bedevilled financial and commercial transactions, the backwardness of French trade and manufacture as compared with those of the Maritime Powers, the end-of-the-queue aspect of French colonial ventures – all problems which France's active participation in the Thirty Years War had exacerbated.[2] In Sweden the long minority of Christina, Gustavus Adolphus's daughter, had entrenched the power of the high nobility, and the Queen, once she became of age, worried lest a plot existed to establish an oligarchic republic on her death. This was one, if not the only reason, for her abdication. (Her secret conversion to Catholicism was another.) Having long ago decided – for complex psychological reasons which have been brilliantly analyzed in Stolpe's recent biography – that she would not bear children of her own body to secure the succession, she felt obliged to manœuvre (and did so with greater skill than he admits) the nobility into a position whereby they permitted her cousin to become Charles X of Sweden without the power of the crown becoming crippled. In the process she utilized the general post-war discontent with the high nobility. Sweden was unique in having three non-noble Estates – the Nobility formed the First Estate, the Clergy and the Burghers the Second and Third respectively, while representatives of the landowning peasants provided a Fourth Estate – and all three lower Estates were seething with indignation at the way in which the nobility had gained land during the period of Swedish expansion. Donation and alienation of crown property had reached such proportions that the post-Reformation balance of land equally divided between crown, nobility and peasants had been destroyed. If Christina's own donations (with which she was lavish indeed) are taken into account, the crown controlled in

1654 hardly 1½ per cent of land in Sweden proper, and inroads had been made also on peasant land. The cry for a resumption of alienated crown land was raised as early as 1648, and, by playing off noble versus non-noble Estates, Christina managed to have Charles X accepted without conditions, leaving him free to begin that 'quarter-resumption' which was completed and extended into a total resumption in the 1680s by his son Charles XI. This happened, however, after yet another minority (on Charles X's death in 1660) had entrenched the power of the high nobility, and their opposition to the resumption was so strong that the King and the reform party had to introduce sovereign monarchy – an idea quite foreign to Swedish political thinking – in order to break their opponents inside the Estate of Nobility. In Sweden the nobility did not rebel – they were loyal to the traditional 'mixed government' and neither *frondeurs* nor commonwealth men, Axel Oxenstierna assured Christina already in the 1650s. But they resisted with all the power at their command the resumption, which was the only generally acceptable solution to the overriding 'problem of the peace': how could Sweden afford an army and a navy strong enough to safeguard the gains of the Thirty Years War and those of the 'natural frontiers' on the Scandinavian peninsula won from Denmark-Norway in the 1640s and 1650s? The nobility as a class had argued that the country's defence could be paid for from the money income of Baltic tolls and dues, and from the subsidies of foreign powers; but the former, though high, did not suffice, and the latter had led to Sweden's involvement against her intention and interests in the European wars of 1672–78. Disillusionment with the government of the high nobility, as well as resentment of its riches and privileges, gave Charles XI the solid backing of the three non-noble Estates for a piecemeal introduction of absolutism. He had support also from would-be reformers inside the House of Nobility (*Riddarhus*) where some of his chief aides were found, and where many of its second and third class* tended to share the non-noble dislike of the high nobility which formed the first class. With sovereign absolutism came much-needed reform. The land-balance was restored by resumption (the so-called 'reduction') of alienated land. With the land returned and from the heavy fines, usually paid in land, levied on those regents of Charles XI's minority who by a judicial 'retrospection' were found guilty of misgovernment, a permanent 'budget' was set up in which the income from given land was set against

* The First Estate had three classes; the first consisted of counts and barons; the second of descendants of members of the Council of the Realm; the third of all the other ennobled families, i.e. the lower nobility.

77 The Swedish *Riddarhus* (House of Nobility), designed 1642 by the French architect Simon de Vallée and completed by his son (Jean) by 1674

specific expenditure. Officers' salaries as well as those of university professors were regulated in this way and were thus protected, as our own age would express it, against a rise in the cost of living. Money income from tolls and dues also formed part of the budget and were set aside for expenditure which needed cash – the cost of the diplomatic service and of the court – and as security for foreign loans when needed. The country in general entered, as France had done, into a period of intense activity in the economic and artistic fields; and if a difference between the two (and there were of course many) impresses itself, it is the one which sprang from the larger population and riches of France. In France Louis XIV, though he complained of having only a few suitable men from among whom he could pick his ministers and high officials,[3] had enough to permit him to restrict the high nobility at large to being courtiers, officers or local estate-owners; whereas in Sweden, crown and nobility had to reach a *modus vivendi* in the administration. Even those who railed bitterly at the wickedness of the resumption found themselves back in government service, since they could not do without the extra income and the King needed trained officials;[4] indeed no Swedish nobleman had the legal right to refuse to serve the crown and withdraw to his estate.

In other countries where absolutism won the day, causes and consequences were similar. The impetus of war (for victor as for

71

78, 79, 80, 81, 82 Some rulers of the period: Leopold, Emperor and head of the Austrian Habsburg state; Frederick William of Brandenburg, 'The Great Elector';

loser) often provided the spur. In Denmark the defeat of 1658 and dissatisfaction with the selfish and backward-looking policy of the nobility brought absolute monarchy into being by 1660. In Brandenburg the victory implied in Poland's relinquishing sovereignty over East Prussia, and Swedish recognition that this was a rightful gain from the Great Elector's participation in the Suedo-Polish war, enabled the Prussian tradition of civil and military administration to be perfected in such a manner that the Elector became an absolute ruler long before the coveted royal title was obtained in 1701. In Russia there was a considerable strengthening of central control in the reign of Aleksey Romanov, but the unsettled conditions with joint child heirs after 1684 made for the kind of pause familiar from French and Swedish history until Peter the Great embarked on a reign of reform in which his favourite words were *Vernunft* (reason) and *vernünftig* (reasonable). Wittram, the Tsar's latest biographer, has noted that these crop up in countless letters, decrees and conversations,[5] as they do in the letters and memoranda of other reforming absolutists and their advisers. A monarch bent on change could always find men willing to work with him, though would-be reformers among subjects were helpless unless they could get support from the crown. In Spain there were many administrators and ministers who, in the last decades of the seventeenth century, felt frustrated and angry that the weak body and mind of Carlos II should rob them of vigour and initiative in the central government even after that King was nominally of age.[6]

Aleksey Mikhailovich, Tsar of Muscovy; William III, Prince of Orange, Stadhouder of the Dutch Republic and (1689) King of England; Charles XI of Sweden

To think of 'absolutism' as regressive and reprehensible, or even as 'feudal' (and that historians frequently do so is easy to read between, if not on, the lines of textbook and monograph alike), is anachronistic. Those who favoured it and worked for it in the second half of the seventeenth century regarded themselves as being in tune with progress, alive to the searching practical problems of the day, for order against chaos, for sound administration in the interests of the whole nation rather than of any one class, for mobilization of the resources of the state and for exploitation of opportunities in Europe and overseas. They were often personally ambitious and not unmindful of their own interests, and an entrepreneur spirit was as common as a bureaucratic one. Often they differed in no perceptible way from those who held office in the Maritime Powers, one of which, England, was a limited monarchy and the other, the Seven United Provinces, a federation usually known as the Dutch Republic or – evidence of its importance in this period – the Republic. Their task differed, however, in one respect. Under sovereign absolutism there were usually groups and factions, holding different views on how to achieve stated objectives as well as being rivals for power, which contended for the ear of the ruler. Where limitations on sovereignty existed, organized political parties developed with, at times, decisive influence on policy and with increasing control over who was to hold office. Would-be reformers or those hungry for office in 'absolute' states therefore worked indirectly, their differences being filtered through the decision-making power of the crown; whereas those in

73

'limited' states fought their battles in the public arena of political discussion in Parliament, Diet or States as well as in the private corridors of power.

CONSTITUTIONAL GOVERNMENT

Constitutional government, whether in the limited monarchies or in the republics and commonwealths, was in some measure regarded by go-ahead administrators as 'old-fashioned' and as weakening the state by party strife. The example most glaringly before their eyes was that of the Polish-Lithuanian Commonwealth: with immense territories, large population and ample resources for trade, the country was sinking in power and prestige and increasingly presented an anarchical face to Europe. The Elector of Saxony, who was elected King of Poland in 1697, entered the Great Northern War because he wanted to 'modernize' Poland by the introduction of hereditary monarchy: he hoped to conquer, with Saxon troops, Swedish Livonia and offer it to the Poles in return for greater power for the crown. For this plan he had the covert support of many Poles, though his efforts were hotly opposed by others who valued the 'ancient liberties'.

In the Austrian Habsburg state the movement towards absolutism was strong enough throughout our period to ensure that though local Diets survived, in practice their political power was nil and their main effect was to render collection of taxes and dues extremely cumbersome and slow, necessitating loans (though not as many subsidies as historians have assumed[7]) from Austria's allies in the wars against Louis XIV. Hungary alone remained in a special position. It had come into the Habsburg fold in 1526 – at the same time as Bohemia, Silesia, Moravia and Lusatia – but it took no part in the unsuccessful revolt of 1618–35 and therefore kept its autonomy in contradistinction to the Bohemian and adjoining districts. The unitary urge of sovereign absolutism made a clash inevitable between the reformers of Vienna and the Magyars as soon as larger tracts of Greater Hungary came to be reconquered from the Turks in the second half of the seventeenth century. The 'German' settlement of the newly conquered territories (which incidentally promoted that spread of serfdom noted above), encouraged by the Emperor Leopold, could not stem Magyar and Transylvanian opposition to centralized government from Vienna, and much Austrian effort during the War of the Spanish Succession was tied down in fighting

Rákóczi's forces. By 1711 the Habsburgs triumphed and the Hungarian Diet, in return for abandoning Rákóczi, was confirmed in possession of rights which enabled it to obtain concessions when circumstances – as they did – changed.

The struggle to conquer foreign enclaves inside the territory of the state and to absorb semi-autonomous provinces was typical of both constitutional and sovereign absolutism. Louis XIV was successful in respect of the principality of Orange, which he was permitted to keep in 1713, but unsuccessful in the case of Avignon, which he dared occupy against papal wishes only for a short while. By 1650 Madrid had defeated the Catalan revolt which began a decade earlier; but as soon as an opportunity offered (in the War of the Spanish Succession) to throw off the yoke of central government, Barcelona reopened the struggle. Philip V did not manage to subdue Catalonia till 1713–15 when he obtained French military help in return for his reluctant consent to the territorial and commercial sacrifices demanded by Great Britain from Spain. Louis XIV was convinced that such sacrifices had to be made for France's, if not for Spain's, sake; but his pressure would have availed little had he not offered his grandson support in a matter close to Spanish interests – the ending of Barcelona's resistance to the centre.

England's determination to keep Ireland subjugated had similar economic and strategic motives; vested interests favoured continued occupation, while fear that Ireland might serve as a base for foreign invasion mirrored fears in Spain, France and Austria. Some parallels can be drawn also with regard to religious unitary policy. Louis XIV disliked having a sanctuary for French Protestants in William III's tolerant Orange; Leopold I did his best to root out Hungarian Protestantism; William III, Queen Anne and George I, rulers of an England in which there was a degree of legal tolerance for most Protestants but none for Catholics, equated Catholicism with support for Jacobitism. The analogy should not be too closely pursued, for the absorption of the whole of Ireland – an island physically separated from the island of Great Britain – was not of the same order as that between adjacent territories. Ulster, however, is proof of the seriousness with which England treated the problem posed as well as of England's power to enforce her policy.

England (Great Britain after the Union with Scotland in 1707) and the Dutch Republic form a special group within the states with a constitutional form of government. They were obviously rich and

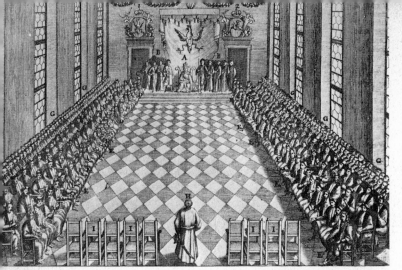

83 A Polish Diet, 1698. Note the arms of Poland to the left, those of Lithuania to the right, with the respective Crown officers of the Commonwealth ranged on each side of King Augustus. In foreground (marked H) the Speaker

84 The English Parliament, 1689. William III to the left (A), the Speaker far right (C)

85 The Sala del Collegio in Venice, the Doge seated in the centre (second half of seventeenth century)

86 The States General of the Dutch Republic, sitting in the Binnenhof at The Hague, 1651

powerful, though absolutists argued that they would have been stronger still if they were governed by sovereign kings. They were both run by oligarchies, and though there is a sense in which, as Kossmann has stressed,[8] we can speak of Parliament in England and the States General of the Dutch Republic as being more 'absolute' than the absolute monarchs, the oligarchic form of government was not in itself thought of as a blueprint for power. The Republic of Venice and other Italian, Swiss and German city-states had long been overtaken in power politics by larger units. There was, however, one field in which contemporaries firmly and justifiably held that 'republics' (a synonym for states and cities with constitutional government) had the advantage over 'monarchies', i.e. those governed by sovereign monarchs: they attracted money. Commercial men, Drummond went out of his way to explain to Robert Harley, would never trust their money to monarchies. Though he may be construed as making a special plea for permitting Dutch merchants and financiers to continue their transactions with France, there is obvious truth in his explanation of the workings of European finance even in wartime: the Paris bankers draw at two months on Amsterdam, then Amsterdam at the two months' end draws on London, then London on Italy, and the Italians of Genoa or Livorno or Venice on Geneva, and 'the Genève Banquier back upon Paris'.[9]

A similar preoccupation with money and property is expressed in Locke's *Second Treatise of Government*:

> The end of government is the good of mankind. And which is best for mankind? That the people should be always exposed to the boundless will of tyranny, or that the rulers should be sometimes liable to be opposed when they grow exorbitant in the use of their power and employ it for the destruction and not the preservation of the properties of their people?

It could be argued that the preservation of property is here more important than tyranny, indeed that the touchstone of tyranny is defined as exorbitant use of power in respect of property (though Locke's definition of 'properties' included 'liberties'). Tyranny in the sense of oppression was deplored also by the theorists of sovereign monarchy. Bossuet in his *Politique tirée des propres Paroles de L'Écriture* (propositions v and vi of article III, Book III) held 'that the true function of a prince is to provide for the needs of his people, while the tyrant thinks only of himself', and 'that a prince who fails to ensure the welfare of his people will be as harshly punished as the tyrant who oppresses them'.

On property Bossuet was reassuring though naturally less emphatic than Locke; but the sentence which most clearly expresses his view is embedded in a section from Book VIII (*De Justice*) which is important enough to render in full since it distinguishes very clearly between arbitrary government and absolute government.

It is one thing for a government to be absolute, and quite another for it to be arbitrary. It is absolute in that it is not liable to constraint, there being no other power capable of coercing the sovereign, who is in this sense independent of all human authority. But it does not follow from this that the government is arbitrary, for besides the fact that all is subject to the judgment of God (which is also true of those governments we have just called arbitrary), there are also laws, in states, so that whatever is done contrary to them is null in a legal sense; moreover, there is always an opportunity for redress, either at other times or in other conditions. Thus each man remains the owner of his property since no one believes that he can possess anything securely if it is in contravention of the law whose vigilance and rectification of violence and injustice is perpetual.

Thus, Bossuet concludes, 'what is termed legitimate government is by its very nature the opposite of arbitrary government.' But though the majority of politically conscious Europeans of the time would have acquiesced in this distinction, the English and the Dutch felt in their bones that absolute government always carried with it the danger of arbitrary government and were confirmed in their belief by Louis XIV's Revocation of the Edict of Nantes. A nation so utterly dependent on trade as the Dutch Republic found toleration essential, while for England, in the throes of the commercial revolution, a toleration which embraced, if not Catholics at home, all Protestants at home and both Protestants and Catholics abroad was becoming essential. When absolutism broke with toleration it was abhorred and the nickname of 'The Christian Turk', with which both nations in their pamphlet warfare saddled Louis XIV, was meant to accuse him of the arbitrary government which Europe at large connected with the Sultan rather than of diplomatic co-operation (which never went as far as political alliance in Louis's reign) between France and the Ottoman empire. The ally of the

Maritime Powers, Leopold of Austria, was no more tolerant than Louis in religious matters; but here political considerations inhibited criticism, whereas in the French case commercial rivalry and fear of an overmighty neighbour intensified the genuine dislike of Huguenot persecution.

The vehemence of the Dutch and the English can be explained also by their consciousness of their own narrow escape from absolute rulers and tyrants. The Dutch oligarchy had resisted attempts of the House of Orange, in 1650 as in 1675, to achieve dynastic status. The English Parliament had denied Cromwell and his Puritans supreme power, put the House of Stuart to flight when James II proved unwilling to keep the bargain implicit in the Restoration of 1660, and laid down explicit terms for their co-operation with William III, who – motivated by his concern for foreign policy rather than domestic issues as such – would gladly have been an absolute monarch. It is therefore understandable that to the majority of inhabitants in England and the United Provinces absolutism was suspect. It spelt lack of control by sensible propertied men over the means by which the armed forces were recruited, forces which could be turned against the inhabitants directly, or indirectly if used for purposes abroad which they deemed unnecessary or even undesirable. It seemed safest to curb the ruler's prerogative whether he be called monarch or *stadhouder*. For this reason the differences between Hobbes (who was by no means so extreme an 'absolutist' as his critics averred[10]) and the continental theorists of legitimate sovereign monarchy on the one hand, and Locke and the commonwealth men on the other, were over-emphasized and what they had in common was ignored – so much so that the propaganda identification of absolute monarchy with arbitrary government has survived into our own day.

GOVERNMENT IN PRACTICE

Quite apart from the common stress on governments being instituted for the needs of the people and the good of the people, and on the obligation for governments to obey the fundamental laws of the state, absolutists and anti-absolutists alike stressed the need to use *reason* in the exercise of power and the execution of policy. Bossuet went out of his way to postulate that the government of the divine-right king was 'subject to reason' and Locke's writings were permeated by his conviction that if ruler and people disagreed, reason was

87 Miniature portrait (by R. Nanteuil) of a French administrator, Jean Baptiste Colbert, Marquis de Croissy, who once remarked 'two months of idleness would surely kill me'. Note the elaborate floral (by Madeleine Boulogne) and bird (by Nicholas Robert) decorations, as the portrait was intended to serve as a frontispiece for a projected 'Receuil d'Histoire Naturelle'

more likely to lie with the people at large than with one man. Those concerned with everyday practical government, cameralists, political economists, ministers and officials, took as their guiding light an emphasis on common sense; on the basis of what could be tested and ascertained, the means whereby the resources of the state could be administered and increased were proposed. The economic aspect of the policies of absolutist states have long been labelled mercantilist (a term not easy to define[11]), implying a dichotomy between a rigid protectionist mercantilism and liberal free-traders to correspond to that between absolutism and constitutionalism. This implication (of nineteenth-century origin and still flourishing) ignores three important factors. Firstly, that all states were protectionist in larger or smaller measure and that even the Dutch Republic, the trading nation *par excellence*, subscribed to the prevalent idea of nations as rivals in the realms of manufacture and trade (that is, in the mercantile life) and imposed tariffs when it felt threatened. Secondly, that no state ignored the non-mercantile aspects of the economy; the fruits of agriculture, viniculture, husbandry and forestry were praised

81

and not only when they served as raw materials for manufacture (as, for example, wool and leather did), but in their own right as the foundation of the well-being of the most precious resource of all, the population. Finally, an element of anti-mercantilism is noticeable in the more economically advanced countries, in France as well as in England, towards the end of our period. Would economic co-operation across frontiers be possible? was a question posed inside as well as outside government circles.[12] An attempt was made by the Anglo-French commercial treaty of 1713 which, however, the House of Commons by a narrow majority refused to accept, mainly because a lobby in favour of Anglo-Portuguese trade disliked competition, but to some extent also because the idea of co-operation with the ancient enemy was too novel.

The late Professor Heckscher rightly emphasized that mercantilism was an 'ideal' government policy, a plan for obtaining as much as possible of the world's manufacture and trade for one's own state, rather than an accomplished fact: ministers and officials might propose, the facts of economics disposed.[13] Recent studies have tended to show that the planners were less other-worldly or falsely optimistic than this might suggest. Certainly for the French economy well-thought-out and patiently enforced methods to improve the coinage, succour local initiative and inspect the quality of goods for export, have been established, while as far as England is concerned the seventeenth-century flexible protectionist system is now regarded as the main reason for the economic growth of the period. On the other hand we have become even more aware than the last generation of historians of how limited were the powers of governments of our period, whether absolute or not. Distances between the centre of government and outlying provinces were often vast and communications were slow. In France the local noble and, at times, even the local official joined the population in revolts which the Marxist historian would wish to explain as a rising of the oppressed peasants alone.[14] In the Dutch Republic, because of the federal nature of the United Provinces, the States General found it difficult if not impossible to control the privateering ventures of the Zeelanders.[15] Successful obstruction to or ignoring of central decrees which proved unpopular have been uncovered in most countries. The failure of Louis XIV's call-up of 'maritime classes' to man the navy is one case in point, as Asher has demonstrated.[16] In Skaraborg province in Sweden, we learn from a recent case-study, aspects of Charles

88 Interior of the Old Exchange at Amsterdam. Each group of merchants had its fixed place of meeting for arranging credits, making payments and other transactions.

XII's taxation policy were circumvented with official connivance for years on end.[17] The necessary control was simply beyond the means at the disposal of seventeenth-century governments, though in general the oligarchies – governing in the interests of a homogeneous section of society – were more successful than the paternalistic absolute monarchies. It is in this sense that we can speak of the English Parliament and the Dutch States General as being more 'absolute' than the nominally absolute ruler; as the policies decided on were acceptable to the oligarchy, there was greater efficiency (some would say ruthlessness) in imposing them on the rest of the nation, but also greater discipline in accepting taxation of self to finance government policy.

There was, both among the Maritime Powers and elsewhere, a feeling that governments had to take the nation into its confidence, that information and explanation were due. Government gazettes, domestic and foreign newspapers, periodicals and annuals had avid readers and provided a good deal of information. Governments naturally tried to popularize their own policies; but no attempts were made to minimize military disasters. In absolutist Sweden

83

89 *The London Gazette* for the week 7 June to 11 June 1694 announcing a commission for taking subscriptions for the Bank of England

the losses of Poltava were freely admitted; in the constitutional Republic the slaughter at Malplaquet and the disaster at Denain were public knowledge and the losses of ships in battle, with names of men killed or wounded, were posted in the relevant one of the five Admiralty colleges concerned. Appeals to the nation at large were relatively rare, as the stir caused by Louis XIV's proclamation of 1709 attests. Addressed to provincial governors, it was read aloud in the churches, a means of communication common all over Europe for government decrees and messages. Indeed, one of the bonds between churches and central government was the need which governments felt for the parish clergy to disseminate information and maintain morale. The church in Catholic countries became in this respect nearly as 'national' as that in the German and Scandinavian states. One example of this is the way in which the French clergy strove for a unitary Gallic Church and initiated conversion of Huguenots at the local level with considerable success. The age was one in which educated individuals thought a union of all churches sensible and reasonable: Queen Christina was strongly in favour of this and Leibniz worked out a specific plan of how union could be achieved. In a more restricted field, John Robinson, Bishop of London, and Swedish divines proposed a union between the Anglican and the Lutheran churches.[18] In France, where priests strove to bring Huguenots back to the mother church, fanaticism entered into what had not initially been so motivated. Louis XIV was persuaded to revoke the Edict of Nantes on being told that it was now 'unnecessary', there being hardly a Huguenot who had not abjured Protestantism. The King, attracted to the prospect of a unitary religious state for personal reasons as well as reasons of state,★ must bear his full share of responsibility for the persecution of the Huguenots which continued once the premise of the Revocation had been shown to be false.

A common punishment for Huguenots who refused even token conversion – condemnation to the galleys – aroused indignation both then and later, but was in fact meant to be humane (and conditions in the galleys were far better than tradition has pictured them) since the age found torture, in matters of faith at least, repugnant and no state had money enough to keep large numbers of men and women in prison for any length of time. In debtor prisons the person who had a man jailed was in theory responsible for his upkeep, if the debtor could not keep body and soul together from his own or his family's resources. If the offence was against the state it was either a serious one (such as treason) which merited execution, or violation of the law, which was punished by physical maiming of the criminal (branding, the loss of an ear or, in worse cases, a hand) that he might serve as a deterrent to others. In some countries (England and Spain, for instance) transportation became an alternative to execution. The number of prisoners was everywhere deliberately kept low and the 'political prisoner' detained in the Tower or at a continental military fort while his conduct was being investigated was more common than the criminal in prison.

★ At this time Louis hoped to gain favour with the Pope, but he seems also to have been influenced by fear of damnation in the after-life.

Governments needed the money they managed to collect for purposes more vital to the interests of the state than an increase in prisons. Chief among these was the improvement of the armies and the navies, which were thought of as providing work for large sections of the population in the building and upkeep of ships, the forging of arms and cannon, the weaving of cloth and the making of uniforms. But it was the utter dependence on the armed forces for security in an age when European problems loomed large and when success in the rivalry for trade ultimately rested on armies and navies which made these the central object of all governments.

The need for money to finance improvements and increases, whether in men or ships, was perpetual. Indeed, the condemning of the Huguenots to the French galleys, or the sale of Hungarian Protestants and Swedish prisoners of war to those of Venice, is partly to be explained by the need of the galleys for manpower to supplement the traditional source, Turkish and other infidel prisoners of war.[19] The galleys as penitentiaries for able-bodied lawbreakers serving a given term had already become an established fact in France as in Spain. In the galley-fleet, officers had to take good care of their men since on active service their own lives depended less on their knowledge of seamanship than on the strength and discipline with which the crew could row. In the big sailed men-of-war the physical condition of the ordinary sailor was less vital to his officers; and the victualling problems, particularly of large squadrons going to the Baltic in times of war, were great since ships had to sail with last season's butter and cheese, and these, as well as beer and other contracted food, often had to be condemned during the voyage with adverse

90, 91 German infantry depicted on a recruiting poster from Zerbst, Anhalt-Dessau (far left); and Watteau's study of French recruits

92 An arms foundry. Note the protective angle of the hats of the workmen (far right) and the spectators, including women (far left)

93 Below, guns in action. Louis XIV at the crossing of the Rhine preparatory to the invasion of the Dutch Republic, 12 June 1672

94 Anglo-Dutch naval battle, 1666

effect on the crew's health.[20] The fleets themselves were so expensive that states grew careful not to risk them lightly in battle. The frequent engagements of the Anglo-Dutch wars of the 1650s and '60s give way to caution after a single engagement (such as the loss of the British Smyrna fleet in 1690 when its convoy proved no match for the French, or Louis XIV's defeat in the battle of La Hogue of 1692) or to the search, as in the Great Northern War, for an overwhelming conjunction of Russian, Danish and British ships in the hope of a 'safe' annihilation of the Swedish fleet. Indeed, storms and shipwreck accounted for more losses than did battles – among them the total loss of ships and men when Shovell's squadron foundered in 1712 off the Scillies – and the French fleet, once the supremacy of that of the Maritime Powers had been demonstrated, was increasingly diverted to privateering ventures during the War of the Spanish Succession.[21]

Armies were less vulnerable to sudden disaster, and were easier to keep in repair than navies, but they demanded even more money to be effective whether they were, as in the case of the Maritime

Powers, partly composed of auxiliaries and other hired troops, or largely national. Armies fighting abroad could be partly provisioned or re-equipped from booty in battle or taxes levied in occupied countries or districts; but it was no longer true that war paid for itself as long as the army was kept outside its own frontiers, though it was truer of the army of Charles XII than of most. This was so because the Swedish permanent budget of the 1680s (discussed above) financed the regular army and its equipment. But even for Sweden long-term war created problems which could only be solved by the methods of the financial revolution. Between 1715 and 1718 Görtz and other advisers of Charles XII mobilized the resources of Sweden in unprecedented ways by government regulation of imports and exports and the fixing of maximum prices, while the taxation and currency problems were tackled along lines reminiscent of those used by the Maritime Powers between 1702 and 1713. The need for the sinews of war was the most urgent one

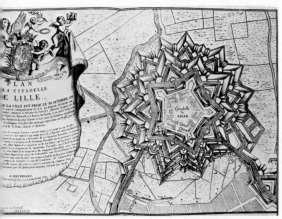

95, 96 Left, the art of Vauban: fortifications at Lille; below left, the Siege of Gibraltar, 1704–05. The victor can be espied on Britannia's shield in the right-hand corner

97 Below, taxes to pay for war: the French poll-tax (*Taxe par Teste*) of 1709

for governments of all the great powers: for armies, for navies and for subsidies to minor allies. Spain was the country most envied by administrators because the Crown of Castile, from its percentage of the output of the mines of Mexico and Peru, possessed bullion to defray the expenses of government – even if lack of initiative from above made it clear that Spain was in temporary eclipse. Other countries had to supplement their store of precious metal and coin by taxes of many kinds from their subjects, and the very wars in which the powers became involved made it in some cases extremely difficult if not impossible to rationalize either the tax-system or the way in which it was administered. Nowhere is this more noticeable than in France. Here useless offices multiplied and became hereditary. Here tax-farmers creamed off money which administrators ardently wanted to divert to the state, though they were prevented from taking the necessary drastic action by the very dependence of the armed forces on a continuous flow of cash. Tsar Peter instigated a system of factory-serfs to equip his armies and increase his exports, but he, like other rulers, suffered from the need for ready money as war-year followed war-year and had to restrict his military operations against Sweden between 1715 and 1721. During the Nine Years War William III was so harassed by his inability to pay his troops that he contemplated (or threatened) abdication;[22] but by increases in the land-tax, as well as by encouraging investment in annuities and lotteries, England was able to finance the War of the Spanish Succession. Such investment was in itself proof of confidence in the government. But it should be noted that by taking on the responsibility for saleable annuities, fixed without taking the age of the original holder into account,[23] England stored up as considerable a debt for the future as did France with her sale of offices: the annual salary to be paid in the future as a consequence of the sale is not so dissimilar to the annuities of the English expedient as might at first glance be assumed. Even those states that had gone furthest on the road of the financial revolution had to face the searching difficulties of post-war crises (the South Sea Bubble in England, Law's crash in France) while the Dutch Republic, the most advanced in the technique of taxing all members of the state, strained its resources to such an extent that it forfeited its great-power position. With no compensatory advantages for the Dutch at the Peace of Utrecht, the Republic between 1713 and 1721 found it necessary to demote itself to the rank of a lesser power.

98 Crown of the Holy Roman Emperor
of the German Nation,
used from 961 to 1792

THE STRUGGLE FOR THE INTERPRETATION OF 1648

One of the factors making for European unrest – however war-weary the powers were after the Thirty Years War – was the determination of the Austrian House of Habsburg that the settlement of 1648 was not to be the final word. The sovereignty which had been accorded by the Treaty of Westphalia to France over Metz, Toul and Verdun was much resented. These three bishoprics, in French possession though not sovereignty since the end of Charles V's reign, had been the reward which the German Protestant princes fighting Charles had promised Henry II of France for his intervention on their behalf after the defeat at Mühlberg. They had been duly handed over by the Peace of Cateau-Cambrésis in 1559. But the old wounds were reopened and salt thrown in by the French claim to sovereignty exacted at the Peace of 1648. The reversal of this clause became one of the desiderata of Austrian policy: the claim for Metz, Toul and Verdun was heard – though never acted on – at every big peace-making in our period and its echo began to reverberate once more during the nationalist struggles of the nineteenth century. By championing a reversal, the Austrian Habsburgs took on a 'German mission' against France which enabled Vienna to recoup in a moral sense some of the prestige lost by concessions on the religious issue. The Empire was divided in religion but unitary, it was hoped, in the opposition against foreign powers which were in possession of German soil. There was, however, nothing equivocal about the 1648 transfer of sovereignty over the three bishoprics to France, nor about the investiture 'for ever' of Wismar, the bishoprics of Bremen and Verden, and part of Pomerania (Swedish Pomerania as it was called in Europe after 1648) in the Swedish crown, possessions which gave Sweden two votes in the Imperial Diet. As a German prince the Swedish King could now be asked to contribute his 'Roman month' (to use the current phrase for contingents agreed to by the Diet in support of the Empire or the Emperor in need); but the prospect of help by one of the foremost military powers of the day was overshadowed by fear of the influence Lutheran Sweden might

91

wield in North Germany where its ruler took part in the rota of directorship of the Lower Saxony circle. Vienna's distrust is clearly signalled by the Emperor's lending the full strength of his power to the town of Bremen when it pleaded that it had not, as Sweden claimed, been ceded with the bishopric of Bremen. It was more than enough that Sweden now held Stettin, a rich port, and Stralsund, that safe harbour protected by the island of Rügen, as *satisfactio* for her effort on behalf of the Protestant cause during the Thirty Years War. If the town of Bremen became hers, she would be able to command the outlets of the Elbe and the Weser as she did that of the Oder. Habsburg opposition prevented this. In the first clash over interpretation of the 1648 treaty Sweden was therefore the loser. Chasing Sweden out of her gains of 1648 became a further objective with which Austria could sympathize, though it was the Elector of Brandenburg who most resented Sweden's possession of that valuable part of Pomerania to which he and his successors regarded themselves (by the will of the last Duke) as having as good a legal claim as to the larger but poorer Eastern Pomerania which he had been permitted to inherit. The Elector realized that other gains stipulated for Brandenburg at the 1648 peace (the bishoprics of Kamen, Minden and Halberstadt – as well as the reversion of Magdeburg) were meant to compensate for the loss of Swedish Pomerania, but the loss rankled all the same; and Hantsch's description of the Great Northern War as *ein später Sprosse*[1] of the Thirty Years War is illuminating.

Where interpretation of the 1648 treaty gave rise to an earlier and more prolonged struggle was in respect of that part of Alsace which the Austrian Habsburgs had ceded to France as compensation for her war effort. Possession of the ten Alsatian towns (the so-called *Décapole*) did not entitle the King of France to a seat on the Imperial Diet; but the question whether the towns had been ceded with or without sovereignty[2] became an issue between Louis XIV and the Emperor Leopold just because the latter wanted to rob France of any basis for interference and influence in the Empire. Louis XIV in his turn took every opportunity to extend his power and his land in Alsace; for him it was a useful base behind Franche-Comté and Lorraine which might facilitate the absorption of these old Burgundian territories into France and thus help to strengthen the exposed eastern frontier. Distrust of the Emperor was a feature of both Mazarin's and Louis XIV's foreign policy; had not Ferdinand III, against his pledge in the Peace of 1648, persisted in sending military help to the Spanish Habsburgs

99 Louis XIV enters Strasbourg, 30 September 1681, accepting the keys of the town from magistrates kneeling in submission. Strasbourg retained, however, autonomy in local and religious affairs and was in effect a free, Protestant town in an absolute, Catholic state

with whom France continued at war till 1659? The reunion policy on which Louis embarked when Leopold was engaged in struggles with the Turks, the very halfhearted way in which Louis, the 'Most Christian Majesty' in the hierarchy of courtesy titles, sustained the fight against the Sultan, is proof of French fears of Imperial designs. So is the occupation of Strassburg in 1681: the town which helped Leopold by opening its bridges for troops invading France in the Dutch War had to become *Strasbourg* so that the 'key to the door of the French house' might be turned. Louis's possession of it was recognized by the Treaty of Ryswick though Austria decided to challenge it as soon as feasible, and did so between 1702 and 1714. French attempts to conquer fortified places on the far side of the Rhine are also evidence of fear of Habsburg revenge; it was not (as Gaston Zeller has shown) the demand for 'the natural frontier' which lay behind such efforts during the wars of our period but rather a policy of reinsurance. Louis needed places to bargain with at the conference table lest he be forced to give up the French interpretation of the 1648 treaty: full sovereignty over the *Décapole* and no reversal of the sovereignty over Metz, Toul and Verdun. In this struggle Louis was successful; at Nijmegen, Ryswick, Utrecht, Rastadt and Baden the French interpretation was upheld however much the Emperor and his diplomats struggled to prevent it.[3] But in the process Louis XIV drew upon himself a general German distrust. At Ryswick in 1697 the French King renounced his reunion policy (a normal enough practice of trying to maximize gains by examining old charters

93

and treaties to see whether one's new possessions had 'dependencies' that could be incorporated) and restored what he had taken, but the damage was done. He could and was pictured in German propaganda pamphlets as the robber of German soil, and Lisola's and Leibniz's warnings against the *monarchium universalum*, which they argued to be Louis's aim, were heeded.

Louis began to realize, since he learnt by experience, that there was as little hope of obtaining Lorraine by the sword as the Southern Netherlands and that his efforts to absorb Lorraine had done him more damage in Germany than his nibbling at the Low Countries and his conquest of Franche-Comté (which, incidentally, Austria tried to reverse both in the Nine Years War and in the War of the Spanish Succession). But even so, and in spite of the considerable success mentioned above, Louis XIV gravely misjudged the German situation. He assumed that the German princes were as alarmed as he was at Leopold's gains in the Turkish wars: he never tired of preaching that their best means of preventing the Emperor from reverting to the *Monarchie* plan was co-operation with himself. They, on the other hand, felt safe enough in their *Landeshoheit*, guaranteed by France and Sweden, to ignore his pleas and were content to reap what advantages they could from Austro-French rivalry. Such advantages were not negligible. Money from Louis XIV flowed into German coffers, and honours and titles from the one true fountain, the Emperor. Only he could make a new elector (as he did in respect of Hanover in 1692) or agree to the title of king for a German prince (as he did for Brandenburg in 1700, upon which the Elector Frederick William assumed, in 1701, the title Frederick I, King in Prussia) as payment for alliance against France; only he had a hold over the German princes in general by delaying investitures and formalities for titles – those for the Elector of Hanover were not complete till 1711 – and, even more importantly, when changes of

ownership of land inside the Empire were concerned. He rejoiced with Hanover and Prussia that Sweden lost most of her possessions in the Empire by 1715, but he maintained a political hold over the Elector by postponing his investiture as Duke of Bremen and Verden and over the King by his delay in recognizing Prussian conquests in Swedish Pomerania.

Charles VI thus had little incentive to respond to the overtures which Louis XIV, in the last year of his life, made for collaboration between Catholic France and Catholic Austria against the growing power of the North German Protestant princes. Louis's hint at mutual concern for the Catholic cause of James Stuart was, correctly, interpreted as springing from French fears that Georg Ludwig of Hanover – George I of Great Britain since August 1714 – might repudiate the Peace of Utrecht and reopen the war against France. Vienna, being well informed of the Elector's determination to use his forces, Hanoverian and British, in the war against Sweden knew that these fears were ungrounded. Indeed, the knowledge that there would be no speedy opportunity to reverse the decisions of Rastadt and Baden led the Austrians first of all to plan for a share of the booty in North Germany (Wismar was what they hoped to gain) and, secondly, to keep the negotiations with Louis spinning to see how they would develop.[4] The Ottoman attack on Venice at the end of 1714, however, reawakened mistrust of France. Was Louis, while ostensibly working for an alliance between Vienna and Paris, secretly inciting the Turks to war? The negotiations were abruptly ended, Louis rebuffed and the 'diplomatic revolution' postponed till 1756.

THE TURKISH MENACE

In the 1630s and 1640s the Turks had been quiescent, but in the second half of the seventeenth century they began to advance once more towards the west of Europe. They were pressed from the Muscovite side. That artificial desert, which had been allowed to develop in the dry steppe between Tartary on the one hand and the Ukraine on the other, became an area of conflict once Khmelnitsky had taken the Ukrainians from Polish suzerainty into that of the Muscovite Tsar. From now on Russian hopes of gaining access to the Black Sea were aroused and the first Russo-Turkish war broke out in 1677. The Russian threat was contained, but seems to have sparked off a movement for expansion in Turkey. The administrative skill of the

101 The Parthenon, used by the Turks as a powder magazine, was severely damaged when a shell, fired on behalf of the Holy League, exploded the stores (see p. 99)

Kuprülü family, a veritable dynasty of able grand viziers, released new forces in an Ottoman empire which had digested the gains of the sixteenth century. Expansion was desired both by land and by sea: Turkish fleets invaded Venetian-held Crete in 1645 – and though the struggle for the island lasted more than twenty years it ended with an Ottoman victory in 1669 – and Turkish armies poured from Greater Hungary towards the heart of Europe. In 1664 they were stopped by Montecuccoli in the battle of St-Gotthard (a battle in which French troops also participated, while a French galley-squadron, under the papal banner, sailed to succour Crete in 1669). But the hordes of Janissaries and Sipahis continued to march, and in 1683 they besieged Vienna itself.

By this time the enmity between Austria and France had come into the open. Leopold renounced his secret partition treaty of 1668 with Louis for a sharing of the Spanish inheritance, and by 1674 openly embarked on his German mission, stung, if not by Louis's invasion of the Dutch Republic (which, since 1648, lay outside the borders of the Empire), then by French interference in Germany and Louis's encouragement of a potential anti-Habsburg League of the Rhine. Even more alarming was the appetite Louis betrayed for Franche-Comté, a territory to which – as to the whole of Spain and its empire – Leopold intended to uphold his claim. He based this on a family arrangement of 1618 which laid down an Austrian Habsburg succession in Spain should the Spanish Habsburg branch die out

96

104 Turkish method of crossing rivers and canals with booty ▶

102 Spahis (i.e. Sipahis) and
Janissaries, Turkish élite forces

103 Prince Eugène of Savoy,
Habsburg commander and victor
over the Turks

(and vice versa) and on various testamentary and other documents, but was also motivated by the pride and ambition he felt at being the father of a son, Joseph, born in 1678 to his third, German, wife. (This wife, Eleonora of Neuburg, bore him a second son, Charles, in 1685.) With rivalry between them so obvious, Louis could not bring himself to support Leopold against the Turks; indeed, he secretly rejoiced at Leopold's being tied down in the east, and his own diplomacy at the Porte made it pretty clear that France would not put obstacles in the path of a Turkish attack on Austria.[5] Moral scruples, as well as concern for his reputation, prevented him from allying with the Sultan or actively helping the Ottomans, and his offer of an armistice and a truce to the Spanish Habsburgs and their allies in the Empire was couched in terms which ranged France with the Christian community of Europe against the infidel.

Louis's reputation suffered all the same. French troops were missing at the defence of Vienna – that great common experience of Austrians, Germans, Poles and a variety of auxiliaries from all over Europe, including some Englishmen in the service of foreign rulers[6] – and Louis was accused after the truce of Regensburg, arranged in 1684 (on terms which permitted France to keep for twenty years what she had taken from Spain and gained by the reunions), of extorting too high a price for refraining from stabbing Leopold in the back as the Turks were driven on to the defensive. In the Nine Years War, the first Grand Alliance against France convinced Louis that the disadvantages of the reunion policy outweighed its gains, and at Ryswick he returned what the Chambres des Réunions had claimed for France, and though he stuck to Strasbourg he had to return Luxemburg to Spain. But he did not grasp the opportunity to bring France into the European preoccupation with resistance to the Sultan and refused to take part in the War of the Holy League, organized since 1684 and for the larger part financed by the Pope, with the objective of driving the Turks out of Europe altogether. The Venetians, the Poles and the Austrian forces under Prince Eugène of Savoy (the would-be soldier of France once spurned by Louis) were the main allies. The rulers of Russia came in by 1686 when Vatican diplomacy had persuaded John Sobieski that it was his Christian duty to let bygones be bygones, to forget Polish losses at the hands of the Russians in the 1660s and to seek, at the side of his traditional enemy, the Tsar, compensation from the Ottomans. Podolia and that part of Ukraine lost to Turkey were indeed regained by 1699, but hopes of further progress – into Moldavia and Wallachia – were not fulfilled. Some fresh conquests at the expense of the Turks were, however, made by the other members of the League. Tsar Peter, using a fleet built secretly inland and transported down the river, secured a foothold on the Black Sea at Azov; Venice gained the Morea and in the process inflicted inestimable damage on the Acropolis when Count Königsmarck, a Swede in Venetian service, bombarded Athens from the sea. The Emperor, who had found in Eugène a general of genius and persistence, overshadowing even the victorious Montecuccoli of the first Turkish campaign of his reign, made the most spectacular progress and became increasingly anxious to turn his attention to the west where, given the frail health of Carlos II, the Spanish succession issue might at any moment enter a critical phase. The Maritime Powers, well aware of this, and also keen to restore peace for the sake of their trade to the Levant, offered mediation. At the Peace of Karlowitz of 1699 the Holy League – in spite of Tsar Peter's protests and those of the Pope – came to terms with the Sultan: the Morea remained in Venetian hands, the Austrian frontier advanced to encompass nearly the whole of Greater Hungary, the Vatican was gratified by the number of Balkan Europeans freed from the suzerainty of Islam. By the summer of 1700 Tsar Peter, who had found alternative plans for expansion during his tour of Europe in 1697–98, made a truce with the Porte which left Azov with Russia for twenty years.

The impetus of Turkish advance had been broken; time was needed for regrouping and preparing a comeback. When a good opportunity offered in 1711 during the Great Northern War the Sultan regained Azov, but the ensuing struggle within Turkey between those who urged greater involvement in Charles XII's war against the Tsar and those who wanted to march west once more was decided in favour of the latter. In late 1714 the war against Venetia was launched and the Morea recaptured, but Austria – drawn in by the hope of new gains – crowned her successes with Eugène's capture of Belgrade in 1718. Louis XIV did not live to see this triumph of the Emperor Charles VI, but even during Louis's reign the *gloire* which came to the House of Habsburg by its identification with the defence of Europe against the Turks was astounding. The Emperor was shown to have a Christian European mission as well as a German one, and French diplomats reported to Louis that the Italians in 1701 welcomed the Austrian forces with the cry of '*Il Imperatore!*'[7]

'This is a war about trade.' Louis XIV's comment on the War of the Spanish Succession[8] might surprise those who prefer a (largely false) dividing-line between the French Sun King, intent on nothing but war and glory, and devoted ministers, principally Colbert, who worked for the peaceful pursuits of trade. That England's wars with France after 1688 were 'in parts war for trade' has long been accepted.[9] Indeed, the very dilemma of the Spanish succession issue lay in the impossibility of solving it in a way which would simultaneously satisfy the Maritime Powers and those who had a legitimate claim on the succession. Before 1688 the rivalry between England and the Dutch Republic had been open and violent. Though the two had obvious interests in common in the 1650s – the Puritan Commonwealth and the *stadhouder*-less Republic being equally anti-monarchical and pro-Protestant – competition in trade, in overseas settlement and in naval power to protect economic interests forced them into war, however much Cromwell and Amsterdam deplored hostilities. The very success of England in the first Anglo-Dutch war (1652–54) contributed to that which broke out in the 1660s;[10]

105 Gobelins tapestry commemorating the marriage of Louis XIV to Maria Teresa, daughter of Philip IV of Spain, 1660

106 Louis XIV and his family, 1670, painted by J. Nocret. Note the cupid- or *putti*-like 'adoring' treatment of the younger children in this, 'the century of the child', and compare Ills. 11 and 151 for other examples of *putti*

LE ROY DE FRANCE.
l'Nome immortel Chef de la St. Ligue

Mon soleil par sa force eclaira l'heretique.
Il chassa tout d'un coup les brouillards de Calvin:
Non pas par un Zele divin,
Mais a fin de cacher ma fine Politique.

107, 108 French figurative plaque of the Sun, an ancient symbol of kings, consciously used in French propaganda for the absolute monarchy; and an enemy caricature of Louis XIV as the exterminator of Protestantism

but the glory of the peace of 1654 (Dutch total acceptance of the English navigation laws) could not be matched by the peace of 1667. Dutch naval tactics had been bolder than in the earlier war. The raid on the Medway was an unpleasant surprise. 'The devil must be shitting Dutchmen', Pepys – grieving for the loss of naval ships and installations – confided to his *Diary*. Plague and fire compelled peace overtures which the Dutch welcomed. The loss of their New Netherlands in North America seemed insignificant compared with the gain of a modified Navigation Act, which improved their trading position in Europe. Their overseas trade was, moreover, improved by their acquisition of Surinam. To the Dutch after 1667, as before, the traditional alliance with France seemed the natural one. The textbook story of their concerted co-operation with England and Sweden stopping Louis XIV dead in his tracks and forcing him to end his aggression in the Spanish Netherlands in 1668 does not stand up to examination. A variety of reasons, however, chief among them the unwillingness of the town of Amsterdam to divide the Spanish Netherlands with Louis XIV lest the Scheldt be opened and Antwerp become a serious trading rival,[11] Louis's own attempt to teach the Dutch a lesson by his invasion in 1672 and the ambitions of William III for the crown of England, did bring the Maritime Powers together in a firm alliance against a France which clearly aspired to equality in naval power and overseas trade and was using prohibitive tariffs against them both to achieve this.

From his miscalculations in 1672 and 1688, Louis learnt that he could not hope to dominate the Spanish Netherlands against the will of the Dutch and that the navies of the two Maritime Powers combined, after the Glorious Revolution, could prevent French expansion overseas into areas which they wanted closed. Here lay the stumbling-block to any division of the Spanish empire in Europe and overseas between Louis and Leopold, the two most powerful claimants, should Carlos II die (as expected) without an heir of his own body. For while Leopold hinted at his willingness to give the Spanish Netherlands and/or land in Spanish America to buy off Louis, Louis knew that these were the areas in which the Maritime Powers would not tolerate the French; while those over which William III and Heinsius were prepared to visualize French suzerainty – parts of Italy[12] – were inalienable in Leopold's opinion and confirmed him in his determination to claim the whole of Spain for the Austrian Habsburgs.

The problem which this posed for Europe, tired and financially exhausted after the long wars of 1672–78 and 1689–97, was recognized by William III and Louis XIV, who hoped by the moral pressure of an agreement between France and the Maritime Powers to force the Spanish and Austrian Habsburgs to accept a solution which would not disturb the balance of power. The novelty of this attempt has been analyzed by the late Mark Thomson, who also wrote the pioneer study of how the co-operation between William III and Louis XIV broke down between 1700 and 1702 due to the latter's mistakes.[13] It could be argued, however, that the initiative lay more with Madrid and Vienna than with Paris, London and The Hague, and that the Spanish determination not to suffer partition or curtailment, aided by Leopold's intransigence, gave Madrid the trump card.[14] Leopold's intransigence, which, superficially regarded, seems foolhardy, is in its turn explained by his conviction (justified, as events proved) that if war resulted he would not fight alone: the Maritime Powers would sooner or later be drawn on to his side since their economic interests clashed with those of France.

The rivalry between Louis and Leopold over the Spanish succession has something of the character of sibling rivalry. They were first cousins, Louis's mother having been the elder daughter of Philip III of Spain, Leopold's the younger. Leopold had been promised the hand of Philip IV's elder daughter, Maria Teresa; but she was claimed for Louis by the Peace of the Pyrenees of 1659, which ended the long Franco-Spanish war (begun in 1635), and Leopold had to be content with the younger sister, Margarita Teresa, who came of marriageable age only in 1666. From the legalistic point of view, Leopold could argue that the renunciation which Maria Teresa had been made to sign before Philip IV permitted her marriage to Louis XIV remained valid, in spite of Mazarin's clever move in specifying nullification if (as transpired) her dowry was not paid within the stipulated time. Judged within the realm of *Realpolitik,* Leopold's stand is weakened, however, when we take into account that he forced the only child of his own Spanish marriage, Maria Antonia, to renounce her rights in favour of her two half-brothers of Leopold's German marriage. In 1698 Louis XIV and the Maritime Powers hit upon the sensible idea that Maria Antonia's son, the young Joseph Ferdinand of Bavaria, should inherit Spain and her empire, with minor consolation prizes for the two disappointed families: Naples and Sicily to go to the Dauphin of France as well as the Guipúzcoa province of Spain, and the Spanish Netherlands to the Archduke Charles, Leopold's second son. Leopold, however, protested strongly at his grandson's prospects; he would have none of them even when Carlos II of Spain adopted the Electoral Prince of Bavaria as his sole heir – that is, without consolation prizes to France and Austria – since he wished for the succession to go to his own sons, preferably Joseph, the elder, though they had less Spanish blood than his grandson.

The Second Partition Treaty between Louis and William, which became necessary after the death of the Electoral Prince in 1699, was even less to the taste of the Spaniards. Since the Archduke Charles was now named the main heir, the Dauphin's share had to be somewhat increased – the Duchy of Milan was added to Naples and Sicily with a secret proviso (lest Leopold should fear the French so close to his own dominions) that it should be offered to the Duke of Lorraine in exchange for France's gaining Lorraine. If that Duke refused, Milan would be offered to the Duke of Savoy in return for part of his territories. This would round off the French south-eastern frontier (though not as satisfactorily as the incorporation of Lorraine) and gratify a ruler who had expectations in Spain according to the will of his kinsman Philip IV. (Victor Amadeus II's great-grandmother had been a daughter of Philip II.)

As it turned out, the Duke of Lorraine accepted the exchange in principle almost as soon as it was proposed to him; and conversations then began between Louis XIV and the Duke of Savoy for a further exchange, that of the whole of Piedmont and Savoy for Naples and Sicily. William III initially opposed this idea, but was converted to favour the exchange once he realized the strength of English resentment (commercially motivated) at the prospect of Naples and Sicily coming under French control. Carlos II's death on

111 Louis XIV accepts at Versailles the will of Carlos II which made Philip of Anjou, Louis's second grandson, King of Spain

11 November 1700 was particularly inopportune, William wrote to Heinsius, since the negotiations with Savoy had not been brought to fruition.[15]

Had they succeeded, they would not have altered the outcome. For Carlos II and his ministers had in October contrived a will which put Louis XIV into a dilemma from which he could, so they rightly argued, escape only by becoming the champion of an undivided Spanish monarchy. The whole of Spain and Spain overseas was left to the Duke of Anjou, Louis XIV's second grandson, a boy of seventeen, whom Carlos's advisers reckoned they could easily turn into 'a good Spaniard' once he became Philip V; though if Louis refused, the same offer would be made to the Archduke Charles or – should the Archduke not be available – to the Duke of Savoy. That the French candidate was top of the list was due not only to the proximity of France's armed forces (she could be mighty in defence of the entire monarchy as well as a tough opponent of an Austrian Habsburg candidate), but also to the hope on the part of some Spanish ministers and officials of regeneration in the administration and economy on the French pattern.

◀ 109 Far left, Carlos II, the last Habsburg King of Spain. The inbreeding of the Spanish with the Austrian Habsburgs (see also Ill. 78 for typical Habsburg lip) made Carlos of the deformed jaw a barren invalid. His death in November 1700 created a serious problem for those concerned with the European balance of power
110 Left, the Archduke Charles of Austria, 'Carlos III' of the anti-French coalition after 1704

Here was the proverbial cleft stick. Louis could not doubt that Leopold would accept if France refused, for the Emperor – alone of the rulers of Europe – looked with equanimity and even hope towards a restoration of the dominions of Charles V, who had ruled the Burgundian, the Spanish and the Austrian realms. While Louis and William and their advisers argued the inadmissibility of such a restoration whether under Austrian or French auspices, Leopold had significantly refused terms which Louis offered him during the Nine Years War: the whole of the Spanish inheritance to go to the Archduke Charles, Louis solemnly renouncing for himself and all his heirs any share of it, the only proviso being that Leopold must agree that Austria and Spain never be governed by one and the same ruler.[16] (In return, Louis wanted the French interpretation of 1648 and the gains of Nijmegen guaranteed.) Nor could Louis expect, were he to refuse Carlos's will, that the Maritime Powers would go to war against Leopold to prevent Austria accepting it on the Archduke's behalf. Against the loss of the territories promised France in the Second Partition Treaty (the Guipúzcoa, Milan and Naples and Sicily) must be set the non-resurrection of the empire of Charles V, commercial opportunities in Spanish America for French trading companies, and the prospect – in time – of frontier rectifications by exchanges of territory: for example, the Guipúzcoa for French Cerdagne and Roussillon. Louis XIV therefore accepted the will. The impossibility of his compensating the Maritime Powers by territorial concessions or even commercial ones on Spain's behalf at a time when the Spaniards were particularly touchy helped to bring war closer. Indeed, as soon as William III and Heinsius found that 'the Spaniards had asked the French into their house' – an invitation they had not seriously envisaged[17] – they encouraged Leopold to march his army into Spanish Italy in the hope of making Louis amenable to concessions. That such compromises were not within Louis's power they found hard to grasp, both in 1701 and during the many abortive peace negotiations in the war which officially broke out in 1702, but which – as far as Leopold and William III were concerned – had started already at the turn of the year 1700–01.

Leopold was thus proved right in his forecast of the great powers line-up in a succession war. That he and his allies did not succeed in imposing the Archduke Charles on Spain as 'Carlos III' was due in some measure to the fact that the main belligerents – France and the Spain of Philip V versus Leopold and the Grand Alliance – were evenly matched, given that the German auxiliaries had their eyes turned towards the Great Northern War and Leopold himself was preoccupied with Hungary. But it was also due to a growing discrepancy between the war aims of the Maritime Powers, the Dutch favouring a compromise peace that would leave Philip V at least Naples and Sicily, while England (mindful of secret promises by 'Carlos III' of separate commercial advantages) stuck to the whole monarchy for the Austrian candidate.[18] When war-weariness at last produced a change of government in Whitehall, the Republic had become identified with Whig intransigence, and the new men in power, Oxford and St John, told the Dutch bluntly that 'England could and would make peace on its own and needed no mediator'.[19] The death of the Emperor Joseph in 1711 (he had succeeded Leopold in 1705) facilitated public acceptance in England of a separate Anglo-French peace which benefited both parties: France obtained the principality of Orange and maintained a Bourbon neighbour, since Philip remained ruler in Spain on sacrificing Gibraltar and Minorca to Britain and transferring to her the *Asiento*, the exclusive right to import 4,000 African slaves per annum to Spanish America for thirty years.[20] This had been granted in 1701 – though for a lesser period – to a French company (with compensation arranged to the Portuguese holders) much to the disquiet of the Maritime Powers since the *Asiento* was supposed to offer brilliant opportunities for a semi-legal trade with Spain's colonies. The Dutch Republic, a former holder of the *Asiento*, was left out in the cold, in spite of Anglo-Dutch wartime agreements to share all advantages. The Tory government also repudiated the one *quid pro quo* which the Whigs had bound themselves by treaty to tolerate in return for Dutch acceptance of British war aims in the critical years 1706–09: namely, the commercial domination of the Southern Netherlands via an enlarged 'barrier' of towns garrisoned by Dutch troops. When this barrier concept had been first mooted at the Congress of Ryswick in respect of a few border towns and brought into being by a Spanish-Dutch agreement of 1698,[21] the chief concern had been security – to guard against a French attack. In course of time, however (and particularly during the Anglo-Dutch *condominium* of the Southern Netherlands after 1706), the commercial advantages which could be gained from such 'barrier towns' were realized and exploited. The Southern Netherlands, by the Anglo-French agreement, was to become Austrian, with provision for a modest Dutch 'barrier', and

Philip V's Spain would also be shorn of all her Italian possessions: Milan, Naples and Sardinia going to Austria, and Sicily to the Duke of Savoy.

The withdrawal of British troops from the Allied armies effectively imposed the Anglo-French terms on the Dutch, the Prussians and the Portuguese by 1713. Charles VI fought on in his own cause and the name of the Empire; but by 1714 he felt bound to make peace with France (partly because of Turkish warlike preparations) though he remained nominally at war with Spain and did not relinquish his Spanish title till 1720. Indeed, he kept a Spanish court of ministers and advisers in Vienna, and tension between the Emperor and Philip V left Italy in an unsettled position for several decades since Spain at large (to say nothing of Philip and his second wife, Elisabeth Farnese) could not reconcile itself to the loss of the Italian possessions. George I defeated Spanish attempts between 1717 and 1718 at the reconquest of Sicily and Naples, fearing that one breach in the settlement of 1713 might bring with it others. The distrust and alarm felt in Britain at the negotiations of Philip V's then chief minister, Alberoni, with the Pretender, contributed to the orders for attacking the Spanish fleet; but concern for all the gains (not only the Protestant succession) of the Peace of Utrecht was operative. Here Parliament was stiffer than George I, forcing him to retract an offer made to Spain to restore Gibraltar in return for Philip's entering into a 'peace plan of the south' worked out by George and his secretary of state, James Stanhope.[22]

The outcome of the 1717–20 hostilities (in which the Duke of Orléans, as Regent for Louis XV, supported Britain) was to settle the outstanding problem of the Spanish succession struggle by the Treaties of Madrid and The Hague. Charles VI renounced his claims to the crown of Spain in return for Philip V's recognizing the Austrian possessions in Italy which now included Sicily, Victor Amadeus having been prevailed on to exchange this island for the less valuable Sardinia. European diplomacy was much bedevilled, though not imperilled, after 1720 by Philip and Elisabeth's efforts to settle sons of their marriage in Italy.* Charles VI's anxiety to obtain international recognition of his daughter's claim (ahead of the daughters of his late elder brother, the Emperor Joseph) to succeed as ruler of the Habsburg territories facilitated the entry of 'baby Don Carlos' into Parma and Tuscany. And during the Wars of the Polish and Austrian Successions (1733–38 and 1740–48), which can be labelled

* Three sons of Philip's first marriage, to Maria Luisa of Savoy, were alive at the time of his second marriage in 1714.

'the Wars of the Italian successions',[23] successful Franco-Spanish military co-operation ensured that the reversion of Lorraine was stipulated for France (it became French on the death of Stanislaus Leszczyński in 1766), that Don Carlos became ruler of Naples and Sicily while his younger brother (Don Felipe) took over Parma, and that Tuscany fell to the Duke of Lorraine's share. But the spirit of the 1720 settlement was upheld, since it was laid down that Don Carlos held Naples and Sicily as a *secundo-geniture* only: he could not keep them if he inherited Spain and, when he somewhat unexpectedly succeeded to the Spanish crown in 1759, he had to leave Naples and Sicily to his second son. This clause he did not challenge. The division of the Spanish succession had become accepted in so far as Italy was concerned: Minorca (regained in 1783) and Gibraltar still rankled.

THE PARTITION OF THE SWEDISH EMPIRE

The Spanish succession problem had been one which was clearly foreseen. Indeed, poor Carlos II, whose disabilities were the result of excessive inbreeding between Spanish and Austrian Habsburgs for the very sake of the family alliance, had been 'an unconscionable time dying'. The causes of the Great Northern War (from 1700 to 1721) were more diffuse and less diplomatic effort was expended in the hope of averting it. That Danes and Swedes distrusted each other was well known. Denmark-Norway had not accepted her losses of territory on the Scandinavian peninsula (Denmark had ceded Scania, Halland and Blekinge and Norway Jæmteland, Herjedal and Båhuslen between 1643 and 1658) and had entered the Dutch War of 1672–78 as soon as Sweden got involved on the French side, in a vain attempt at reconquest. Since it suited France and the Maritime Powers that the northern crowns share control of the Sound, Denmark looked around for other allies to restore the good old days when the Sound could be looked upon as 'a stream that runs through the dominions of the King of Denmark', with no exception for Sweden in the payment of Sound dues. Sweden now possessed Bremen and Verden to the west of Jutland and Wismar and Pomerania to the east, and had, moreover, an alliance with the Duke of Holstein-Gottorp which amounted to a protectorate. Successive dukes could withstand Danish attempts to reabsorb ducal lands in Sleswig and Holstein in their knowledge of a Swedish guarantee of possessions and sovereignty;[24] but Sweden would not welcome any real relaxation of tension between the dukes and the crown of Denmark since it was by virtue of the Holstein-Gottorp alliance, which linked Swedish territories in the Empire, that she possessed a back-door entry into Jutland. It was by this door that Torstensson in 1643 and Charles X in 1655 had forced gains on the Scandinavian peninsula. The 'natural frontiers' on the peninsula could be and were demanded at the conference table when Copenhagen was threatened from the south. Once the new frontiers were achieved, the Swedes were able to defend them between 1675 and 1678 and again in 1709–19. Sweden thus saw the Holstein-Gottorp alliance as the first defence line of her great-power position, a means to curb, by the prospect of invasions on the earlier pattern, Danish ambitions for reconquest of provinces lost, expansion into the Empire or a resumption of her East Baltic ambitions.

The Holstein-Gottorp problem was advertised to the world at large by forceful Danish attempts to deny the ducal (and Swedish) interpretation of the sovereignty Denmark had accepted in 1658, and in particular of the *jus armorum* aspect of it. This quarrel led to long conferences at Altona between 1682 and 1692 which, when William III and his allies desired Sweden's participation in the Nine Years War, brought a guarantee by the Maritime Powers and the House of Hanover of the Duke's sovereignty. Danish resumption of the struggle, as soon as continued Swedish neutrality in that war became obvious, caused a conference of guarantors at Pinneberg; but while it deliberated, Danish diplomacy was actively preparing a coalition to attack Sweden.[25] The moment seemed opportune, since Charles XI had died in 1697, leaving a son not yet 15 to become king. The Swedish high nobility was assumed to be dissatisfied to the point of making common cause with Sweden's enemies. Augustus of Saxony* was won for the coalition – though he cleverly managed to lull Stockholm's suspicions – and hard preparatory work in Moscow bore fruit when Tsar Peter accepted that his allies in the War of the Holy League were determined on peace with the Turks. Russia had never regarded expansion to the Baltic and to the Black Sea as mutually exclusive; they were both desirable, but would have to be pursued as and when opportunity offered. The memory of the years between 1560 and 1590 when Russia had a foothold in Estonia was kept alive and, whatever treaties had been signed admitting Sweden's possession of Estonia and the ancient Muscovy lands of Ingria and Karelia, Tsar Peter argued in terms of inviolable rights. Already the role which a 'window towards the west' would play

* His name as Elector was Frederick Augustus, but it would be pedantic not to use Augustus after his election as King of Poland in 1697.

for the future of Russia was shaping in the Tsar's head under the stimulus of his first tour of Europe: a Muscovy in direct contact with the great trading powers would become a modern Russia and the Baltic German population, experts in commerce, would contribute to this. Russia, so long cut off from technological and economic change by conscious Polish and Swedish policies, would be thrown open to European influences.

The only way in which Sweden could avoid war was by a sacrifice of the Holstein-Gottorp alliance, to be signalled by a marriage between Sophie, a princess of Denmark, and Charles XII. The Swedish advisers of the young King were quite keen on the marriage but unwilling, since they regarded vital interests to be at stake, to pay the price asked. With this refusal the die was cast and the coalition dovetailed their plans for attack. Augustus would march his Saxon troops into Livonia and attempt to surprise Riga, Frederick IV would clear Sleswig and Holstein of ducal troops and their Swedish auxiliaries preparatory to an attack on Scania; the Tsar would fall upon Ingria as soon as he obtained his truce with the Turks. Other powers were asked to join the coalition; Brandenburg-Prussia was interested, but her first priority was the western theatre of war where she was tied to the Grand Alliance as 'payment' for her royal title and by hopes of territorial gains. But as the Great Northern War continued beyond the War of the Spanish Succession, opportunities recurred for German princes, resentful of Sweden's gains of 1648, to join in the struggle for the partition of her trans-Baltic possessions. In 1715 Prussia and Hanover officially became enemies of Sweden, both having taken the decisive steps which divided belligerency from neutrality in 1714. Many attempts, before and after 1714, had been made to end the Great Northern War by mediation, but these had foundered on the strength of interests which could not be reconciled. Sweden, the attacked party, did not want to sacrifice territory and the anti-Swedish coalition were determined on solid gains – hence the appeal to the dice of war could not be withstood.

The very length of the war (1700 to 1721) proves the strength of Sweden, but also the tenacity of the opponent who emerged as the most determined one, Tsar Peter of Russia, who fought hardest when he fought alone between 1706 and 1709. After the Russian victory of Poltava in that year the anti-Swedish coalition, depleted by Denmark's separate peace of 1700 and Saxony's of 1706, was reconstituted and efforts to recruit new members redoubled, while

Charles XII spent five years in Turkey: a captive, first, of his wounded foot, then of the Habsburg closure of the Ottoman frontier during the plague years. His attempts, in collaboration with his Polish ally Stanislaus Leszczyński (elected King in 1704 on Augustus's deposition), to push Russia further east by regaining for the Commonwealth at least some of the *avulsa imperii* signed away at the Treaty of Andrusovo (1667) had, at least for the moment, failed. His efforts to gain a new ally in the Sultan were crowned with success in so far as four declarations of war by the Porte on Tsar Peter were issued between 1710 and 1714. The non-arrival of the army Charles expected from Sweden prevented him, however, from utilizing the Turkish and Tartar campaigns for his own war aims.

In September 1714 – the Habsburg frontier open at last – he hurried within the fortnight, by post-chaise and on horseback, to Stralsund in Swedish Pomerania. The Tsar was helped, as was Denmark-Norway, particularly in the crucial years 1715-16, by the use which Georg Ludwig of Hanover made of the British fleet in his capacity as George I of Great Britain.[26] Luck was with the Tsar, as with the rest of the Allies, when Charles XII was killed in the trenches before Frederikshald in the early stages of his big new offensive of 1718. The Swedish war effort slowed up. Norway was evacuated so that the domestic issues of a contested succession and return to limited monarchy (the *monarchia mixta* of old) could be settled. The will to continue the war in order to achieve 'a reasonable peace', that is one which would not impair the great-power position, survived Charles; but his successful playing-off of Russia and Great Britain for such terms between 1716 and 1718 could not, for a variety of reasons, be continued. Frederick, husband of Queen Ulrika Eleonora of Sweden, and elected King on her abdication in 1720, felt bound to choose between George I and Tsar Peter. A German prince by birth (he was heir to the Landgrave of Hesse-Cassel), he had shared the disquiet occasioned by Russian troops in Mecklenburg between 1716 and 1717 as well as concern lest the Tsar's virtual protectorate over Poland become permanent. It was natural, therefore, that he should choose to make sacrifices to Hanover (and to Hanover's allies, Prussia and Denmark-Norway) in order to gain George's diplomatic and naval support against the Tsar.

But once more luck was with Peter. The formation of an anti-Russian coalition with the objective of reconquering for Sweden at least Livonia and Estonia was blighted by the bursting of the South

112 The Duke of Marlborough (painted by Kneller), Allied commander in the War of the Spanish Succession

113 Peter the Great, main victor in the Great Northern War, 1700–21

114 Charles XII's Danish enemy, Frederick IV (participant in war 1700, 1709–10)
115 George I of Great Britain (participant in Great Northern War as Elector of Hanover 1715–20), who skilfully utilized the British fleet to further his Hanoverian purposes

116 Allies in the anti-Swedish coalition of the Great Northern War: Augustus of Saxony-Poland (participant in war from 1700–06 and 1709–19) and Frederick William I of Prussia (participant 1715–20)

117 Verse on the belligerents of the War of the Spanish Succession; copy sent by Ralph Palmer to his nephew Ralph Verney in 1704

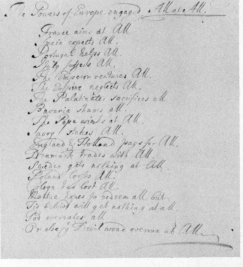

Sea Bubble in England. (There were other contributory factors, but this was the basic one.) Without the king-pin of British naval strength at George's disposal the other interested powers, Saxony-Poland, the Emperor and France, fell away and Sweden faced the onslaught of Russian superiority in shallow galleys which executed lightning raids on her coast without sufficient naval, military or moral force to counter-attack. The result was the Peace of Nystad of 1721 which transferred Ingria, Estonia and Livonia to Russia and restored most of the Karelian territory previously ceded to Finland. The Tsar had long ago intimated his policy of leaving the urban (mainly German-speaking) Baltic population, with their colonies of merchants from western countries, a great deal of freedom in arranging their own affairs. Only in this way could they play the role he envisaged for them in drawing Russia towards the west.

By 1721 the Swedish empire was lost. Sweden was permitted to keep Wismar and part of Swedish Pomerania (with Stralsund and Rügen). These might serve as some restraint on Denmark if she contemplated future attacks on the Swedish peninsular provinces; but the main security – the alliance with Holstein-Gottorp – had to be renounced and the freedom from Sound dues for the Baltic sacrificed. Complete Danish incorporation of Sleswig took place, under English and French guarantees, in 1720. If Frederick IV profited relatively little from the war, his original partner Augustus of Saxony came out of it empty-handed. The gains went to Russia with her greater strength in manpower and the single-mindedness, not to say ruthlessness, of the Tsar in channeling all human and economic resources to the war effort, and to the two latecomers, the King of Prussia and George of Hanover-Britain. In each case significant gains were made. Prussia obtained Stettin and was at last a German naval and commercial power (her only previous port had been Königsberg in East Prussia, outside Germany proper). Hanover, by absorption of Bremen and Verden, became the second state in North Germany, while for Great Britain these duchies were thought of as giving ready access to the Continent for British goods as well as a direct seaborne route of communication between George's electorate and his kingdom.

The settlement of 1648 had indeed been undone as far as Sweden was concerned. Her position as a European great power had rested on her right to station troops close to the heart of the Empire and within striking distance of Denmark, the Low Countries, France, the Habsburg dominions and Poland. Now this was lost. The Swedish people at large did not mind. They had wearied of the burdens of empire. Even before the long war, administrators had complained that the German provinces contributed nothing and cost a great deal; and the post-1715 years of mobilization of Sweden's resources for the war effort brought with them an absolutism, effected through virtual 'cabinet' government, which was repugnant to the traditions of the Swedish bureaucracy. The loss of the East Baltic empire, which had become Swedish between 1561 and 1661, was, however, deplored since the prosperity of the nation had been so heavily dependent on it and on the attempted exclusion of direct Russian and Polish trade with the west.

The partition of the Swedish empire between 1719 and 1721, seen from a European point of view, meant an increase in the number of states which could be regarded as great powers. Hanover and Prussia had already benefited from the War of the Spanish Succession. In the sense in which that war was also a war of the Protestant succession in Great Britain, Georg Ludwig of Hanover was one of the main victors, and Prussia – apart from the royal title which was now internationally recognized – increased her territories in the west of Germany by Upper Guelders (Spanish Gelderland), long coveted by the Dutch Republic. Tsar Peter had knocked in vain on the doors which would gain admittance to the Grand Alliance during the war and to France's inner circle of friends after the war; these efforts, though their foremost purpose was to weaken ties with Sweden, were also genuine attempts at becoming part of the European system of states. But Russia demonstrated that she was a power to be reckoned with when she succeeded in holding on to all three Baltic provinces, in spite of all Sweden could do, and against the Tsar's own reiterated treaty obligations that Livonia should go to either Augustus of Saxony or to the *Rzeczpospolita* as their share of the war booty.

There were those who assumed that Russia, on Tsar Peter's death, would weaken to such an extent that the process of advance could be reversed. They pointed to the loss of Azov in Peter's lifetime after the disastrous Prut campaign of 1711 and emphasized the favourable circumstances which had facilitated Russian successes against Sweden, not least a plurality of allies. But like many prophets of history in the making they were proved wrong: after 1721 Russia was a European, not only an eastern power.

V THE ARTS

Victories in war were celebrated by the ringing of church bells, by solemn and stirring *Te Deums*, by the illumination of buildings and whole cities, by lavish expenditure on non-lethal fireworks and by congratulatory poems. The triumphant march with which Tsar Peter gave thanks in Moscow for Poltava was considered somewhat barbarian since not only Swedish officers and men taken prisoner in that battle were ignominiously paraded through the streets, but also those (a much larger number) who had capitulated at Perevolochna on what they assumed to be honourable terms. Of more permanent nature were triumphal arches, displays of booty such as fine cannon or Turkish tents of exquisite workmanship, commemorative medals, engravings, tapestries and paintings of battle scenes, and monuments or even buildings of celebration. On these, architects and artists expended their gifts so prodigiously and skilfully that they have provided us with treasures of our civilization as well as with evidence of the material aspects of their own age.

Such commemorative activities at times occasioned indignation. The story that the Dutch offended Louis XIV by depicting, on their medal celebrating the Peace of Aix-la-Chapelle, Joshua 'bidding the sun stand still' is – alas – apocryphal, but the inscription on the medal the States General did cast to commemorate 1668 was not calculated

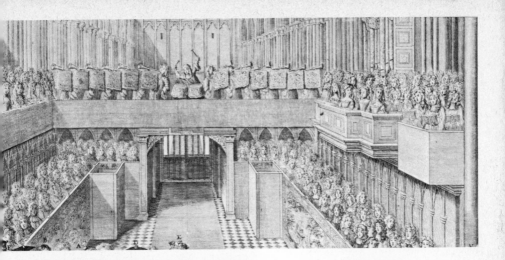

118 Opposite, fireworks at Vienna after the raising of the Turkish siege of 1683. Note the Imperial arms

119 Top, choristers and musicians at the coronation of James II, 1685

120 Left, the Town Hall at The Hague, illuminated to celebrate William III's stay in 1692

121 Above, medal commemorating the Treaty of Aix-la-Chapelle, 22 June 1668

to please either the French, the Spaniards or the Austrians in its proud boast that at Aix the United Provinces 'had forced three nations to make peace'.[1] Louis XIV's Place des Victoires caused offence to former enemies and allies alike. The design for a French monument to celebrate the Peace of Nijmegen had to be modified after representations from Charles XI,[2] who could be worked upon in later years by stories (which the French ambassador took great pains to prove false or at least exaggerated) of Louis's self-glorification at the expense of Swedish honour.[3] In Franco-Austrian relations there was some tit-for-tat (Viennese sculptors depicted Frenchmen in chains being trodden underfoot by a triumphant Emperor); but the height of presumption was perceived by the Huguenot La Motraye in 1715 when he examined the plinth that supported Queen Anne's statue outside St Paul's Cathedral – did it not show Great Britain as master of all the continents of the world?

Irritation with local customs sometimes interfered with appreciation of buildings travellers had come to admire. French visitors were scandalized at the presence of apple and oyster-sellers in Westminster Abbey: how could they view the building in the right frame of mind with so much bustle and irreverence, with people talking shop on 'Sunday's Exchange'?[4] But in general, joy and admiration, or curiosity satisfied, compensated for the considerable trouble and expense to which people put themselves in order to view new buildings and monuments.

In the plastic arts a broad division can be noticed between the Baroque of the southern Catholic countries and the more restrained Protestant north. Baroque church and monastery architecture had begun in Spain and Italy long before our period and spread beyond the Alps into Germany and Poland with the Counter-Reformation and Jesuit proselytization; it spread also to Spanish America via the Jesuits. With its avowed missionary purpose, its profuse ornamentation, its sensuousness and even sensational theatricality, the Baroque religious building shocked most Protestants and even Catholics if they happened to be averse to devout mysticism. But it exacted admiration both then and later by its superb handling of masses, by the spiritual content of its message and by the organic whole which its best exponents achieved. Their compositions were powerfully modelled, curves were daringly used and cunning foreshortening compelled upward perspectives. The present-day purist may regret that Bernini, commissioned by successive popes between 1629 and

1655, masked Michelangelo's work by marble facings, gilt stucco, outsize statues and colossal 'furnishings' inside St Peter's; but this was as much part of the spirit of the age as the piazza and the double colonnade which, between 1655 and 1673, he made its splendid setting. Bernini, like Borromini and other architects of the time, was personally devout and the 'triumphal' aspect of the glorification of God pervades the whole range of Baroque church architecture, decoration and sculpture which can be traced as far east as the Orthodox Church of pre-Petrine Russia. Towards the end of the seventeenth century a version of the Baroque known as Churrigueresque (after a family of architects who developed this form) developed in Spain, which has been described as 'architecture devoured by ornamentation'.[5] The heavily ornamented altars of Spanish Baroque laden with paintings and sculpture are not admired by our own age though the workmanship is impressive and the *trompe-l'œil* realism of the carved figures with their enamelled or jewelled eyes, real hair and eyelashes, startle us as they did contemporaries. It is the more restrained examples, such as the clock-tower at Compostela of 1670, which please us. So do some of the outstanding examples of religious architecture north of the Alps: the monastery of Melk on the Danube (built between 1693 and 1724 by Prandauer) is among the finest of the Baroque. The building to the glory of God, influenced (sometimes only half-consciously) by the joy in creation of patron, architect and workmen alike, was the driving motive behind the burst of building after the 1648 peace. The skill and daring involved in Baroque architecture appealed to the age and an element of competition entered into the building programme – between town and town, prince and prince.

From church architecture Baroque spread to secular buildings, first in Italy. Guarini's textbook *Architettura Civile* was not printed till 1737, but it circulated widely in manuscript copies from 1668 onwards. Foreigners came to Rome to learn the secrets of the new style in religious and public buildings, in villas and magnificent fountains with their superb bronze sculptures. Tessin, the 'Bernini of the North' as he was called on his return to Sweden,[6] was deeply influenced by his years in Italy, and so was the Austrian Fischer von Erlach who in 1687 became architect-engineer to the Emperor Leopold. The masters of the Italian Baroque were also invited abroad; Bernini, for example, was called to France to design a new façade for the Louvre and to make an equestrian statue of Louis XIV.   119

122 Top, St Peter's, Rome, with Bernini's colonnade built between 1656 and 1667

123 The Karlskirche, Vienna, designed by Fischer von Erlach; the first stone was laid by Charles VI in 1715

124 A carousel at the Zwinger Palace, Dresden, on the completion of the palace (by D. Pöppelmann) in 1719

125 G.L. Bernini's third project for the Louvre, 1665

126 'Place des Victoires', Paris. The Place was designed by Robert de Cotte (see Ill. 131)

It is typical, however, that architects returning from Italy had to modify the new style (or even suppress it) to suit the personality of the ruler they served. The best-documented discussion between prince and architect is the correspondence of Charles XII and Tessin from 1709 to 1714 when the King, during his 'lazy-dog-days' in Turkey, had time to become aware of his mature taste. He favoured rich materials and impressive colonnades, but he desired the lines and restraint of the Classical manner, abhorred the idea of sculpture and fussy ornamentation in churches, and compelled changes in building plans which Tessin, with his Italian leanings, regretted. Bernini's design for the Louvre of 1665 was modified and restrained by Perrault, and his statue of King Louis was relegated to an unimportant position in the grounds of Versailles, the palace and gardens about which it has truly been said that they have nothing of the Baroque except the colossal scale on which they were planned. Louis XIV preferred a style modelled on the Antique, the one we think of as French Classicism and which evolved during his reign after 1661. Before Louis's personal control of the government, Baroque influence can be seen, for example in the elder Mansart's Invalides; and the argument has been put forward that it is Louis's absolutism which explains his Classicism – his concern for order and restraint to keep chaos and anarchy in check extending from the realm of politics to that of architecture. French Classicism certainly celebrated the glory and majesty of church and state (symbolized by the King) by emphasis on grandeur in size, costliness in material and regularity and symmetry of design. That there was a distinct fashioning of the style by the ruler is undeniable, but it would also seem to have suited something in the French temperament which distrusted the unbridled Baroque appeal to the emotions.

It has been argued that the whole of Atlantic Europe resisted the Baroque, from Portugal in the south to France, England and the Dutch Republic in the north. The religious division would, however, seem to be the stronger denominator. When John V of Portugal, after the Peace of Utrecht, was free to use his Brazilian gold for building, the monastery-palace of Mafra which he began in 1713 was in the Baroque style. No Lutheran ruler succumbed to the Baroque though Augustus, the Catholic Elector of Protestant Saxony (and elected King of Poland), did and commissioned Pöppelmann to build the enchanting Zwinger Palace in Dresden between 1711 and 1722. The burghers of Brussels in the Catholic Southern Netherlands

127 The Apotheosis of Prince Eugène of Savoy, sculpture in wood by B. Permoser, 1718 to 1721 (see p. 125)

128 Louis XIV as an Augustan general, sculpture in bronze by F. Girardon, 1680

richly ornamented in Baroque style the houses of their Grand' Place, rebuilt after 1696. The Karlskirche, the very climax of Habsburg Baroque, was commissioned from Erlach in 1715 by the Emperor Charles VI, who had spent some of his most impressionable years in Spain fighting for the Spanish crown. Erlach himself, the chief architect of Vienna's replanning and rebuilding after the Turkish siege of 1683, was interested in the history of architecture and even in non-European styles. He wrote an *Entwurf einer historischen Architectur* (published in 1717) and used features from pagoda and mosque in some of his work. In his designs for the Habsburg palaces, 'imperial' Classical themes were introduced. Here, as in France, the symbolism of the Roman Empire★ was brought into play; and it is worth noting that French Classicism as formulated at Versailles became the model for palaces in Prussia and Russia in the eighteenth century when these countries were able to display their status as great powers by large-scale building or rebuilding. It would indeed seem as if the conscious and subconscious harking back to Roman and Greek history, architecture, dress and symbolic emblems helps to explain

123

★ The title of the Emperor's first-born son – if the Electors could be persuaded to grant it and thus automatic succession – was 'King of the Romans'.

129 H. Pellé's marble bust of Charles II, 1684

130 J. M. Rysbrack's bust of Robert Walpole, early 1720s

131 A. Coysevox's bronze bust of Robert de Cotte, architect to Louis XIV

the choice of 'Classical' motifs in court building, decoration and statuary. Generals and politicians frequently chose to be depicted in sculpture and painting, the former with Roman accoutrements and the latter with Roman togas. The extent to which the educated classes were steeped in classical history for the sake of its literature, and their real admiration for Roman and Greek temples and statues – scattered over large areas of southern Europe – must also, however, be taken into account.

Political considerations often played a role in choice of style. Bavaria, the ally of Louis XIV, proved more resistant to Baroque than its neighbours, presumably because the Elector Maximilian chose a French architect. Englishmen began to sing the virtues of the 'free English garden' just because it was so different from the gardens of the political opponent France. The architectural gardens of Le Nôtre with their clipped hedges, stylized flower-beds and out-door 'apartments', so much imitated on the Continent, were not considered fitting to the 'free English spirit', though his use of statues and fountains was admired. The fame of French sculpture of the reign of Louis XIV has stood the test of time: the bronzes of Coysevox show exquisite characterization, and Girardon is superb in his Classic-inspired treatment of mythological figures. Even a formal task, such as the large equestrian statue of Louis XIV as an

Augustan general finished in 1699 for the Place Louis le Grand, he fulfilled so splendidly that though the statue itself was destroyed during the Revolution (along with most other royal equestrian pieces) the small-scale models which have survived are among the treasures of museums in Europe and America. That England resisted the Baroque seems, however, to have few political implications, whether those of imitation before 1688 or opposition thereafter. The firm entrenchment of the Palladian style through Inigo Jones's work is probably the main reason. Indeed, an edition of Palladio's work on architecture annotated by Inigo Jones was published as late as 1715. Roman influence can be traced in St Paul's Cathedral which Wren consciously modelled on St Peter's; but in Wren's other churches, as in those of his pupils Hawksmoor and Vanbrugh, there are only restrained echoes of Baroque influence. Classical and Palladian patterns predominate also in secular buildings, in the many small manor-houses, in Wren's rebuilding of Hampton Court and in the Vanbrugh design for palace and bridge at Blenheim. In sculpture the Classical was equally admired in England. Obelisks were used for commemoration of victories, as at Schönbrunn and Versailles, with inscriptions in the style of the Classics. Statues were as eagerly sought as on the Continent – whether antiques or modelled, more or less successfully, on Classical lines. In commemorative church tablets and carved decorations a discreet Baroque influence is noticeable. Extreme pieces are rare, but one of them, the carved bust of Charles II made by Honoré Pellé in 1684, epitomizes the Baroque ideal of catching the fleeting moment. The curls of the wig seem to move in the breeze as do the folds and draperies, and the King's proud and lively expression is strongly conveyed. Even here there is no trace of the apotheosis-like form which statues sometimes took on the Continent – that of Prince Eugène by Permoser being a good example of the genre; and the tombstone skeleton sculpture so typical as to be called a favourite motif in Catholic countries in the Baroque period is totally absent in England and in other Protestant countries.

132 J. Vanbrugh's original design for the Grand Bridge at Blenheim

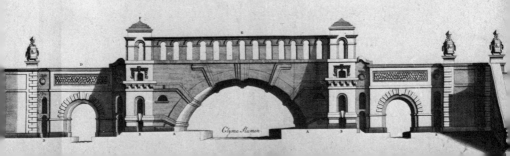

The distinction between 'Baroque' and 'Classical' must not be overdone, and in one aspect of architecture, that of town planning, European countries in our period adopted similar solutions irrespective of religion or latitude. The ideal of a town centre with public buildings grouped round it, and streets and squares and quays laid out in a pleasing and regular pattern, with statues and monuments to embellish it, was one which rulers, administrators and civic authorities had in common all over Europe and which they carried out to the extent their purses permitted and opportunities offered. The large-scale fires to which most towns were prone often supplied such opportunities, both to speculators who laid out alternative sites (as in London while the City was rebuilt after 1666[7]) and to governments that wanted to regulate and beautify. Differences within the pattern were dictated by climate and social need. The Dutch towns in the *stadhouder*-less periods had a less grand aspect than those of monarchies which planned even in towns to celebrate or symbolize the power of the dynasty. The *plazas mayores* of Spain could, because of the climate, be used as open-air theatres in the way that French and English squares could not. The balconies of Spanish houses (sometimes regularly numbered) served as boxes for entertainments: bullfights and plays of religious or secular nature. (In the time of the Counter-Reformation they had been used also for *autos de fé*.) In more northerly climates carousels and displays had generally to take place indoors, in magnificent riding-schools specifically built for the purpose, while theatres were more frequently constructed for popular use.

126

133 Opposite, town planning: Wren's design for London after the Great Fire, 1666

134, 135, 136 Left, medal to commemorate the founding of St Petersburg, 1703; below, St Bride's Church built by Wren 1671–78, steeple completed 1701–03; bottom, Vermeer's *View of Delft*, 1658

The princes of Europe gave work to a great number of artists for the decoration of their palaces, and so did the authorities of the Catholic Church. Rich patrons, such as Queen Christina in her exile in Rome, supported veritable colonies of artists and formed collections of paintings, specializing sometimes in painters or themes which particularly appealed to them. In Christina's case the strong (possibly unconscious) attraction she felt for the naked or near-naked male body can be seen to have influenced her choice of pictures.[8] Other collectors on the grandest scale, royal personages, were in our period of the male sex and had emotional ties more diverse than those of the Queen who lived in self-imposed chastity and exile. Though their collections often indicate a natural delight in the female nude, such pictures were part of a whole in which family portraits, favourite castles, horses, dogs and falcons, faithful servants or ministers, Biblical and historical scenes, floral and architectural compositions intermingle. In a few countries there was a religious or socially motivated aversion to the naked human form, whether male or female, and hence also to the mythological paintings in which that form was generally displayed. Dutch and Spanish artists avoided the subject, and it was only towards the end of his life that Velázquez painted for the Escorial the nude now known as the *Rokeby Venus*.

137 *The Toilet of Venus* by Velázquez, *c.* 1650

Even below the royal rank there were collectors in plenty. Italian and Flemish painters of the sixteenth and the early part of the seventeenth century were eagerly sought for and the art-dealer's profession was already a thriving one. Some dabbled in paintings as a sideline to their ordinary business, and diplomats and educated men residing and travelling abroad were often used as amateur buyers on behalf of collectors. For those who had recently started collecting, books such as the *Polygraphice* of 1675 (with several later editions) offered advice on how to display pictures. Those who had not the means to collect still followed the general custom, which spread from court and noble circles, of having their own portrait or that of their family as a group painted. The good court-painters set the standard: Velázquez in Spain, Lely and Michael Dahl in England, Largillière and Rigaud in France, Krafft and Swartz in Sweden, and a host of painters, often of French or Italian nationality, at the German courts and at Warsaw. When these men, as they sometimes did, painted at second-hand someone famous whom they had never seen, the results are elegant paintings which fail to convince: a case in point are the portraits of Charles XII by Dahl and Rigaud which should be compared with those from life by Swartz or Wedekind. The amount of excellent portraiture in our period is impressive enough to permit us to characterize the age as one in which the character-study flourished, and certainly more people below royal, high noble or official rank than ever before sat for their portraits. The representative portrait, such as Largillière's of Louis XIV or Rigaud's of Augustus of Saxony-Poland, may by the pomp and circumstance of setting and robes obscure the personality of the sitter; and it is no doubt true that a fashionable artist, then as now to some extent, imposed a fashionable face. Lely certainly did so in the case of many female sitters, and Kneller perfected, for both sexes, the polite and urbane 'mask'. But even rulers could demand to be depicted warts and all, as Cromwell did of Cooper and Charles XII of Swartz; and convincing portraits are the rule rather than the exception below the rank of royal personages. Many are brutally frank, or seem so to us today; for example, Gennari's portrait of the Duke of Lauderdale in the 1670s, or the portrait (by an unknown painter) of the Swedish Count Gyllenstierna from the same period. But the age must have welcomed realistic portraits if the artist was able to provide them. An admirer of the Duchess of Marlborough, when she was old and reckoned herself ugly, begged for a portrait of her, 'just as you are,

which I hear is mighty well for a grandmother'.[9] Charles XII and his companions in Turkey found 'wonderfully true to life' an amateur portrait by the officer Axel Sparre which emphasized the King's receding hairline and the plump jowl which was the legacy of the years of enforced inactivity.[10] Where the painter was moved by the subject or when he felt entirely free – as in self-portraits – the results are often masterpieces: we need think only of Kneller's portrait of Newton of 1702 or that of Locke in the late years of his life (now in the Hermitage), or of Rembrandt's series of self-portraits painted in his unfashionable years after 1656. Portraits of well-known people were engraved for mass sale. Prints of rulers and generals or statesmen with a European reputation were found in most inns and coffee-houses, and Pepys tells of the rush to buy prints of the female beauties of England as soon as they were issued.

Apart from portraiture the period is rich in Biblical, mythological and other decorative or allegorical painting. In every country, irrespective of whether the Baroque had triumphed or been resisted in architecture, the Baroque's concern to catch the fleeting moment influenced this kind of painting. Le Brun, Louis XIV's *premier peintre*, is a typical exponent of the decorative painting of the age:

138 Far left, Largillière's portrait of Charles Le Brun, Louis XIV's *premier peintre*, 1686

139 Left centre, Rigaud's 1707 portrait of Louis XIV in full regalia; note the realistic elderly face with sunken mouth

140 Left, Largillière's portrait of Augustus the Strong, Elector of Saxony and King of Poland

141 Top right, Charles XII, King of Sweden, detail of portrait by D. Swartz, 1707; note realistic receding hairline

142 Above, the English Duke of Lauderdale, *c.* 1674

143 Left, the Swedish Count Gyllenstierna, *c.* 1675

symbolic, allusive, concerned with the technical means whereby the movement of bodies and clouds could be transferred to canvas and stucco. We find his opposite numbers at courts all over Europe, where ceiling paintings executed by the 'first painter' and his pupils celebrate the apotheosis of the reigning dynasty. This kind of painting has obvious resemblances to the Baroque religious paintings of the Spaniards, Murillo and Zurbarán, which in their turn go back to the Genoa school influenced by Rubens and van Dyck.

The prevalence of flowers and fruits in decorative painting – to suggest the prosperity and joy which dynasties brought to their subjects or to set off the figures of allegorical designs – encouraged the kind of minute observation characteristic of at least part of the Dutch school and forms a link both with the Northern Netherlands and with the realism which derived from Caravaggio's break with the mannerist tradition towards the end of the sixteenth century. The humble models chosen by him, his powerful frankness and popular lyricism, his characteristic use of light and shade had influenced French painters in the first half of the seventeenth century – artists like de la Tour and the Le Nain brothers – and in the Dutch Republic in the second half his heritage can be seen in Rembrandt and Vermeer, though the fluid mellow light which suffuses their paintings is typically Dutch. The Dutch Republic supported an astonishing

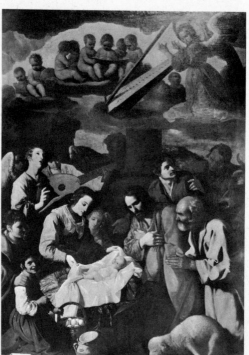

132

144 Zurbarán's *Adoration of the Shepherds*, an example of Spanish religious Baroque painting

145 Glorification of the Protestant Succession, an example of English political Baroque painting, by Sir James Thornhill

number of painters outside princely or noble patronage. William III had cared as much for Het Loo and his other Dutch palaces in respect of pictures and decoration as he did for Hampton Court; and the above-mentioned van Ellemeet possessed famous collections in his country seats as well as in his town house, as did other rich men. But Dutchmen far lower down the social scale also bought pictures; it was not uncommon for artisans and farmers of very moderate income to buy paintings and carpets at fairs, and the habit was widespread among those slightly better off.

It may have been the very large number of painters active which encouraged the specialization typical of Dutch artists of this period, particularly those of the second and third rank. Some did winter scenes only, others seascapes, landscapes with cattle or landscapes with figures, others again flowers, animals or insects, or *nature morte* compositions. The exquisite detail of many of these paintings was

146 Velázquez's *Las Meninas* ('The Maids of Honour') gathered round the Spanish infanta Margarita Teresa, *c.* 1656; note dwarfs to the right

much admired, and a vogue for 'naturalism' spread either via Dutch painters who went abroad or through foreign painters who had their training in the studios of the Republic. Towards the end of Louis XIV's reign several young painters at his court began to specialize in naturalism: Desportes and Oudry were already choosing the motifs for which they became famous in the post-1715 period. Chardin worked at Fontainebleau by 1720 and Watteau (of South Netherlands stock, the family name being originally Vato) lived his brief, but from a painting point of view prolific, life wholly within the period with which we are concerned: born in 1694 he died in 1721. His *fête galante* themes and his many drawings tell us much about the fashions and the amusements of the age.

147 Detail from Watteau's *Assemblée dans un parc* ▶

148 Hondecoeter's birds, typical of the mastery achieved by Dutch specialized painters

When we consider painting within the framework of European art as a whole, we are likely to respond less to the decorative artists, however much they illuminate our particular period, than to those painters who seem to us to be artists for all times and have enriched our civilization: those who compel our attention because they struggle with the eternal problems of humanity or because they solve technical problems (however placid their themes) in a way that is, artistically, absolutely right. Something of the mystery of life comes across to us whether we ponder the transcendental quality in Zurbarán's paintings or marvel at the composition and the light which characterize those of Vermeer. We ask ourselves why Velázquez was so convinced of (or haunted by?) the rightful place of evil and imperfection in God's creation that he felt impelled to remind us of our condition by painting freaks and dwarfs. We stand abashed before the courage and the powers of self-analysis in Rembrandt's portraits of himself and feel moved by the evocativeness of his use of chiaroscuro and colour. All these painters died between 1660 and 1675, not long after de la Tour and the Le Nains, and we may be justified in concluding that the age of the giants was over long before the seventeenth century had ended. At the time, however, they were not generally

149 Vermeer's *The Music Lesson*, c. 1655 ▶

appreciated. The humble models chosen were often disliked, and the painting of Christ in defiance of accepted conventions (as Rembrandt did) was considered shocking. Of those who gained wide acceptance, apart from portraitists, we should note the two French painters Claude Lorraine and Nicolas Poussin. Both worked mainly in Italy, where they died in 1658 and 1665 respectively, and both perfected a largely constructed landscape based on acute observation. Their pictures convey a Classical, delicately Arcadian mood; and their reference to antiquity, in temples and statuary, in its turn (as we have already mentioned) influenced landscape-gardening. Their appeal was to an educated taste and, as Anthony Blunt has shown in Poussin's case, the intellectual content of their work can be studied with profit. Poussin emerges as a painter typical of the Early Enlightenment, one who equates reason with nature and with the natural virtue of man. This message struck chords of response with buyers, but even those who did not fully grasp it were attracted (as were buyers of Vermeer's paintings[11]) by calm beauty in an age of war and uncertainty.

Many of those who made their living from pictures might be called artist-craftsmen rather than artists. The successful painters had pupils at their studios who did not always establish independent reputations; most engravers and etchers were essentially craftsmen. The best of them were highly regarded and their number increased as the demand for prints and illustrations grew. Scientific and travel books were thought incomplete without plates; and for teaching purposes, as well as for decoration, engravings were much in demand. The market for other pieces of craftsmanship which can be classified as applied art was also expanding. Churches and monasteries, courts and colleges, noble families and municipal authorities had always valued heirlooms of precious metals, and continued to employ designers and craftsmen to replenish their collections of plate, jewellery, coins and medals and *objets d'art*. The 'monstrance of a thousand gems' of Cadiz Cathedral is an example of what such craftsmen could do when given an unlimited supply of precious stones. The glorification of hereditary absolutism in our period created a particular demand for craftsmanship on the grand scale; for halls of mirrors, for silver furniture, for fine ironwork for balustrades and staircases. Louis XIV's Versailles was the supreme example, and French gold and silversmiths were invited to foreign courts to execute particular items of French design. Charles XI of Sweden, austere in his own habits, went to a great deal of trouble and expense to bring back to Sweden jewellery which Queen Christina had taken with her into exile and sold or pawned when she needed ready cash; and he spent a considerable sum on a French-designed and executed silver font for the christening of children of the royal house. Though it is easier to find proof of concern to have lost treasures restored in the case of corporate institutions or powerful individuals, we should not assume that delight and pride in heirlooms or in new acquisitions were not experienced lower down the social scale. Rural parishes in some countries had what amounted to communal worldly treasures in possessions such as bridal crowns and gold cups. The amount of gold and silver ornaments which were passed from one generation to another even in modest rural and urban society is not negligible: from widely separated areas of Europe we know of brooches (often made from coins) and rings used as betrothal and marriage symbols, of belts and chains which decorated both male and female traditional costumes – particularly at the performance of country dances – and

150 Silver furniture in Louis XIV's Grande Galerie (later Galerie des Glaces), Versailles

of the silver buckles which formed part of a man's Sunday and feast-day best whether as ornaments on shoes or in the hatband. In their money-value such ornaments were far inferior to the necklaces and hatbands studded with pearls and diamonds which even 'common' Europeans wore in the Eldorado of New Spain,[12] but from examples which have survived we notice good if simple design and persistence of local motifs.

The major part of the work of silversmiths was made for men and women higher up the social scale, and here a cosmopolitan influence is evident. Acanthus leaves, and other decorative devices, spread from one country to another; the designs of French craftsmen, like Daniel Marot, were copied in Germany and from there copied in Scandinavia, though in England a specific style, so-called Queen Anne, developed fairly independently. Foreign motifs were modified to suit domestic purposes: a bridal crown made by the Bergen silversmith Johannes Reimers the elder (a master between 1704 and 1725) is composed of ten panels, each showing a central male figure flanked by lions and topped by an unmistakably French fleur-de-lis. Jewellery, often very intricate in design, was also influenced by European-wide fashions. Necklaces and earrings (or 'ear-

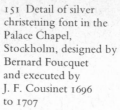

151 Detail of silver christening font in the Palace Chapel, Stockholm, designed by Bernard Foucquet and executed by J. F. Cousinet 1696 to 1707

152 Covered goblet from Saxony, engraved in Dresden, with the cypher of Queen Anne of Great Britain

153 Spanish bodice ornament: cut emeralds and diamonds set in gold

154 Norwegian bridal crown (see p. 139)

bobs', as they were sometimes called) for the rich and discerning were beautifully done, and miniature portraits were set in rings or fixed to bracelets. Pearls and diamonds which could be used for jewellery were always welcome presents, and portraits, when in frames decorated with precious and semi-precious stones, were royal presents indeed. So were watches and small table-clocks of exquisite workmanship. For the individual family, expenditure on jewellery and on articles of silver and (for the very richest) gold represented investments as well as adornment of person and house on grounds of prestige or status. This is particularly true of larger articles which were treasured by weight as much as for visual delight. A retiring diplomat reckoned himself unlucky if he had to return the plate with which he had been issued in order to represent his ruler with a dignified table abroad, and Saint-Simon proved reluctant (as did many of his fellow dukes) to respond to the appeal for families to sacrifice their heavy silver in the time of France's need during the War of the Spanish Succession. The larger pieces, the representational ones, tended to be the more ornate: the obligatory test piece whereby the journeyman proved himself a master was on the Continent particularly showy, as were most guild-cups and much of the church silver in Catholic countries. It is in the smaller, more everyday articles that we get an insight into the growing popularity of simpler design for domestic use in households below those of the high nobility – in table-silver, in candlesticks, in chocolate- and coffeepots, in sugar-basins and condiment-sets, in the little dishes for sweetmeats, even in the silver beakers and tankards which, though they follow traditional shapes, are given cleaner lines and less heavy decoration. In itself the greater production is proof of a wider diffusion of money above and beyond what was needed for the absolute necessities of the family. Fine candlesticks for card-table and keyboard instruments, chessmen carved from ivory, inlaid and bejewelled boxes for trinkets, spectacles, snuff and mathematical instruments, casings for telescopes and other working equipment of naval and military officers – all become *objets d'art* through the perfection which went into their making.

Furniture and decorative devices for houses also approached to applied art because of the excellence of craftsmanship. Contact with the Far East influenced taste in various ways. The lacquered, or japanned, cabinets and boxes brought to Portuguese, Dutch and English ports in the 1680s set a fashion, as did the porcelain teapots, cups and plates from the east. Lacquer-work from Japan was more highly regarded than that of China,[13] but since the expense of articles brought from such a distance was great, imitation of 'japanned' work soon began and many fine pieces were made from the 1690s onwards in Europe. The same kind of imitation – or rather a twofold one – can be noticed in the case of porcelain. The search for the special clay which would enable Europe to produce porcelain was unavailing till the very end of our period when the Dresden and Vienna factories were successfully launched. Up to then, those who could not afford imported china ware bought Dutch and French pottery, frequently of a type decorated with eastern motifs. It is interesting to note that in China attempts were simultaneously made to cater for the European market by the choice of decorative motifs supposedly popular in the west: the Don Quixote and Sancho Panza figures are unmistakable though in Oriental dress.

European furniture in general tended to become lighter and more elegant towards the end of our period. The heavy oak and the solid cupboards and chairs of the pre-1680s begin to give way to varied woods (principally fruit) and to a greater variety of design of chairs and tables, bureaux and mirrors. This was in large measure the effect of the domestic style of Louis XIV as expressed in the places in which he lived for preference as a private person when he got older, at Marly for instance, in contrast to the Palace of Versailles which symbolized the power of the state and the work of running the

156 Left, lacquered cabinet on stand, c. 1670

157 Above, Chi'en Lung ware: meat dish showing Don Quixote on Rosinante with Sancho Panza in attendance

government. Here the designers and craftsmen created a style (which is sometimes erroneously called Louis XV) of elegant simplicity, with large windows, fine mirrors strategically placed, elegant bureaux, more comfortable chairs and sofas. A similar style evolved in England during Queen Anne's reign, and from England and France it spread into domestic architecture and craftsmanship on the rest of the Continent.

MUSIC AND OPERA

The patrons of music, as of the other branches of art we have so far considered, were church and court and, occasionally, private individuals rich enough to afford orchestras and pay for composers, who usually played, sang and conducted from the harpsichord. Well known among private patrons in England is Brydges, Duke of Chandos after the accession of George I, who kept a large orchestra at Canons, had a German *Kapellmeister*, Pepusch, from 1712 onwards and later commissioned Handel to compose and conduct for him. The Duke of Marlborough paid the salary of the Italian composer Bonancini in London. Every German and Scandinavian court had its *Hofkapelle* (usually with German musicians who became naturalized in time) and one of Charles XII's relaxations in Turkey was to assemble a large orchestra for concerts. His servant wrote nostalgically in his 143 memoirs about the 'wonderful musical evenings we then had'. In England music came into its own after repression during the Commonwealth when (though Cromwell himself enjoyed music) ballad singers and fiddlers were forbidden in public places as 'sinful', religious services were mute and even singing at funerals was prohibited as 'a popish custom'. After 1660 the waifs of Sheffield and other towns in their cloaks and badges were paid for going about town singing on a 'ffaire Evening'. Festive music for all kinds of civil and royal occasions was commissioned and much sacred music was composed. Many church organs, destroyed during the Puritan period, were not restored till the nineteenth century, but string and percussion players formed small orchestras in church galleries to enrich the singing. French hautboys (i.e. oboes) and clarinets were introduced, and the new form of entertainment which had swept Europe since the mid-century, the opera, was given a trial. Before the end of our period, the English compromise, the oratorio, was already taking shape.

Music was truly inter-European. Italy was reckoned the Mecca of composers, singers and instrumentalists alike. There the choirs of great churches were supported by rival city-states. There the opera developed from the Florentine 'chamber opera' and the Roman palace performances into fully-fledged public productions. There the spate of theatre-building for operas was most rapid. There Amati and Stradivarius perfected the violin to serve opera. There the provision of masters under whom to study was most abundant. French and German composers and singers sought their inspiration in the south (even if they modified what they had learnt on their return home) and the compositions of those non-Italians who did not travel, for example Johann Sebastian Bach, were nearly unknown in their own lifetime because they worked in isolation. Bach achieved early local fame as a brilliant organist; but when he played harmonies, preludes and fugues which we regard as our musical treasures, he was accused of confusing the congregation. His counterpoint and fugue were in the seventeenth-century tradition, but his mastership was such that the ordinary German churchgoer found it strange to the point of non-comprehension. His chorales, like those of Buxtehude, were more easily assimilated: they moved even those who did not grasp the technical ingenuity both composers possessed.

In our period there were obvious similarities in the construction of sacred and secular song and music. Motets and madrigals balanced

158 French musicians, playing a composition of Michel de la Barre (probably the flautist, far right) of 1707

each other; variations and fugues, whether four-voiced or more complicated, were common to both. The influence of popular dance tunes (the pavane, the galliard, the coranto or *courante*, the jig or *gigue*, the hornpipe, the saraband, the borry or *bourrée*, the allemande and the French minuet which became so popular towards the end of the century that it was danced in all countries) can be traced in both the *Sonata da Camera* and the *Sonata da Chiesa*. The former had recognizable dance tunes as the foundation of its four sections; the latter had four movements in which the first was slow and majestic, the second lively, the third slow and graceful and the fourth *presto*. Both have been labelled 'Baroque Sonatas' to distinguish them from nineteenth-century sonatas. They were written for orchestras of viols, violas da gamba, flutes, oboes, trumpets, trombones, harps, harpsichords and organs. Embellishments, the so-called figurations, were permitted and expected though not usually indicated by the composer. Instruments were improved and new ways of combining them worked out. A good deal of specialization must have existed, since high trumpet passages, apparently commonplace then, have been found to be outside the capacity of modern players. The sonata form was also used in compositions for single instruments of the clavecin, harpsichord or organ type. (The piano proper was invented in Italy in 1711, but not exploited musically till much later.) Fine examples are those by François Couperin, court musician to Louis XIV, who published four volumes of clavecin pieces, the subtle feeling, sensuousness, *esprit* of which are such that they have been called 'some of the finest music written by a Frenchman',[14] and

145

Domenico Scarlatti, whose clavecin compositions are showier, but with daring harmonies. Characteristic of the period is also a liking for descriptive music: battles and animals were imitated in sound and the German Kuhnau became famous for his sonatas depicting Bible stories.

An important development in the second half of the seventeenth century was the Concerto Grosso in three or more movements, composers becoming intrigued by the effect achieved when contrasting a small group of instruments (the so-called *concertino*) with the rest of the orchestra, the *tutti*. These proved very popular, though many of them later disappeared from the European repertoire only to be rediscovered in recent years. Vivaldi is a good case in point: the wonderful vitality and freshness of his music is now as well known as that of Handel and Bach. The impact of music, church and secular, on seventeenth-century society after 1648 was general. The fiddlers at fairs and peasant weddings, the fife and drum of the military march, the fanfare of public processions, the religious and court concerts – all were part of everyday life even among those who had no musical education. Those with musical aptitude were trained, chiefly through choir schools; and musical teachers were engaged for their children by the well-to-do. The demand for musical compositions was seemingly insatiable since, besides card-playing, social gatherings were entertained by music whether at the dance or at the concert.

159 Boy playing the flute, detail from painting by Judith Leyster

160, 161, 162, 163 Composers: J. S. Bach, G. F. Handel, A. Vivaldi (presumed), F. Couperin

Most striking of all musical innovations of our period is the opera. The fashion for it began in Italy soon after the beginning of the seventeenth century when certain composers and singers rebelled against music so contrapuntal that it was impossible to hear the words sung. The first score that has survived with the new style of musical recitatives is Monteverdi's *Orfeo* of 1607. For several decades opera remained a private and courtly entertainment, but after the 1637 opening in Venice of an opera-house admitting the general public there was a rush to do the same elsewhere. Rome, Naples, Florence, Parma and Palermo rapidly followed suit; Paris had its first opera-house by 1671 and its second in 1715; Hamburg had a permanent theatre in 1678 which opened with the *Singspiel* 'Adam und Eva' by the German composer Theile; Dresden had an early opera-house and Vienna got its theatre at the Kärtnerthor in 1708. But long before this, Vienna had a court opera, and visiting Italian and French companies carried operas all over Europe, principally to court theatres, often built specially for them: to Warsaw in 1613, Munich in 1653, Berlin in 1688, Ghent in 1698, Stockholm and Copenhagen shortly thereafter; London in 1705 and Dublin in 1711. Spain and Russia lagged somewhat behind. Madrid and the Escorial saw many private operas but no permanent opera-house till Farinelli, Philip V's court singer, built one in 1739; and Petersburg had no court opera till 1737. Royal patrons were again important. Queen Christina

147

164 Setting for A. Cesti's *Il Pomo d'Oro*, opera performed in Vienna, 1667

commissioned an opera from Alessandro Scarlatti when he was only nineteen years old; Władysław, who became King of Poland in 1632, inaugurated a reign of regular opera performances of the kind he had grown to love in Italy, and a Dowager Queen of Poland was a generous patron of Domenico Scarlatti during her stay in Rome after 1709. The Emperor Leopold commissioned Cesti to make an opera, the *Pomo d'Oro*, to celebrate his marriage to the Spanish infanta Margarita Teresa. This opera was performed early in 1667 and its elaborate décor – twenty-three complete sets were used – brought the cost to 100,000 Reichsthaler. The Emperor, an amateur singer and composer, was motivated by more than ostentation, and to the next Cesti opera performed in Vienna he contributed the prologue himself. Later he commissioned Burnachini to design a court theatre in the Hofburg and both his sons, the Emperor Joseph I (1705–11) and Charles VI (who succeeded Joseph), continued the family tradition. Dynasties of architect-designers for the Vienna opera were established, court composers rewarded and the orchestra increased to 134 players, as against the 40 used by Monteverdi in 1607. In France Louis XIV's patronage encouraged the new art form

148

165 Charles II in exile dancing at The Hague with his sister, Elizabeth, Princess Palatine. Through her the Protestant Succession was secured (daughter: Sophia; grandson: Georg Ludwig, Elector of Hanover) ▶

and brought it before the public: Lully, the master of Louis's music, composed his first opera, *Fêtes de l'amour de Bacchus*, in 1672 and followed it with thirteen more before 1687, often in collaboration with Molière whose plays were frequently transformed into operas. Another musician-collaborator with Molière was Charpentier who composed and produced seventeen operas at the Théâtre-Français on his return from studies in Rome. Racine's plays were also turned into operas; composers – who often had to produce a commissioned work within a short time – liked having their libretto to hand with a story familiar to the audience.

The opera as it developed in the second half of the seventeenth century had roots not only in the Italian *opera camera* but also in the masques and ballets of an earlier age, and ballets formed a regular part of the spectacular court opera, above all in France. The staging became extremely elaborate in capital cities. The public demand for novelty and 'spectacle' could at times stifle the musical genius. It has been suggested that this is the case with Purcell, whose later works never equalled his fine first opera, *Dido and Aeneas*, staged in 1689.[15] When Handel, following his years in Italy, settled in London in 1710, he introduced Italian singers, some of them very famous, for his operas, in the hope of rekindling musical interest, but the 'spectacle-opera' had driven the music-lovers away and his genius found better expression in other forms of music. In the late 1720s he turned increasingly to oratorios (some of which were lifted from his operas) and concertos.

149

The opera of this time in any case had negligible action and it depended - in so far as it was not the spectacle or the ballet that appealed - on virtuoso singers who embellished their grace notes with Baroque trills and turns. Each singer left the stage after his or her *aria de capo* to return for applause; there were few choruses and ensembles for the main characters. The *bel canto* style was fully developed in the early eighteenth century in Naples (where Porpora, the composer of many operas, started a school for singers), but even in the seventeenth century it was the beauty of the sound and the impeccability of technique rather than dramatic expression that mattered, and music was specially composed for the virtuosi, male and female, of the day. Most famous among the virtuosi were the *castrati*, the male sopranos or mezzo-sopranos produced by a pre-puberty operation on promising singers. *Castrati* singers (who formed part of the chorus of the Vatican church and other churches in Rome till late in the nineteenth century) had voices stronger and more flexible than female sopranos or contraltos and were capable of astonishing technical brilliance. The tone, according to contemporary listeners, was both voluptuous and spiritual, other-worldly, angelic. The Melani brothers, of whom three were composers and five singers (four of them *castrati*), were perhaps the most talked-of musical family in the second half of the seventeenth century, while towards the end of our period Farinelli, whose songs alone could keep Philip V's melancholia at bay, made his début. Most operas, from Monteverdi's *Orfeo* onwards, demanded *castrati* singers, but fine tenors, baritones and basses were also eagerly sought by opera-houses. Female singers became increasingly important as audiences (in some countries anyhow) demanded looks as well as voice.

The themes of most operas were mythological and historical; the characters of Greek and modern drama and contemporary plays also served. Sometimes operas were commissioned for a particular occasion that dictated the theme: the first opera in the Dutch language by Hacquarts, *De triomfeerende Min*, was produced to celebrate the Peace of Nijmegen of 1678–79, and when the Hanoverian opera-house was inaugurated in 1689 it was with Steffani's *Heinrich der Löwe (Enrico Leone)*, specially composed to link the ducal house with this heroic historical Emperor.[16] In general German operas were considered more dramatic than those of Italy and France. Composers like Keiser and Mattheson (who sang in his own operas, male and female parts, stepping straight from the stage to the harpsichord to form part of the orchestra) were well known and Johann Hasse, whose first opera was produced in Hamburg in 1719, became so beloved in Italy as a singer that he was known simply as 'il caro Sassone'.

In the main stream of European music, most mysterious of all art forms since we cannot define why music moves us, our period is one in which important changes were being prepared. Handel started to take the tone of individual instruments more systematically into account by scoring for specific instruments; Bach began to note embellishments to bend instrumentalists and singers alike to the composer's will; the contrapuntal tradition was weakened by various developments, among them the growing number of preludes, elegies and études which were of that free form which owed something to the older church mass. The modern symphony was foreshadowed by the *sinfonia*, the Italian name for the opera overture with its three movements. This overture was tied neither to the musical nor to the dramatic theme of the opera itself. It was simply a curtain-raiser for the opera proper and was perfected, first by Alessandro Scarlatti in a fast-slow-fast pattern, and then by Lully who preferred a slow movement followed by a fugal passage and dance. By the mid-eighteenth century the *sinfonia* had become established as an independent musical form. The modern sonata, evolving from the concerto already described, was only a generation away, Bach's son being reckoned its creator.

In their own right, however, the second half of the seventeenth century and the first decades of the eighteenth are increasingly appreciated as part of the European musical heritage, as forgotten compositions are rediscovered, played and enjoyed. The most original contribution of the period, it will be generally admitted, is to opera as an all-inclusive art: here we have for the first time the sung story, broken by set musical pieces, including orchestra, solo voice, chorus and ensembles, incorporating ballet and even pantomime. *Opera buffa* or *opéra comique* is already being divided from *opera seria* since the *intermezzo* has begun an existence separate from the main work. All over Europe the theatre, with its proscenium stage, its orchestra-pit and row of lights, its elaborate sets and its curtain, is there to stay. It never lacked an audience whether for operas or plays in the years we are discussing though courts strongly influenced by Pietism sometimes closed the theatre and forced the audience back to private performances or the reading of plays in their own houses.

166 Left, Racine's *Bérénice*, first performed 1670

167 Below, Jean Racine (1639–99), the French playwright whom Louis XIV made his historiographer

168 J.B. Molière (1623–73), the French playwright to whose son Louis XIV stood godfather

VI LITERATURE AND LEARNING

It was in the second half of the seventeenth century that plays, comedies as well as tragedies, came into their own in the sense that they were reckoned part of the literature of the age. The playwright had formerly been suppressed, as in Puritan England, or reckoned a social inferior by contamination with the strolling players who performed his plays on the Continent, or prevented by an insatiable demand for popular entertainment from paying much attention to the construction of his pieces: only the Spaniard Lope de Vega (d. 1635), whose output of comedies is known to have been some 1,300 (of which 500 have survived), could produce, for Madrid audiences demanding at least one new work a week, plays which convince us of his talent. But with the Restoration comedies in England and intense court patronage in France and Spain, the position of the playwright improved all over Europe, and plays which were successful in Paris and Versailles – especially those of Corneille, Racine and Molière – were speedily known in German and Scandinavian educated circles.

Themes were frequently common to opera and theatre since librettists, composers, ballet masters and playwrights alike chose popular subjects from Classical mythology. But whereas opera and ballet depended on professional performances to re-create the ideas of their begetters, the fashion of printing plays meant, first of all, that amateurs who would find it difficult to stage an opera (even if they secured libretto and music) were quite ready to embark on the private performance of a play. Indeed, student and courtier amateur groups in countries remote from France helped to create a demand for professional theatre which was largely satisfied before the end of the seventeenth century. Secondly, individuals could and did read plays as literature even if they lived far from capitals, court and theatres. The alexandrines of the French tragedies made them particularly suitable for reading aloud, and the eternal dilemmas of human existence with which they concerned themselves offered more opportunity for general discussion than did the comedies.

169 Setting for Spanish play (by Calderón), *c.* 1680

But we have evidence to suggest that both were read and talked
of far beyond the confines of their actual place of production – in the
French provinces, on the Continent in general either in the original
French or in occasional translations into German. Plays formed
part of travelling libraries of diplomats and officers and, in the case
of the latter, became an important source of relaxation during sieges
or on campaigns when they found themselves removed from polite
society and its comforts. During Charles XII's stay in Turkey the
King, his officers and officials, visiting diplomats and travellers,
often read French plays, analyzed plot and characterization, and
debated the motivation of playwright and characters alike.[1]

Since knowledge of French was practically universal among educated men, while that of English was not, it is natural that the plays of
Corneille and Racine should have exercised the greatest fascination
on the European reading public. The fact that the Restoration
comedies satirized society and were meant to provoke laughter,

170 French and Italian actors in composite painting, *c.* 1670 (Molière, far left). Note the
candelabras: the length of the act was initially determined by the time it took
candles to burn down; the entre-act enabled new candles to be fitted ▶

whereas the French dramatists were concerned with the effect of human passions on character (irrespective of the period of history chosen for the setting of the play), probably also had something to do with the more pervasive appeal of the latter. Even Molière, who did not bother much about the construction of his plays, exhibited a 'Classical' grasp of the fact that it is the flaw in the individual character which brings disaster and retribution. Ludvig Holberg, a native of Bergen, who studied the theatre in both England and France, was a good-humoured satirist who learnt from the Restoration comedies as well as from Molière. His plays were not written down till the early 1720s (fifteen plays in fifteen months) and performed in Copenhagen where he was professor of *eloquentia*. But they are relevant for us in that they make fun of recognizable European 'types' of the turn of the century: the social climber of both sexes, the would-be politician with inadequate grasp of affairs, the boastful traveller, the superficial scholar. His social comment is not restricted to negative criticism. On the plight of the Danish peasant he pointedly put the following words into the mouth of one of his characters: 'Everyone complains that Jeppe drinks: no one asks *why* Jeppe drinks.'[2]

While Holberg, Molière and the comedy writers as a class liked to dash their plays off quickly, the Classical dramatists and the so-called Baroque playwrights tended to put prodigious intellectual effort into their work. Racine's *Phèdre* took two years to write, and recent research has patiently reconstructed the intricate system used by Calderón for the image-making of his allegorical plays.[3] This Spanish playwright wrote some seventy plays, many of which are still read for the fine poetry in which they are couched, and some are classics of the Spanish stage. They are all enlightening for the purposes to which plays were put in Spain and other Catholic countries. Calderón's secular plays, the so-called *zarzuelas*, were for entertainment only, but the one-act *autos sacramentales* were commissioned by the Church to illustrate Catholic dogmas to the masses. They had evolved from *tableaux* set on floats during processions and were now presented on fixed, but temporary, stages. In the hands of a skilled exponent of the morality or instructive play these were remarkably effective. In the *zarzuelas* Calderón's themes are interesting since they touch on the contemporary European debate about the relationship between the individual and society. One popular device (used by him as by others) was to centre the play round a child who is accidentally brought up remote from civilization (for example, in a cave among primitives) and who, when fate carries him back to society, questions both his own and its purpose. After Calderón's death in 1681, Spain had no playwright of real importance; it would seem that the financial and political decline of the last decades of the century affected even the art of the theatre.

This was to some extent true also of Italy, where the intense absorption with opera lessened interest in the theatre proper and the *commedia dell'arte* had begun to deteriorate. But in Germany, which caught up with the rest of Europe after the stagnation of the Thirty Years War, we find Baroque dramatists, even a whole school of them in Silesia. Best known is Lohenstein who wrote his first tragedy, *Ibrahim Bassa*, when he was fifteen and had it published three years later (in 1653), basing it on Madame de Scudéry's novel which he had read in the German translation of 1646. The French Classical drama also had its devotees. Johan Velten, who translated Corneille and Molière, was influenced by them in his own plays and made German theatrical history by insisting that women play the female roles: in this respect, too, there had been isolation from the general European development.

Poetry was the vehicle of most serious plays, and even when the plays themselves have been forgotten, since they have no appeal for modern audiences, the poetry has in part survived because of its intrinsic beauty or force. Apart from this – the main use of poetry in our period – poets expressed their gifts also in occasional verse, in satires and in propaganda of various kinds, and in the words of the hymns of Protestant countries. The Swedish revised hymnbook of 1696 gives us a particularly good insight into the established values of a whole community. Charles XI commissioned the theologian Swedberg (who was interested in linguistic studies) to produce one hymnbook to replace the many different hymnals in current use. He was free to include new hymns. The result, though acceptable to the Diet of the Estates and printed in 1694, had to be withdrawn when the clergy denounced it as insufficiently traditional. A committee of bishops cut out some of the offending items; but the end product of 413 hymns published in 1696 still contained hymns by secular poets, administrators and officers as well as by theologians, and fitted the Caroline spirit of the age in its emphasis on duty to God and the King. The language used, even in hymns translated from the German, expressed the temperament of the nation: direct, realistic, forceful. For this reason it remained *the* hymnbook among ordinary people long after the 1819 version had been commissioned and accepted by the Church. In all Protestant countries, the words of hymns and prayers are significant as sociological documents, and though the Caroline hymnal of 1696 may represent the Swedes at that time as they wanted to see themselves rather than as they really were, we learn – or get confirmation – of their class distinctions, their preoccupations and joys, what they regarded as human and national weaknesses, and discern the propaganda value (or moral strength) which the hymns possessed, with their stress on patience and faith to endure grim times of famine and war.

Propaganda or moral teaching is also noticeable in the satires and rhymed epigrams of the period. The German epigrammist Logau, who published 3,000 *Sinn-Gedichte*, has much of the same force as Protestant religious poets of the second half of the seventeenth century, though not the beauty of the best of them, such as Gerhardt whose hymns are still in use. Logau tried to develop a specific German consciousness strong enough to resist the encroachment of French manners, fashion and language. The fear of political domination is evident in his

171 *The Inspiration of the Epic Poet,* by Poussin

Diener tragen ingemein ihren Herren Lieverey
Solls dann seyn, dass Frankreich Herr, Deutschland aber Diener sey
Freyes Deutschland, schäm dich doch dieser schonden Knechterey.

(Servants usually wear the livery of their masters
Shall it then be said that France is Master, Germany Servant?
Free Germany, be ashamed at this low servitude.)

The Italian painter and poet Salvator Rosa wrote six satires in *terza rima* which castigate the peninsula at large: the muses accept lavish patronage while the masses starve and suffer; the evils and horrors of war are too placidly accepted; hypocrisy covers corruption and lax morals in church and state.

Rosa's contemporary, Francesco Redi, may be taken as a fairly typical writer of occasional verse in our period in that his profession was not that of a man of letters. A physician with a busy practice among the well-to-do, he found time for worth-while scientific experiments, investigated Italian dialects and lectured on them at the University of Florence, collected manuscripts not only from Italy but from all over Europe (he is probably best known as the man who saved the manuscript of Cellini's autobiography for posterity) and wrote fluent verse. His *Bacco in Toscana* – a thousand-line dithyramb – is still read for its perceptive comments (supposedly made by Bacchus) on the different local wines of Tuscany. Other countries offer similar examples of men – and even women – who graced social life by light verse composed for specific occasions, though none were professionals in the sense that patronage (whether royal, noble or bourgeois) permitted them to live from their pen. One who had what is now thought of as an undeserved reputation for her moralizing poems in French, Latin and German, was Sophia Brenner, known in her lifetime (1659–1730) as 'the Swedish Sappho'.

NOVELS AND PROSE

Women also made an impact in novel writing at a time when prose writing was only beginning to embrace entertainment. The tradition of 'rhetoric' or prose, including only *eloquentiae*, church and secular history, and learned writings in general, died hard. The first breach on a European scale came with the growing popularity of Cervantes' *Don Quixote de la Mancha*, published in 1605, and translated, in part, into German in 1648 and in full into French in 1683. Parts of the work appeared in English as early as 1620; these, as well as later complete translations, were frequently reprinted. Here was something deeper and truer to life than the previous *contes* and romances. Subsequent novel writing profited from the disillusioned but optimistic Spaniard whose plot had unity, whose characterization was subtle and who used dream sequences to reveal hidden or suppressed motives. The essence of his appeal was the quickly moving story which entertained while yet inviting reflection by drawing, in Brenan's phrase, 'our thoughts towards their frontiers'.[4]

Next in importance, from the point of view of popularizing the novel as a form of literature came the *salons* of the *précieuses*. The talent for good talk which was the passport to the *salons* from the time of the Marquise de Rambouillet (who died in 1665) onwards, the number of important figures from political and literary circles who congregated in them, the amount of analysis of the subtler shades of friendship and platonic love which took place there gave impetus to the novels of Madeleine de Scudéry, Honoré d'Urfé and Madame de La Fayette. Their novels were popular because they were *romans à clef* in which (as in Scudéry's *Le Grande Cyrus* and *Clélie*, La Fayette's *La Princesse de Clèves* and – at a lower level – Mrs Manley's *New Atlantis*, which featured, in light disguise, Queen Anne, the Duchess of Marlborough and Mrs Masham) those inside the charmed circle could recognize friends and notabilities, but also because they showed psychological understanding of character which made them acceptable to those who read the stories of love without

172 French authoress:
Madame de La Fayette

bothering about the real persons who might have served as models for the authors.

The same element of escapism may have been present, at least for superficial readers, in the popular novel by Aphra Behn, *Oroonoko, or the Royal Slave*, published in London in 1688 and in the whole German genre known as *Schelmenroman* in which the adventures of the hero are piled one upon the other. The authors, however, usually intended to convey a message, as well as to tell a story. Grimmelshausen's *Der Abentheurliche Simplicissimus Teutsch* (1669) has a theme in common with Abraham a Sancta Clara's *Judas der Erzschelm* (published in instalments between 1686 and 1695) – the child brought up out of contact with his own parents. Both authors share a belief that blood or fate will tell: Simplicissimus turns to a life of meditation and books, pondering the lessons learnt from the hermit at whose feet he sat for two years in his youth without then knowing that this beloved sage was his own father; Judas, thrown into the sea in a basket when his mother dreams that he is destined to commit a terrible crime, cannot escape his fate of patricide, incestuous marriage to his own mother and – when remorse on learning the truth has made him a disciple of Jesus – betrayal of Christ. But whereas Abraham a Sancta Clara (a South German who had become court preacher in Vienna in 1677) had for his chief purpose moral instruction, Grimmelshausen was concerned to paint a realistic picture

of society as he had experienced it. Simplicissimus is carried off
by soldiers while guarding the flock of the simple peasant whom he
believes to be his father and enters the same raw and rough world of
soldiers and crooks which Grimmelshausen as a child had been
forced into by abduction. His own adventures, when fighting in
turn for and against each of the two ideological camps in the Thirty
Years War, as well as his own meditations, are mirrored in those of
his hero. German adventure stories after *Simplicissimus* continued
to make social comment, frequently with the help of satirical laughter.
The genre had little effect in France where social change was reflected
more straightforwardly in novels with bourgeois themes and story-
telling was satisfied by the translation of Sheherezade's tales in
twelve volumes. English fiction, however, was not immune to
the influence of the continental novel of adventure. This is clearest
perhaps in Defoe whose realistic treatment surpassed his models in
Robinson Crusoe (1719) and *Moll Flanders* (1722). In their turn Defoe's
novels brought forth a spate of imitations: *Robinson Crusoe* was
immediately translated into German and throughout the 1720s
there appeared 'local' Robinsons – Saxon, Silesian, Thuringian,
Swabian, to say nothing of the German, French and Italian Robinsons
and even a Miss Robinson – which borrowed the name to cash in on
the popularity of the original. The appearance of children's stories
should also be noted. The fables of Aesop and Reineke Fuchs had
long been favourites of children in educated homes; but these were
in reality allegories for grown-ups and La Fontaine's were even more
definitely of this kind. For children's entertainment only, however,

173 French letter-writer:
Madame de Sévigné

Perrault published in 1697 his *Les Contes de ma mère l'Oye*, the precursor of a whole branch of literature.

Instant history in the form of journalism was rapidly expanding in our period. Official gazettes and independent newspapers multiplied and the sumptuously illustrated and well-documented yearbook *Theatrum Europaeum*, published in Frankfurt from 1633 onwards, had many subscribers. More widely ranging was the weekly or monthly journal consisting of a collection of essays on contemporary topics, which made its appearance towards the end of the period. England's *Tatler* and *Spectator* were pioneers in this field and had imitators on the Continent. The Hamburg *Vernünfftler* which started in 1713 consisted mainly of translations from the English, but forerunners to the English monthly can be found in Leipzig as early as 1688–89 and the Dutch periodicals – though more specialized than the English weekly or monthly – had a high reputation, the more important ones appearing in both French and Dutch editions. Directly utilitarian were the many publications which catered to the demand for information. Travel guides and descriptions of countries (sometimes culled from diplomatic reports without the author's permission[5]) were popular. There were innumerable books on gardening and on the qualities which made 'the ideal ambassador'. Books of etiquette and encyclopaedias which popularized research in the humanities and in science sold well in a society anxious to be *au fait*. They were often written for an avowed purpose. Encyclopaedists attempted to put across a point of view, more or less discreetly, and played a significant part in the struggle against orthodoxy which was so characteristic of the intellectual climate of the age. More openly biased were the stream of pamphlets which formed part of party or national propaganda. Lisola's *Le Bouclier d'État* of 1667 against Louis XIV and Swift's venomous *Conduct of the Allies* of 1711 are the best known, but their numbers were legion. Many books have been compiled analyzing the polemical writings of the anti-French propaganda of the period,[6] and a recent analysis has shown that the word 'Europe', as a political concept, was brought into current use as part of the Allied pamphlet warfare against Louis.[7] Jacobite and anti-Jacobite propaganda flourished, as did the pamphlet warfare between Whigs and Tories; and any absolutist ruler ran the risk of being cruelly caricatured in the penned missiles of those in favour of limited sovereignty.[8] Beside these must be put the many pamphlets of anonymous authorship, usually entitled *Letter from Monsieur de B. – allegedly of Rotterdam or Hamburg – to his Friend Mr. A.* which, when investigated, are found to have been commissioned by diplomats less neutral than they wished the author to appear.

Another group of prose writings on the popular level were books of religious moral instruction – Bunyan's *Pilgrim's Progress* of 1678 being the most famous of them all – or pious meditations. These often

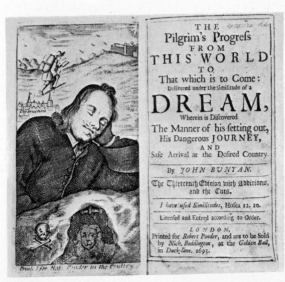

175 Frontispiece of a much-read book (thirteenth edition, 1693)

found their place beside the Bible which was the one certain item of prose literature in most Protestant homes, the book on which generations were brought up and in which the births and deaths of the family were listed. Books of meditation, with popular lives of saints, were widely bought in Catholic countries. Clergymen everywhere published their sermons, usually in a form which must be classified as scholarly debate rather than prose writing, though in England, where theological literature was prevalent, the standard was high enough to cause universal admiration.

Men and women wrote journals and autobiographies, but these – though they have become literature in many cases – were not often intended for publication. A kind of autobiography was published in 1657 under the title *Freund in der Noth* by the Hamburg pastor Johann Balthasar Schupp. He had wandered on foot through large parts of northern Europe and felt moved, when his son went to the university, to write down his experiences in order that the young man should not have to learn his lessons from life the hard way. And the satire which was printed in the same year, *Comoedia vom Studenten-Leben*, by Johann Georg Schoch, a German administrator, seems to have autobiographical traits. But those autobiographical writings that have accidentally been preserved and published later have for us greater appeal, either because they were meant only for an inner circle of family and friends and the writer therefore could be very open, or because they were written to ease or please the writer alone and compel our attention for their conscious or unconscious revelation of character, or for the information they convey about the life of different types of men and women in that age. Pepys's *Diary* is perhaps the best example of the uninhibited self-revelation which at the same time teaches us much about everyday life of the seventeenth century. We eavesdrop on his temptation to sell an office his noble patron has procured for him and note his refusal – out of fear of the patron's reaction; we hear his confession that he does not at all like his wife 'painted' though rouge is now all the fashion. Through the journals of Locke and Temple we learn how the scholar and diplomat were formed. Letters and memoirs, not printed till long after the writers' deaths, help to enlarge our understanding of the period: from well-known letters such as those of Madame de Sévigné to her daughter, and from less accessible ones (for linguistic reasons) like those between Peder Dass, Norwegian vicar in the far north, and the blue-stocking Dorothea Engelbretsdatter in Bergen; from famous

176 Page of a private journal: Edward Barlow's 'Life at Sea 1659 to 1703', with his drawing of a ship in a storm, 1671 ▶

memoirs like those of Saint-Simon at the court of Louis XIV to the relatively unknown (in the west) anecdotes and memoirs by the Polish seventeenth-century nobleman, Jan Pasek. Journals and other papers of men who travelled to or lived in the East Indies, China, Japan and the New World permit us to see with their eyes and be astounded, as they were, at the riches and the ancient civilizations of the east and to assess the opportunities and trials of the West Indies and the Americas. English accounts of attempts to find a safe passage round the Horn, French reports of explorations in the Southern Seas, Austrian reminiscences from a visit to Moscow, the *Journey to Peking* by a Scottish doctor who between 1719 and 1722 travelled overland from Petersburg and back in the suite of a Russian embassy from Peter the Great to the Chinese Emperor K'ang Si – there is no end to the material at our disposal for the less visited parts of Europe and for the wider world.

177 Right, the first English road atlas of 1675, making (typical) use of older engraving, by W. Holler (1607–77) after F. Barlow (1626–1702)

Autobiographical writings offer glimpses of universal moods and types. Edward Barlow, in his journal, labours the theme that beggars had 'a far better life of it' than sailors; they had 'their bellies full of better victuals', could sleep their fill at night while the sailor had four hours at most in one stretch, and shared neither the monotony nor the dangers of the seaman's lot.[9]

A Swedish noblewoman of ancient lineage, Agneta Horn, neither well educated nor particularly intelligent, kept a record of her hard and loveless childhood and the rebellions of adolescence: the slights (real and imaginary) she suffered, the revenge (executed or merely plotted) she wrought on stepmother, aunts, governesses and maids before, with pride tamed and heart thawed, she married her 'brave soldier' Lars Cruus.[10]

In his memoirs, Axel von Löwen, an old officer, looking back on service in many European armies, marvelled how times had changed and how the 'heroic virtues' admired in his youth had gone so totally out of fashion.[11]

ACADEMIES AND HUMANISTIC LEARNING

In 1635 Richelieu had founded the Académie Française to promote the French language and to hold a brief, so to speak, as the public guardian of taste and correct usage. The predominance of Latin as the intellectual language of Europe was already slipping, at least in the more populous nations, and it is noticeable that Descartes published his *Discours de la Méthode* in 1637 in French. One task given to the Académie was to produce a French dictionary, but preparatory work was time-consuming and it was not complete till 1694. The need for dictionaries, glossaries and grammars was felt all over Europe and enough were published to justify their being enumerated among the 'blessed inventions of our time'.[12] The Dutch Republic was, from a publishing point of view, multilingual. The nations with tongues not widely spoken retained Latin (though French and German were also used) in order to maintain their participation in the intellectual and scholarly life of Europe. The Swedish grammar, the *Grammaticae suecenae* of 1694, was in Latin, and even Swedish poetry was lectured on in the universities of Uppsala and Lund in Latin, since the academics argued that the use of Latin for all subjects was what distinguished the universities from the schools. Not till the reign of Charles XII did a conscious improvement of Swedish begin, strongly encouraged by the King himself. The German philosopher Christian Thomasius began to lecture in German at the University of Leipzig as early as 1687–88 and wrote his scholarly works in German. The increased academic use of the vernacular became possible everywhere as the indigenous language rose in esteem thanks to the work of grammarians and propaganda from above.

Linked with the concern for language was critical advice on how to use it. Boileau-Despréaux' *Satires* were directed against bad writing and his *L'Art Poétique* of 1674, though didactic enough to earn him the nick-name *législateur de Parnasse*, set standards and gave rulings which

178 Queen Christina of Sweden conversing with Descartes

were widely accepted even outside France. In Rome an academy named the Arcadia was founded in 1692 by men of letters (who had earlier met under the patronage of Queen Christina) to continue their avowed purpose 'to exterminate bad taste and to see to it that it shall not rise again' – a shaft directed against the extravagant and 'Baroque' poetry of Marino (1569–1625) and his imitators. After 1700, when the Bourbon dynasty had been established in Spain, Luzán popularized Boileau in an attempt to cure the Spanish language of the twin diseases of obscurity and turgidity which, he held, it had contracted. The War of the Spanish Succession delayed the setting up of bodies which could help the process; but the Biblioteca Nacional was founded in 1711 and the first part of a Spanish dictionary was published in 1726. In Germany Leibniz preached the founding of academies as foci for learning. He helped to establish that of Berlin in 1700, but the Russian Academy he planned for Tsar Peter had to be postponed, because of the Great Northern War, till 1724. The same war prevented the realization of Tessin and Charles XII's pet project of a Swedish Academy till 1735.

The historiographers-royal at the various courts fulfilled some of the functions of academies in sorting manuscripts, evaluating evidence and writing history with critical use of source-material. Leibniz's work at Hanover is a good example of this, though his main commission – a history of the House of Hanover – was delayed because of his genealogical researches, his wide intellectual interests (he was, in Cassirer's phrase, the last universal scholar before eighteenth-century specialization set in), his vast correspondence and his many journeys to collect material. Indeed, it was only his desire to become the historiographer of George I in his capacity as King of Great Britain which spurred Leibniz on to finish two volumes of the *Historia Domus*, and he had reached only the year 1005 when death overtook him in 1716.[13] An interest in genealogy and heraldry, motivated in part by practical considerations, was typical of all courts, large and small; but it was only powerful and ambitious dynasties that commissioned contemporary history. The campaigns of Louis XIV, Charles XII and Tsar Peter were covered in this way, as were the reigns of Leopold, Joseph and Charles VI. Some of the distinguished thinkers of the age became interested in general history. Pufendorf, who as historiographer, first of Sweden and then of Brandenburg, had written histories of Charles X and of the Great Elector, wrote a history of Europe which was an immediate success.

It dealt with all the major states and discussed their conditions and objectives. It became the first modern textbook in European history. Statesmen studied it and Louis XIV's theory of the harmonizing of interests of states was possibly affected by it. The cosmopolitan interests of the age found expression in attempts at writing universal history and universal geography going beyond the confines of Europe. The effect of more critical standards can be noticed even in Bossuet's treatment of religious history; in the third edition of his *Discours sur l'Histoire Universelle* he changed the date of the creation of the world since he accepted information from Egyptian and Chinese history brought to his attention by Father Perron.

Jesuit missionaries and other travellers had increased the body of knowledge of and from non-European continents, and in the *Description de L'Universe* by Manesson-Mallet, a profusely illustrated work published in 1683, the information conveyed on the geography, government, social structure and culture of all known countries was such as to encourage speculation whether Christian Europe possessed a monopoly of truth and civilization. The power and riches of Far Eastern states had been respected and admired (as well as coveted) from the first days of contact: now a sympathetic understanding of their religions and civilizations had a broadening influence on European thought.

Such notions of the relativity of religious truth could not be freely expressed in the academies which enjoyed court patronage, for in Catholic as in Protestant countries the church buttressed civil authority. It was expressed, with specific attacks on the church everywhere as an obstacle to rational search for truth, by the French Huguenot Pierre Bayle (who had left France in 1681) in the *Dictionnaire historique et critique*, printed in 1697 in Rotterdam where he held a chair of philosophy specially created for him by William III. This he lost, since even in the tolerant Dutch Republic his 'impious comments' could not be officially stomached; but his book proved immensely popular and influential. It laced erudition with invective and stirred enough snippets of unsubstantiated 'facts' into the brew to expose him to the charge that he did not apply critical standards to his own work. The importance of it, however, lay in the way he challenged accepted authority and encouraged others to join him in his search for the truth wherever reason might lead. It ran to nine editions and was translated into English and German. In 1719, Ludvig Holberg tells us in his memoirs, there was a queue, stretching

179 Criticism: Pierre Bayle,
author of
*Dictionnaire historique
et critique*, 1697

all round the corner of the Bibliothèque Mazarine in Paris, of scholars waiting to consult it.[14]

Bayle was no atheist, but after his wanderings between the Catholic and Protestant churches he came to rest in a vague kind of deism. The dissatisfaction of many contemporaries with the split between the churches led to plans for reuniting them. In this they were unsuccessful, but in their other quest, that of erecting a philosophical structure which would accommodate the discoveries in physical knowledge while yet permitting a belief in God, considerable progress was made.

TECHNOLOGY AND NATURAL PHILOSOPHY

The investigation of nature had made great strides before the mid-seventeenth century. The needs of the state had contributed to this. Land-drainage schemes created an interest in tides, and the first scientific tables appeared as early as 1590. Artillery promoted the study of the laws of ballistics. Mining of precious metals and iron ore encouraged investigation into pumping machinery. Navigational problems gave impetus to research into magnetism and astronomy. Precision instruments of observation and measurement were invented and perfected: compasses, the telescope, the microscope, the barometer, the thermometer, the pendulum clock and balances that were accurate to within one five-hundreth of a grain. The Aristotelian picture of man's physiology, of the elements, of the universe itself burst its framework as Galileo proved Copernicus right beyond doubt, Harvey discovered the circulation of the blood, and Boyle, by his law of gases, proved that four elements were not sufficient to explain the nature of matter. Nature itself seemed to be on the side of the wreckers of the old system. The bright star which appeared in 1572 had dented the Aristotelian picture of the finite unchanging universe; the comet of 1577 – which so obviously passed through Aristotle's separate and immutable crystalline spheres – smashed it for ever. And when the comet of 1682 appeared it caused less concern than Halley's prediction that it would be visible once more in 1759 since it, like the earth, moved around the sun on a regular path. Comets, indeed, were no longer objects of awe; when an English diplomat wanted to express his annoyance at Louis XIV's arrogance, he ridiculed the King as 'this Great Comet that is risen of late and expects not only to be gazed at but adored.'[15]

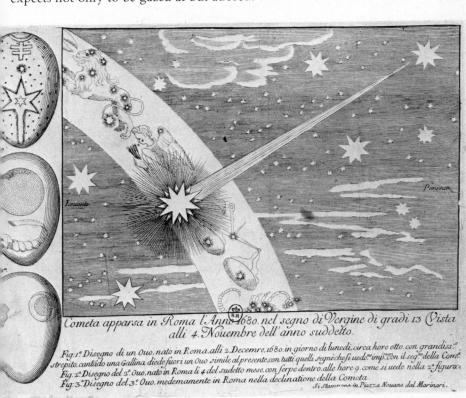

Cometa apparsa in Roma l'Anno 1680. nel segno di Vergine di gradi 13 Vista alli 4. Nouembre dell'anno suddetto.

Fig.1ª Disegno di un Ouo, nato in Roma, alli 2. Decemre, 1680. in giorno di lunedi, circa hore otto, con grandiss.º strepito, cantado una Gallina diede fuori un Ouo simile al presente, con tutti quelli segni, che si uedo.m imp.ºn il seg.me della Com.ta Fig.2ª Disegno del 2º Ouo, nato in Roma li 4 del sudetto mese, con serpe dentro, alle hore 9. come si uede nella 2ª figura Fig.3ª Disegno del 3º Ouo, medemamente in Roma nella declinatione della Cometa. Si Stampano in Piazza Nouano dal Marinari.

180 Superstition: Italian print on the comet seen in Rome, 1680–81

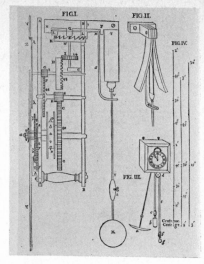

Generally speaking, however, it was the technological applications of scientific discoveries which made themselves more widely felt. These were often made by men whom we would call scientists, but whom contemporaries thought of as natural philosophers. Most of them worked in academies and societies, such as the famous Accademia del Cimento of Florence, founded in 1651, where several of Galileo's pupils, among them the famous Torricelli, worked, and which from 1667 onwards published results of its members' experiments. Colbert's Académie des Sciences, started in 1660, and the Royal Society for Promoting Natural Knowledge (to give it its full title), begun in London in 1662, are outstanding among the societies expressly founded for the purpose of contributions to practical knowledge; indeed the Royal Society was divided into eight 'committees' according to the field (mechanical, agricultural, etc.) in which the scientists wanted to concentrate. The Swedish Laboratorium Mechanicum where Hjärne and Polhem worked was as utilitarian in purpose, and the many Dutch scientists – though they organized themselves less frequently into societies – were eminently practical in their approach. The Huygens brothers improved on Galileo's telescope in the 1650s; Leeuwenhoek, carrying on from where Malpighi of Bologna left off, increased the magnification of the microscope three hundredfold. Christiaan Huygens, when in the service of Louis XIV, introduced the pendulum as the controlling device for clocks and achieved accuracy for the first time: not a minute lost in the test period of four months.

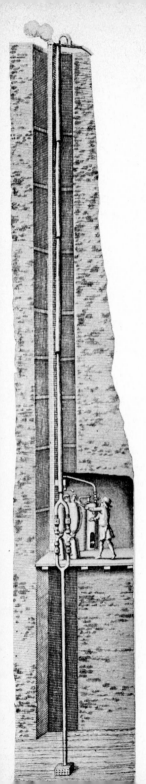

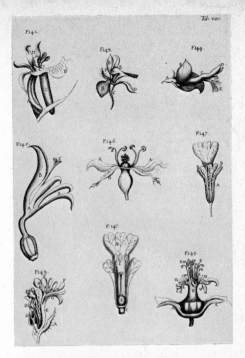

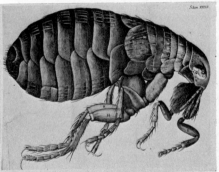

181 Opposite left, laboratory at the University of Altdorf, *c.* 1720

182 Opposite right, drawing of pendulums by Christiaan Huygens, published in 1673

183 Left, steam pumping machine for mines, designed by T. Savery, published in 1702

184 Top, botanical drawings by M. Malpighi, published in 1675–79

185 Above, drawing of a flea by R. Hooke, published in 1665

There was a response to society's needs. Pumping machinery for mines was perfected, accurate almanacs and tables of tides were produced; the repeating watch enabled people to tell the time at night without lighting a candle and made unnecessary such exotic expedients as having each hour-number indicated by a different spice which could be touched and then identified by smell or taste.[16] Not all inventions were popular; the Dutch looms caused riots among the ribbon-weavers of England when they were first introduced. Others were ahead of their time; the ingenious seed-drill of Jethro Tull was not immediately successful and the delicious dinner prepared for members of the Royal Society in a receptacle operating on the pressure-cooker principle did not lead to its commercial exploitation.[17] On the other hand, some problems for which society keenly desired solutions were beyond the scientists of the time; in spite of the high prizes offered and the many attempts made, the exact determination of longitude, vital for mariners, had to wait for a later generation.

Advances in medical science (the diagnosis of illnesses such as diabetes, for instance, and important discoveries in the field of embryology) were much discussed, though those dealing with botany and geology (where classification became surer) were limited to a relatively narrow range of near-specialists. The observations, calculations and speculations of the natural philosophers regarding the universe and the laws that governed it also made an impact on society at large, though only men familiar with mathematics could grasp the formulation of the arguments involved. Two central problems agitated educated men once they had accepted Galileo's thesis of the sun as the centre of the universe. One was a scientific one that related to the problem of gravity. Aristotle had

186 Experimental blood transfusion in the 1680s (see p. 61)

187 Louis XIV and Colbert visit the Académie des Sciences ▶

taught that gravity pulled all objects to the centre. Why then were not the planets, including the earth, pulled towards the sun and burnt to cinder in its heat? The other was an issue of faith. How could the new theory be reconciled to the teachings of the church and the Bible: where did God fit in?

In the search for answers the philosophers had decimals, algebraic equations, logarithms and the slide-rule to help them in their calculations. Descartes invented co-ordinate geometry and Leibniz and Locke – independently – discovered the formula for infinitesimal calculus. The road was now open for the completion of Galileo's work: Kepler, inheriting Tycho Brahe's papers and calculations, charted the elliptical movement of the planets; Borelli, in 1665, argued that the planets would gravitate towards the sun but for centrifugal force; Huygens published his mathematical formula for that force in 1673 though he did not apply it to the planets; and in 1674 Hooke of the Royal Society postulated that all heavenly bodies exerted attraction upon one another. By that time Newton had already formulated his law of universal gravitation though he did not publish it till 1687. Newton's law restored mathematical order and certainty to the universe and replaced for most scholars the earlier Descartian theory of the vortex, though this persisted in France till about 1730. Newton did not claim to have explained the universe, or even gravity itself: 'Pray do not ascribe that notion to me, for the cause of gravity is what I do not pretend to know.' What he did feel he had contributed to was the reconciliation between God and natural philosophy, for did not his universal law constitute a proof of the existence of a God who had designed and created the universe?

This search for unity between the physical and spiritual worlds had become increasingly the concern of scholars who felt the dualism of Descartes to be unsatisfactory and even anti-God, however much Cartesian philosophy denied this. Descartes had proved God to his own satisfaction by the formula 'That all things which we clearly and distinctly conceive are true, therefore God must exist since we clearly and distinctly conceive him.' But the distinction made by Descartes between the 'thinking substance' of the spiritual and the 'extended substance' of the physical created a dualism with no visible link between the two; and his scepticism was put into use only for 'extended substance'. From this, deism could easily be construed – and Spinoza and other philosophers did so to the regret of those who

PROSPECTVS INTRA CAMERAM STELLATAM.

188 The Royal Observatory at Greenwich: astronomer royal (Flamsteed) at table, his two assistants making observations

could not accept the dictum that God's existence cannot be proved. Leibniz tried to solve the problem by harmonizing matter and spirit. He postulated a unit of consciousness, the monad, which possessed spiritual potentiality. In this system he found proof of a preordained God-given harmony of the kind Newton conceived as proved by his law of gravitation. To later ages his philosophy has seemed closer to Platonic idealism; but it needs stressing that the majority of the philosophers of the seventeenth century wanted to find room for God in the structures they erected, and managed to do so in a way that satisfied their intellects as well as their emotions.

Yet, if they were not content to leave God as the creator who had merely set the universe in motion, they were challenged towards the end of the century by the new interest in psychology. Descartes had argued that there were certain innate principles common to all mankind and placed there by God. Locke in his *Essay concerning Humane Understanding* of 1690 denied this. He used the growing amount of information gathered about non-European peoples to make his point by contrasting different customs and moral tenets in different parts of the world. 'What, then,' he asked, 'are those innate principles of justice, piety, gratitude, equity, chastity!' But Locke also strove to obtain mathematical certainty, and believed this to be possible in politics and ethics – i.e., in the social as in the natural sciences. 'Where there is no property there is no injustice is a proposition as certain as any demonstration in Euclid,' is a typical example of the way in which he phrased an argument. This particular proposition may at first glance be as difficult for our own age to grasp as the definitions, widely accepted at the time, that liberty was freedom to enjoy property and privilege was exemption from a duty or charge which fell on others. The significant point about Locke's conviction that society was subject to laws as demonstrable as those of mathematics was that he, more than any other thinker of the period, helped to create an intellectual climate which promoted interest in reform of society; if the laws governing society could be discovered, as they had been in natural philosophy, then rational improvement of society would follow.

189, 190 Kneller's portraits of Sir Isaac Newton, 1702, and John Locke in the last years of his life (see page 130)

VII THE INTELLECTUAL CLIMATE

Until the mid-seventeenth century most educated Europeans tended to subscribe to the belief that man's progress must be in a downward direction. God had created the perfect world, man had sinned and been thrown out of Eden; ever since, man's history was one of universal decline, however slow, from the state of perfection. Analogies were drawn between the individual's progress through life – he flourished, weakened and died; the universe in its turn must fade and fail. In God's own time, after the Day of Judgment, man and universe would be reborn into a new and perfect state.

The challenge to this belief came first in the field of religion from the Anglican divines of the 1620s, but the debate which ensued spread to scholars in all fields and developed into a European-wide controversy, usually labelled 'Ancients versus Moderns', which raged till the early decades of the eighteenth century. The intensity of the debate varied according to country and to the subject discussed, but there was hardly any aspect of culture and learning which escaped the fashionable bisection: drama, poetry, sculpture, architecture, painting, eloquence, medicine, music, philosophy and natural philosophy, which we would label the 'natural sciences'. The debate had significant consequences. It tended, as it progressed, to separate theologians from other scholars; it developed history as an independent branch of knowledge; it accelerated the momentum towards the natural sciences and provided a tie with the social sciences; it influenced the educational theories of what future generations ought to learn and shaped the intellectual climate of the age in such a way that we can speak of a revolution, broader than the word 'scientific' alone would convey, about 1660. Indeed, the word *Frühaufklärung* has now been coined to link the period we are studying firmly to the familiar 'Enlightenment' of the eighteenth century. The accepted English translation of the new label, the 'Pre-Enlightenment', is not fully satisfactory since it hints only at the chronological connection, and a literal translation, the 'Early Enlightenment', is to be preferred.

At the centre of the debate stood the idea of progress. Not perpetual or linear progress, but the possibility of progress as well as regression in the history of mankind. The theological motivation for this optimism was first expressed by G[eorge] H[akewill] in *An Apologie* of 1627. The idea that God had condemned His own creation to a perpetual decline was repugnant to Hakewill and he substituted the idea of a cyclic process: civilizations flourished and failed, but rebirth and renewed flowering were possible even within the allotted time-span of the universe. Hakewill himself distinguished between three periods of relatively recent history in which man had records and other evidence to help him. Greek and Roman history constituted a period of 'flowering civilization'. The Middle Ages had brought 'decline and darkness'. With Petrarch revival had started in Italy and since then Hakewill could only find improvement everywhere: truer knowledge of the Bible and the Classics from grammatical and textual criticism; better history because of surer chronology; gains in medical and scientific understanding; practical innovations such as aids to navigation, the publication of dictionaries and 'the invention and perfection of stenography'. Even the advent of improved artillery might serve, he argued, a progressive purpose in 'that by the cruel force and terrible roaring of it, men might rather

191 *Historiography* from *Theatrum Europaeum* of *c.* 1650. The study of history made great strides: documents were collected, source material criticized and Vico laid down the guidelines for sympathetic (indeed empathetic) understanding of the past

192 On the side of the Moderns:
title-page of Glanvill's *Plus
Ultra* of 1668

PLUS ULTRA:
OR, THE
Progress and Advancement
OF·
KNOWLEDGE
Since the Days of
ARISTOTLE.
In an ACCOUNT of some of the most
Remarkable
LATE IMPROVEMENTS
OF
Practical, Useful Learning:
· To Encourage
PHILOSOPHICAL ENDEAVOURS.
OCCASIONED
By a Conference with one of the
NOTIONAL Way.

By *JOS. GLANVILL.*

LONDON,
Printed for *James Collins* at the *Kings-Head*
in *Westminster-Hall.* 1568.

193 Making fun of the controversy between
'Ancients and Moderns': title-page of Swift's
Battle of the Books (ed. of 1710; first ed. 1704)

181

be deterred from assaulting one another in a hostile and warlike manner'.[1] Other Anglican divines took up his theme and it was echoed also on the Continent, particularly after 1648 when religious peace was restored. Here Descartes's *Traité des passions* (1649) played an important part, as did notions latent in Renaissance writings. The discussion spread outside religious circles, partly because there was as yet no particular dividing-line between theologians and other scholars; but also because there was in this period, in Herbert Butterfield's phrase, 'a colossal secularisation of thought in every possible realm of ideas at the same time'.[2] The impact of the experimental sciences also promoted the idea of progress. When Joseph Glanvill, in his *Plus Ultra* of 1668, listed improvements much in the manner of Hakewill, he gave as a specific example the advances made by the natural philosophies of Vieta, Descartes and Dr Wallis, and looked forward to fresh gains from the newly founded Royal Society.

By the 1670s the debate became lively enough in France to erupt into print. Significant contributions are Fontenelle's *Une digression sur les Anciens et les Modernes* of 1688 (after which the debate has been named), since it evolved the theory of 'necessary improvement', and Perrault's grandly conceived *Parallèle des Anciens et des Modernes*, published between 1688 and 1696, in which comparisons were made along the whole range of arts and learning. Perrault even argued that the poetry of the Moderns must be better than that of the Ancients since the physical knowledge of the heart, the seat of emotions, was now surer. Others took up the challenge on behalf of the Ancients, among them Sir William Temple in 1690, though his point that the Ancients had once been Moderns might be thought to reinforce rather than combat the idea of progress. By this time, however, there are signs that the battle was over. Temple admits the justification of regarding the mid-seventeenth century as a watershed because of the improvement in the methods of scientific inquiry; Wotton, in 1694, tried to divide honours between Ancients and Moderns; and Swift, by 1704, ridiculed the protagonists in *The Battle of the Books*. The idea of inevitable and perpetual decline had largely vanished; that of progress had come to stay and with it optimism. Those who fought only with words were now left behind, and fruitful speculation and discussion began on how knowledge is absorbed and how the behaviour of individuals or groups is motivated. Before 1700 the object of investigation takes on a new slant: from the nature of things, or 'extended substance', to use Cartesian terminology, attention is directed to human nature. Would it not be possible by the exercise of human reason to discover laws which governed man in society to correspond to the laws which had been established for the circulation of blood in the human body by Harvey and for the structure of the universe by Newton?

Neither the men of the *Frühaufklärung* nor those of the Enlightenment were as optimistic or irrational in their belief in rationality as later ages have sometimes assumed,[3] but they either believed in a universal design – with or without a God as the great Geometer who had set the whole in motion – or, if sceptics, argued that reason was the only means known to men whereby improvement could be brought about. In either case the road was open for hopeful reform in all aspects of human life.

RELIGION AND CHURCHES

During the intellectual revolution sketched above, what we would call sensibility became a noticeable trend, emphasis being placed on the individual as opposed to the community. Such ideas were expressed by believers and sceptics alike. The optimism of the Moderns, if they were religiously inclined (as most of them were), stressed God's universal benevolence. God's love for man rather than his punishment of man was preached by Anglican divines after 1660; the Jesuits in the same period showed a compassion for the individual which their detractors interpreted as the virtual dethronement of God and His replacement with man. The Pietist movement which spread so rapidly throughout Germany and into Scandinavia carried a message of divine love, the kernel of which resided in the individual's emotional relationship to God rather than in corporate church worship. The Quietist and Molinist movements in Catholic countries had something of the same character.

The stoicism so much admired in the early part of the century was now derided as hard and unfeeling and untrue to man's character. Man, it was argued, is a social creature who naturally loves his own species and is full of pity, tenderness and benevolence: indeed, it is these very qualities which distinguish man from other creatures. 'The Stoics', wrote Lowde in 1694, 'would make men so wholly rational, that they will scarce allow him to be sensible'; if man was permitted to be sensible, that is, to let his natural affections and passions guide his behaviour, these, when duly regulated by reason, would give 'Vigour and Wings to the Soul in its pursuit of Virtue'.[4] George

Stanhope, in the same year, thought equally well of the passions: 'These are indeed the secret Springs that move and actuate us; and all the Care incumbent upon the Governing Part of the Mind, is to set them right.'[5] Frenchmen expressed similar thoughts even earlier. Antoine le Grand argued in 1662 that charity was preferable to stoic insensibility and Simon demanded tolerance for the Jews in his *Histoire critique du Vieux Testament* of 1679.

Tolerance was also demanded on intellectual grounds. The contact with peoples outside Europe who had never heard of Christianity produced, as stressed before (see p. 169), a degree of relativity in the assessment of culture and religion. All religions could, however, be reconciled if one looked upon them as embodying one essential truth which could be discovered once 'local' myths, accretions and perversions were removed. Such an attitude had predictable repercussions in a Europe divided into several religious camps. If Christianity had as its basis the one universal truth, 'natural religion', it would be sensible and reasonable to get rid of the 'local' differences that separated Catholic and Protestant, and reunite them. Queen Christina of Sweden, encouraged by discussions with tolerant Protestant and Catholic thinkers, hoped for such a union and, when she found herself disappointed by orthodoxy in both camps, turned towards Molinism for a time. Leibniz, who publicized his optimism in *Nouveaux Essais sur l'entendement humain* and his belief in God's benevolence in *Essais de Théodicée sur la bonté de Dieu*, formulated a detailed plan for the reunion of the churches – including the Greek Orthodox – but was equally disappointed.

Individual tolerance was the rule rather than the exception in Protestant countries, at least from the side of the ruler. The Hohenzollern dynasty turned Calvinist but did not interfere with the Lutheran Church of Brandenburg-Prussia; Saxony was unaffected by its Elector's conversion to Catholicism in 1697; there was tolerance for foreigners in Russia, and Swedish clergymen with Pietist leanings had no higher praise for Charles XII than their conviction that, had he lived, he would have continued to champion their cause against intolerant Lutheran bishops. Such tolerance proceeded either from lack of genuine religious conviction, the rulers themselves being influenced by the process of secularization mentioned above, or from an intellectual conviction of the relativity of revealed truth. In Charles XII's case a tolerant attitude to religion and ethics is noticeable after his stay in Turkey, where he learnt at first hand that the moral standards of most Moslems were equal to, if not higher than, those of many Christians, however much the followers of Islam were dubbed Unbelievers by the European churches. But tolerance was harder to come by inside the hierarchy of any particular church. Limborch's famous treatise of 1686 condemned intolerance, not only in respect of the Catholic–Protestant dichotomy but also inside each church, including that of the Reformed or Calvinist one. On the whole, Catholic countries fared worse than Protestant ones if the ruler, like Louis XIV of France and Leopold of Austria and his sons, achieved a vested interest in conformity. This happened when the security of the state was concerned.* Louis, who had laughed at Molière's ridicule of *la vie dévote* and who, according to Madame de Maintenon, did not possess a religious temperament, found himself not only worried about the punishment to come, which she preached, but obsessed with the way in which the Protestants in the enclave of Orange and in the neighbouring Piedmont-Savoy could be made to work with the enemies of France. William III's principality provided a haven for those Frenchmen who defied the religious unity envisaged by the Revocation of the Edict of Nantes, and Louis's fear of a Protestant crusade to free the suppressed Huguenots of *l'église du désert* of the south-east were not entirely groundless as the War of the Spanish Succession showed. Leopold, like Joseph and Charles VI after him, was determined to tie reconquered Hungary as firmly as possible to Austria, and the extermination of Protestantism was one means to this end. Their Protestant allies proved at times an embarrassment to the Catholic Austrian Habsburgs. The infamous Ryswick clause, the fourth in the treaty of 1697, which decreed that the religion in the 'reunions' returned by France to the Empire should remain the Catholic one, was generally blamed on Louis XIV, though it was Leopold who had secretly insisted on it;[6] and Charles – as Archduke claiming the throne of Carlos II – found himself reviled by the Catholic Spaniards because he was supported by foreign heretics, the English and the Dutch, a cry taken up by the Spanish Church as well as by Philip V. The Spanish Church was in any case particularly alarmed at divisive influences, having purged itself of Moslem Spaniards and hispanicized Jewish *conversos* at a considerable cost to Spain's economic prosperity. Attempts by government circles in Spain (instigated by Oropesa and Macanaz) to weaken and even abolish the Inquisition towards the end of the seventeenth century were unsuccessful, though the temper

* Oppression founded on reasons of state was not of course confined to Catholic countries; post-Cromwellian England continued, for religious and secular reasons (though less crudely), that suppression of Catholicism in Ireland which in the Protector's time had witnessed 500 leaders hung, 10,000 sold as slaves and 11 million acres of land confiscated. Nor were fears of divisory forces entirely absent: William Penn founded Pennsylvania because Restoration England was not sufficiently tolerant of Dissenters. But generally speaking tolerance increased after 1680 and Penn himself found no difficulty, in his later years, in reconciling himself to living in England and attempting to govern his colony from afar.

of the 'Holy Office' became milder after the accession of Philip V.

Even inside the Catholic Church tolerance and rationalist thought were preached, particularly in France. Some of the opposition to Jansenism can be explained by the God of the Jansenists appearing a 'barbaric tyrant' to the Jesuits, and Fénelon criticized monks who would possess nothing in this world but demand 'all' in matters of faith. The Jansenists Pierre Nicole and Antoine Arnauld attempted to rid the church of superstition and ridiculed clerical tyranny in all their work. When the conservatives closed their ranks, Nicole and Arnauld counterattacked by delving deeper into the psychology of belief and exposed supernatural events as self-deceptions and illusions, denied the efficacy of prayers and condemned the sacramental teachings of the church as 'mystical'. Such attacks helped to undermine belief in a revealed religion and train a generation

194, 195 Jansenist philosophers: Antoine Arnauld (1612–94) and Pierre Nicole (1622–95)

196 Right, Miguel Molinos, a Spanish Quietist condemned and imprisoned for life by the Inquisition in Rome, 1687, for heresy, alarm having been created by the sexual immorality fostered by Molinism

Mme de Guyon, French Quietist

198 The religious hypocrite attacked: Molière's *Tartuffe* of 1664

199 The Freemasons of England

200 Above, Pope Clement XI (1700–21)

of sceptics. The very raging against freethinkers and atheists in English and French religious pamphlets at the end of the seventeenth century proves that deism and atheism must have become vocal. The natural philosophers, genuinely motivated – as were Descartes and Newton – by a desire to prove God's existence, had by their very work opened the door to deist and atheist theories. The scepticism of Bayle and Malebranche, the rationalism of Nicole and Arnauld, nourished them, and so, unwittingly, did Locke's *The Reasonableness of Christianity*. In retrospect we can see that many who at the time thought of themselves as Christians, for example Molière, were in reality deists. Fénelon has been accused of creating his own God, 'who may or may not have been a Christian one',[7] and Bossuet has been categorized, on the evidence of his own writings, as a 'subjective pan-hedonist'.[8] This may be going too far, since what a man believes himself to be has a validity of its own and Bossuet's insistence that God creates happiness is not far removed from the Anglican idea of God's benevolence. But though scepticism was rife, the open expression of deism and atheism was a rarity and contemporaries did, in any case, often confuse the two. The best-documented examples are from London where a group of deists held regular meetings under the leadership of John Toland between 1696 and 1699 and where the Masonic Order was founded by 'freethinkers' in 1717. Attacks on the authority of the churches which claimed to interpret religion were, however, common enough, and criticism of the Church of Rome by Frenchmen and Spaniards can be paralleled in Germany where the philosopher Thomasius castigated Lutheran metaphysics and sectarians were protected by the Electress Sophia of Hanover in the name of freedom of philosophical enquiry. This habit of questioning the authority of the churches spread beyond the educated classes, who criticized on rational grounds, to popular sectarian emotional movements. The emphasis here was on freedom to worship as one felt right, but mysticism and ritual far removed from rationalism were easily introduced. In Russia, for example, sects originated when in time the 'Old Believers', who would not accept changes in ritual, found it impossible to obtain bishops or even priests within the established Church. Splinter-groups then developed, each with its own particular cult, some reminiscent of the more visionary sects of English dissenters. It was among the dissenters in England that the cry of complete separation between church and state was first raised.

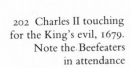

Consulting an astrologer in
70, still an important part of
ryday custom at some levels of
iety

202 Charles II touching
for the King's evil, 1679.
Note the Beefeaters
in attendance

Though the word 'psychology' was not used in Europe till 1749, thinkers in our period were preoccupied with 'the passions', the driving forces of human behaviour. Dryden pondered what passions are in themselves and how they are produced. Nicole and Arnauld developed, in the words of a modern scholar, 'a rough psychology model which lasted for two hundred years',[9] cataloguing, in their attacks on the supernatural, the self-deception and illusions, the egoism and concupiscence to which man is prone. Thomasius's teachings at Leipzig spread far enough to make Charles XII of Sweden compose a 'thesis' in 1718 about the delights of the senses and the delights of the soul, based on what he had learnt of the German rationalist's theories of the *Leidenschaften* via a courtier in the service of Frederick of Hesse.[10] The spirit of rationalism was applied in assessing the probability of man's behaviour and in questioning his motives. William III refused to touch for the King's evil because belief in the efficacy of the custom seemed to him superstitious and was therefore repugnant. Queen Anne restored the custom; George I abandoned it once more. Tsar Peter of Russia was always asking whether a given policy was 'reasonable'. In 1698 Charles XII, as a young king of fifteen, queried whether it served any purpose to use torture: might not an innocent man be likely to confess just because he was being tortured and wished his pain to stop? This was an idea

189

he may well have picked up from discussion of French writings, since in France torture had been condemned in print as early as the 1670s, or he may have been unable to grasp (if he had ever heard of it) the theological justification of torture: that God would be on the side of the innocent and help him to stand up to this, the most severe test of the truth of his testimony. The problem of evil was much discussed in England, France and Germany. How was it that moral virtues and intelligence were so unequally distributed, to say nothing of worldly goods? Were the wide differences observed in class and property justified? Were the curricula of universities and schools sacrosanct? Was the inferior position of women pre-ordained?

The challenge implied in these and similar questions, and the greater understanding of motives, had repercussions on education. Instructions for the guidance of the teachers of royal princes and young men of high noble family have survived for our period. They all stress the importance of making the lessons come alive: the boy must feel that he is present at the historical events which his Latin and Greek texts depict. When he gets older and receives the training in mathematics indispensable for a future general in the field – a task for which tradition decreed that those who showed aptitude should be educated – past battles, including those of his own ancestors, must be used to illuminate the art of war, and serving officers should be brought in as part-time teachers. Bossuet, entrusted with the education of the Dauphin, tried to make geography lessons as exciting as travel. Ideas of this kind were found also in wider circles and are known to us from treatises on educational principles. The teachers at Port-Royal strove to make lessons 'more palatable than play', and the Jesuits devised a system of competitions which permeated their schools and had a nearly hypnotic effect on pupils and teachers alike. Some non-Jesuits believed that the frequent and semi-public competitions encouraged pride. Port-Royal would have none of them, though Pascal insisted that those robbed of the competitive incentive became 'nonchalant' and stressed that the *gloire* gained in the striving for the best piece of poetry and the cleverest dialogues was beneficial: 'L'admiration gâte tout dès l'enfance.'[11] Mnemonics of various kinds had long been used for Greek and Latin grammar; now verses were employed to teach modern subjects like geography. The one beginning 'La Hollande ou plutôt les Provinces Unies' might well serve as a reminder for today's students only too willing to let the name of one province serve for the federation of seven.[12]

In England the dissenters were particularly open to new ideas in higher education. They wished to establish colleges for the 'advancement of experimental philosophy'. The model one proposed in 1661 with a staff of twenty professors and sixteen assistants, where pupils from the age of thirteen would have access to laboratories and museums as well as to libraries, and where the curriculum would offer mathematics, mechanics, medicine, anatomy, chemistry, the history of animals and plants, agriculture, military art, navigation, gardening, plus the 'mysteries of all trade' and the 'manufacture of all merchandizes,'[13] never came to pass. Many dissenting schools were, however, founded with a more 'practical' range of studies than the classics, and foundations were laid for new colleges which in their turn influenced the studies of the old universities. It used to be held that there was an affinity between the dissenters and the 'new science' – some historians even hold that the Puritans 'created' the scientific revolution[14] – but this is no longer generally accepted. The 'modern' subjects of dissenting schools and colleges are sufficiently explained by the fact that their founders had no vested interests in the Oxford and Cambridge system. At Catholic Rouen in 1715 we find a school not very different from that of the dissenter ideal. There is no Latin in the syllabus; it has been replaced by living languages and natural sciences.

203 J. A. Comenius (Komensky), 1592–1670, the Polish educationist of European-wide influence

204 St Cyr girl pupils visited by Louis XIV, 1704

205 Above, a lady at her
dressing-table, listening to a secretary
or tutor reading aloud

L'ART DE PLAIRE
DANS LA CONVERSATIO

206 Right, conversation manual

Some interest in the education of women and in improving the position of women in society can also be noted. In English and Russian dissenting circles women could speak at meetings and hold posts of honour or office; and, at least in England, it has been argued that this significant breach with male monopoly, as compared with the established church, had more general repercussions. If woman was not man's inferior, had she not a claim to educational and social equality? In France the *salons* had made men aware of what women could contribute to polite and intelligent conversation if given equal status. Louis XIV and Madame de Maintenon founded St Cyr as a school where girls could obtain a secular education, that is, not one which ignored religious teaching but one which gave girls the opportunity of advanced studies without being members of a religious community. Fénelon drew up the curriculum, and though the St Cyr experiment proved relatively short-lived, it did function for several decades as an establishment where girls were educated 'for the world', to become intelligent wives and mothers if they felt no vocation for the religious celibate life. Before the end of Louis's reign it became clear that the majority of girls taught at St Cyr

207 Above, a seventeenth-century bluestocking

208 Right, coming down to the women's level: popularization of the new science

entered religious orders on the completion of their studies, but the popularizing of the new knowledge specifically for women had by that time taken firm root among the educated classes in France. The secretary of the Académie des Sciences, Fontenelle, was particularly active in publishing books which explained the theories of the scientific revolution. His *Entretiens sur la Pluralité des Mondes*, cast in the form of conversations between an astronomer and a lady, is perhaps the best-known work of the genre. Public lectures in Paris on geometry, chemistry, and astronomy were attended by men and women. The wider curricula and the concern for female education, however, made slow progress if viewed in a wider context. Girls all over Europe picked up higher knowledge, if at all, from learned women in religious schools, male relatives or friends. The general emphasis was on useful practical education which – in Protestant countries – was usually received at home from resident tutors and visiting teachers, and consisted of music and languages. The lack of a formal education did not, however, necessarily imply a low standing for women's position in society. All the evidence we possess seems to indicate that she shared that of her husband and family in general. She ran the household and often his affairs – be it farm, shop or estate – if he were absent on travel or campaign; she bought her own shares and signed for them at the transfer-office.[15] Letters and diaries make it clear that she was usually a most valued and beloved helpmeet; and there are plenty of warnings (and complaints) that men in power were swayed by the opinions and prejudices of their womenfolk.

Educators were on the whole more intent on keeping their charges, male and female, away from the contamination of the world till their standards were formed than with bringing them in touch with the latest speculation and theories. Teachers who belonged to religious orders were particularly anxious lest bad example prove contagious. The boarding-school élite of the Jesuit colleges were hardly permitted holidays at home where lax moral standards, among servants if not parents, might be observed and copied. Breaks from study there must be, but play and exercise in the fresh air under the watchful eye of the teachers was substituted for vacations. The boarders were, all the same, a small minority; Catholic day-boys and most Protestants were not so physically shielded from the world. But all schools tried to inculcate high moral standards. Religious teaching played its part here, and so did the study of Greek and Roman history. This history was not realistic, but a contrived idealized set of examples which stressed certain virtues in a glamorous context. Known faults and weaknesses of character in the heroes of antiquity were suppressed in the interest of creating models for the child. The bravery of Alexander, the willingness of Themistocles to forgive those who had hurt him, the love of the Romans for their city and their clemency in governing their empire – these and other 'good' traits were emphasized in the hope of preventing that materialist, selfish outlook which, in the opinion of most teachers who have put their views on paper, governed the world. In an era of absolutism some questioned whether concentration on the history of the Roman Republic was desirable, but Bossuet averred that the Roman love of liberty could not weaken the monarchy since both the republic and the monarchy rested on law – Roman liberty being defined as 'un état où personne ne fût sujet que de la loi et où la loi fût plus puissante que les hommes' ('a state in which every person is subject only to the law and in which the law is more powerful than all subjects'). He admitted that injustices might take place in the monarchy as in the republic, but this would have to be suffered in the belief that God will remedy matters since He is just and benevolent.[16] The need for endurance was also emphasized at schools in which modern subjects and less idealized history were taught. One must not complain of one's fate since history shows us the vicissitudes to which men and nations are subject. The Roman virtues were absent – or less prominent – in this teaching; but since the problem of providing the young with good precepts for the future remained they were replaced by idealized stereotypes of the 'noble savage', the 'wise Chinese', the 'unselfish Quaker' of North America, or the Paraguayan Indians in their Jesuit-inspired Utopia.

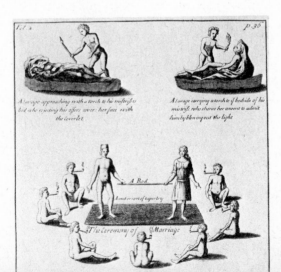

209 Savages and
their mores
observed

195

Once out of the schoolroom the young people met a less idealized precept of the grown-up world, that of the *honnête homme*: that is, of men and women who lived in the world and who, while not especially religious or moral, yet maintained standards which allowed them to live within a framework which they thought of as 'honourable'. What the concept implied varied according to class and calling, but it generally meant that one kept one's word if pledged, that one strove to be useful and to educate oneself. The virtues connected with the concept were taught in service: in the hard work of the administrator, in the self-sacrifice of the officer's code, in the pursuit of knowledge or the exercise of art, in the supply of goods that were up to standard, in the punctuality and probity of financial transactions. At the royal level it was absorbed into the *gloire* concept. This was, in my opinion, less concerned with glory or magnificence than is generally assumed today, and far more with the reputation of a ruler and the verdict of history upon him.[17] Duty to his subjects governed the ruler, but even more the duty to the state with which the dynasty was entrusted. To strive for its prosperity and for its standing among nations was all-important; to leave it weakened, its territory reduced, without having tried one's utmost to prevent this, was dishonourable. The young soon discovered that there were those in all walks of life who were self-seeking, grasping and deceitful and that some rulers were more concerned with the outward appearance of keeping their pledged word than with the reality. But the idea of the *honnête homme* guarded against too placid an acceptance of anti-social behaviour, just as the *gloire* concept (which was not restricted to royal personages) inculcated the ideal of service to the state. The precepts were in part consciously transmitted. Young men were sent in the service of a nobleman, a diplomat, a king, a trader or banker who was known as 'honourable' in order that they might imbibe ideals along with the professional training and the opportunities for later advancement which the connection was meant to supply. In part, however, the precept of the *honnête homme* was unconsciously transmitted by the way in which the age had begun to look upon society.

THE CONCEPT OF SOCIAL JUSTICE

The intellectual revolution had freed history from the reins of the church and had produced a more realistic appraisal of the past. Men became absorbed with the chain of causation, since many of

210, 211 Left, Jean de la Bruyère, writer of satirical fables; right, Mandeville's anonymously published *The Fable of the Bees* of 1714, expanded version of his 1705 pamphlet *The Bumbling Hive*

them believed in a mechanistic universe created by a benevolent God who did not interfere in everyday life. Man's responsibility for his own actions was, often joyfully, accepted. History was studied for its own sake, but also for the sake of the useful precepts which might be gleaned from it. The need for secular ideals was strongly felt, for if society was no longer held together – at least at the level of educated men – by a common belief in damnation and salvation, what should replace the older bond? Social utility was the most acceptable answer. How it was to be achieved was another matter. It was easier to criticize than to be positive. In his *Caractères*, published between 1685 and 1694, La Bruyère satirized behaviour that was becoming socially unacceptable: the parasitic self-satisfaction of the idle nobleman, the expectation of the stupid and vicious of office if they had the advantage of family connections. In *The Fable of the Bees*, printed (anonymously) in 1705, Mandeville posed a moral dilemma by his paradox of the prosperous but immoral hive which disintegrates when a party among the bees enforces a policy of 'virtue', ruining in the process the social cohesion of the hive. Locke stipulated more hopefully that once the needs of society were determined, the required moral code would evolve and be honoured

197

by most members of that society. He thus pointed to the road of rational reform.

Social utility had also a more immediate positive impact. Since belief in the rectification of injustice in this world by the bliss of a supernatural heaven had become weakened, it seemed essential to improve life on earth and discover how happiness for the greatest number could be achieved. Already the ruler was being transformed into the first servant of the state in his paternalistic role of mediating between the different classes of society, and seeing that justice, in so far as this was possible, was done to all.

The greatest obstacle to such just paternalism was vested interests, sometimes those of the rulers themselves, but more often those of individuals who had bought offices or inherited rights and privileges which they were unwilling to forego. Administrative reform, which was essential for the imposition of a fairer tax burden, for example, was blocked by long-established practices, chief of which was the bought or farmed office. The *venalité des offices*, which has often been assumed to be due to absolutism, was, in fact, a legacy which absolutism abhorred, but which it was forced to tolerate since no ruler possessed enough money to indemnify the holders of offices in local government and jurisdiction. Indeed, pressed for money with which to defend the country in time of war – or to gamble for the gains which an offensive war might bring in terms of enlarged territory and resources in Europe or overseas – some rulers were forced to go beyond condoning the practice and sold offices themselves in order to finance the war effort. Louis XIV was worst hit in this respect. The kernel of his administration (the *intendants*, the secretariat and the higher army commands) was not for sale and the inherited judgeships produced better judges than might be expected; but rational reform of the taxation system proved impossible since his own need to raise money prompted the sale of minor offices and titles on a vast scale. Even in countries where the sale of offices was practically unknown – as in Sweden – the tax-free (or nearly tax-free) privileged nobility proved a hindrance to reform. Charles XII introduced a tax on the Dutch model in 1713 to tap the capital resources of the well-to-do, but it met with strong opposition by all propertied men and was abandoned on the King's death in 1718. This tax reform was motivated apart from the obvious concern to obtain the sinews of war, by a conviction that 'the ordinary man' carried a disproportionate burden. Similar resentment at a social injustice can be traced in the writings and letters of theorists and practical administrators all over Europe. The respect for property rights and inherited rights was strongest of all in England. Here William III was prevented from creating offices (not intended for sale) since judges upheld the right of those who had paid for theirs in the past not to suffer diminution of income by having to share given fees with new entrants.[18] Though the bought office in England (where it lasted longest) hindered the 'career open to talents' in many fields, the taxation system was not ossified by it as in so many continental countries – a fact which made it easier for William III and Queen Anne to wage war than for Louis XIV and Charles XII.

The bought office created another form of social injustice in England as on the Continent. Since it had been bought for investment but usually carried a small salary in relation to the capital expended, the holder was intent on getting for it as much in fees and other perquisites as possible. Consequently he tended to bear hard on those with whom he came into official contact, whether his post was in town or country or at court. Even where he was manifestly extortionate it was difficult for the central administration to control him (except perhaps at court) if he had bought his office for life, for he could sell it any time and usually did so to provide himself with a pension for his old age. This lack of control was resented by many ministers and bureaucrats, but little could be done about it in the larger states where the system had taken firm root. In a few cases we note at least partial reform. In 1713 the citizens of the town of Hamburg forced through a decision that the proceeds from sales of municipal offices should go to the town coffer, an arrangement already in use in some towns in the Dutch Republic.

If the office-holder was not too overtly greedy (or sadistic as in the case of some bought offices, such as jailers, where this trait might be given free rein) there was little resentment in society at large, that is, outside the sphere of would-be reformers in the central administration. It was a time-honoured system of letting the customer pay directly in fees of various kinds for services rendered; it enabled the key central administration, salaried in full by the government, to remain small; and it solved, in a simple but effective way, the problem of providing for minor and even menial officials in their old age or for their widows and children if they died before selling their office.

Nor was the system of patronage, which to our own age seems suspect if not corrupt, considered a social injustice. Judged by the standards of the time it was the accepted manner in which people obtained posts or received pensions permitting them to carry on those professions which did not pay well enough to afford a living commensurate with educated needs. The lawyer and the notary, the doctor and the apothecary, the portrait-painter and the architect could make such a living; but the poet, the man of letters, the man of learning outside the universities and the church, could not unless he had a court sinecure, or a royal or noble pension, or was sure of government rewards – as were Defoe and Swift – for the writing of political pamphlets. Voltaire was the first European writer to make an independent living from his pen, and his first book was published in 1732. A man who showed himself too greedy in extorting payment for his patronage or for services rendered was regarded as failing to measure up to the precept of the *honnête homme*; he was made fun of, but he was not thought of as one who offended against society. The one exception was in some (but by no means all) cases of receiving money from foreign rulers: this could at times be tantamount to treason and if a man took money from more than one foreign state at any one time he was looked upon as dishonourable.[19]

NATURAL LAW AND INTERNATIONAL LAW

Fundamentally men's attitude to what was permissible or not in society and in international society rested on their concepts of natural law and international law. Such concepts are not immune from general changes within the society. In the age of Louis XIV they were modified by three main factors: the memory of civil war and large-scale ideological warfare; the development of the mathematical and mechanical sciences; and the secularization trend which we have already stressed. That man possessed some irreducible rights deriving from a primitive past when each individual was his own 'state' had never been contested; nor had the fact that this *jus ad omnia* must be merged when individuals formed a society. But the relationship between 'natural law' (*lex naturalis*) and the 'positive law' by which society regulated its affairs had been a matter of debate throughout the ages of recorded history. Reformers always tended to stress the primacy of natural law since this would permit reform in positive law and bring it into line with their ideas for improvement of society.

A first step in the secularization process of law was taken by Grotius when, in his *De jure belli ac pacis* of 1625, he postulated that natural law would continue even if God ceased to exist. The mechanistic theories which Hobbes, Spinoza and Pufendorf accepted from natural philosophy worked in the same direction. They argued that just as physical objects, which had been shown to have atoms as their irreducible components, were held together by a natural force which prevented the atoms from flying apart, so individuals were held in society by a global force which prevented the divergent forces from destroying the whole. From here the road was not long to a postulated antithesis between a rational 'natural law' and a 'supernatural law', identified with positive law, which stood in need of examination and change. If aberrations and accretions were removed, a universal beneficial natural law would, it was assumed, be discovered, analogous with the universal natural religion which would emerge once the 'supernatural' accumulations deposited by different ecclesiastical hierarchies had been cleared away. The object of the reformers was therefore to improve positive law so that it would express natural law more convincingly and rationally and thus command readier acceptance by the reasoning individual.

The legal attitude to witchcraft is a good example of how the law became more secular and rational in our period, as a result of the growing understanding of psychology and lessening respect for the church. It was superstitious to believe in 'witches', the reformers argued; there were no such creatures and it was time that women accused by neighbours who feared or disliked them should – however malicious or hysterical the accused might be – keep their lives. Trials of witches now disappeared: first in the Dutch Republic, then in England and Sweden and on the Continent in general, though they persisted in the two Calvinist strongholds, Scotland and

212 A fine example of contemporary map-making of 1690 by F. de Wit (detail, showing western Europe)

201

Switzerland, till far into the eighteenth century, as also in parts of North America.

The demand for collection of codes of law and revision of old law-books was, in part, stimulated by the new rationalism. There was sometimes a need for revision because the language of the old statutes was such that none but the very learned could understand them; and administrative facility was another common motivation for attempts to achieve uniformity. But wherever codes were collected and published, as in Louis XIV's France for civil, criminal and commercial law, or revised, as in Sweden by a commission which sat between 1686 and 1734, some removal of the 'supernatural' took place in the process, and a more compassionate spirit frequently inspired changes. In the French Code des Nègres, to give but one example, slaves received rights which they were not accorded outside Spanish America. Slaves were protected from families being separated and had the right to appeal against injustice. They were also guaranteed religious instruction so that their owners should not be able to treat them as heathens, that is, in an uncivilized manner. Generally speaking, however, it was easier to modify application of the law than to change the law itself; but where changes were made they were all in the direction of greater tolerance and less ecclesiastical control.

In their concern for the individual the rationalist reformers were influenced by memories of civil war and international warfare. Hobbes's argument in the *Leviathan*, that the sole purpose of the state was to guarantee peace and security and that for this purpose the state needed power, was welcomed by a generation that had experienced the anarchy of civil war in much the same manner as the French jurists who preached absolutism were welcomed after the Fronde. Spinoza, who in his earlier works had praised the Dutch pacific oligarchy of the federal Republic, changed his tune after the shock of the French invasion of 1672. In his *Tractatus Politicus* of 1677 he reflected that the price of peace might be stronger central government with greater military preparedness. His 'It is not wisdom but authority that makes the state' differs little from Hobbes's theories, and his admonition that one should not weaken the guarantor of security, the sovereign, would not be out of place among the French jurists. Locke's right of the individual to rebel against a tyrannical monarch was not as live an issue in his own lifetime (aside from its significance as an 'Exclusion tract' against the Catholic Duke of York) as after it,

and was – as recent research has stressed – backward-looking, attempting a vindication of the rebellion against Charles I, rather than preparing for the Glorious Revolution of 1688.[20] What interested contemporaries most was his theory of the innate rights of the individual and the demand that positive law should concentrate on realizing as much of the *lex naturalis* as possible.

Among these innate rights, the rights to life and property were central. A man's life was his own and so was his property, unless the central government could show good cause, namely a state of war, why a town or country should take on extraordinary burdens of tax or men risk their lives as conscripted soldiers and sailors. Men could, however, forfeit their lives and their property by treason or by other offences which, according to the law of their town or land, carried the death penalty. In England such penalties were much concerned with property; theft and arson were punished by death, though in practice sentence was sometimes commuted to transportation. In most other European countries treason and desertion in war were the only crimes which in practice brought the death penalty. It is symptomatic that many French Huguenots in exile argued that if they stayed loyal to Louis XIV and refrained from service in the armed forces of his enemies in wartime – that is, if they avoided treason – the King would eventually be forced by public opinion to listen to their entreaties and let them return to France. (Though no official reversal of the Revocation of 1685 took place, a considerable number of Huguenots returned to France before the end of the reign and those who had stayed behind began to practise their religion openly if discreetly.)

Offences against the vital economic interests of the state were tantamount to treason and sometimes punishable as such, as the following example (from 1707) shows in relation to England's monopoly of fine quality wool. The Secretary of State's office was anxious to follow the advice of an individual diplomat, supported by the Duke of Marlborough, and present a foreign minister with a ram and ewe of English stock. The Judge-Advocate counselled refusal, referring to a statute from Elizabeth's reign which decreed that anyone who exported a ewe or a ram would lose the right hand at the first offence and life itself at the second. The present of politeness was thereupon changed to a pair of earrings for the minister's wife.[21]

Even where treason had actually been committed, a nobleman was at times permitted to escape abroad and the sentence (if passed) was not effected unless he happened to be caught in the service of an enemy after war had been declared and all loyal subjects had been told by proclamation to quit the service of a particular monarch or state. If the death sentence was then not put into effect, it was argued, the law itself would fall into disrepute.

It was in tune with the growing humaneness of those who administered the law that in cases where the infliction of pain was the essence of the punishment, quick death was consciously engineered (for example, the *peine dure* of English prisons where the slow increase of pressure on the accused was speeded up to crush life in the name of mercy). The prevalence of torture on the Continent was assumed and rumoured in stories such as those about Louis XIV's mysterious prisoner, 'the man in the iron mask'; but in reality it was no longer a regular feature of the legal life of the civilized nations.

Respect for the law was generally regarded as the distinction between civilized and barbarian society. The difference between the English legal system with its lay juries, open court and savage penalties once the accused was found guilty, and the continental procedure which was generally more lenient but was conducted in utter secrecy, was one which caused much comment among travellers from one to the other; but both sides regarded each other as 'civilized' because both possessed bodies of law that were respected and upheld. The further east one got the less certain were Europeans that there was a rule of law. There was a mistaken impression that Russia was a 'barbarous' eastern kingdom where the Tsar administered law as he thought fit. Charles XII was once heard to remark that he would rather be the meanest peasant in Sweden than the highest noble in Russia where government was not subject to the law.[22] Peter's plan to re-codify the law of 1649 and to teach law at the universities is proof of his desire to bring 'civilization' to Russia. A country's law went abroad with its people if they left the confines of Europe for its colonies or trading-stations overseas, and to the realms of Islam if the Sultan could be persuaded to grant the foreign community such rights via its consuls. The conception of 'natural rights' was, however, still limited to their own society, and we ought not to be shocked (though we are likely to be so) that Locke, to whom we owe so much clear thinking on the subject of political rights, had no objection to enslavement of non-Europeans and indeed himself profited from the slave-trade. And Louis XIV, who abolished slavery in New France, and who – as we have just seen – promulgated a humane code for Negro slaves in the French West Indies, was as anxious as the rulers of other states to obtain for his countrymen the *asiento* for trade in slaves[23] and regretted the contract's becoming one of Great Britain's spoils from the War of the Spanish Succession.

The European warfare, and particularly the ideological warfare, of the first half of the seventeenth century encouraged jurists to attempt a structure of international law which might for the future limit war or at least regulate it. The breakdown in diplomacy during the century of the wars of religion[24] was looked upon after 1648 as an unnecessary calamity. Rules and regulations for the smooth operation of diplomatic intercourse became a common preoccupation while treatises on the craft of diplomacy multiplied. These processes were influenced by the current philosophical trends in much the same way as we have seen for the 'natural law'. Grotius tried in his *De jure belli ac pacis* to produce a chain of reasoning sufficiently exhaustive and systematic to prove 'mathematically' that there was a common law among nations which remained valid in peace or war. The humanitarian desire to prevent war 'being a riot or fury' inspired him, as it did other jurists, and they hoped by the use of right reasoning to deduce a natural 'law of nations' which governed the actions of sovereign states in their relations with each other as part of the universal natural law. Best known among these jurists is Pufendorf, whose *Of the Law of Nature and Nations* (to use the title of the English translation) of 1672 became the textbook of generations of foreign chancellery officials all over Europe. From this and other works a secular code of international law became gradually accepted. The state was sovereign and the ruler (or rulers of a federated state such as the United Provinces) therefore totally responsible for state acts committed in its name. War was 'just' only if defensive; the state that carried on a just war was entitled to compensation from its attacker in the form of a *satisfactio*, though it could declare itself willing to accept a bare restoration of the *status quo ante bellum*. Examples of applications of this code are numerous throughout our period. Louis XIV admitted that he had been the aggressor in attacking the Dutch in 1672; they were therefore entitled to *satisfactio* at the peace-making in 1678, and the 1667 French commercial tariff which had been so obnoxious to them was therefore greatly modified. The young Charles XII, fighting a just war of defence, worried his advisers by an unwillingness to enter into negotiations with Augustus of Saxony: both he and they had proof that Augustus was insincere in his professed intentions of leaving the anti-Swedish coalition, but it was still necessary to negotiate lest Charles put himself outside civilized behaviour. In the Nine Years War (1689–97) and the War of the Spanish Succession (1702–13) negotiations were, so to speak, continuous in that the campaign seasons lasted during half the year only (May till October-November) while in the winter seasons the negotiations – which had not languished even in the summers – became the main preoccupation of the belligerents.

The actual conduct of warfare in our period gave rise to less trouble than might be expected, since the behaviour of regular armies was better controlled than before by growing administrative machinery, while individual officers were generally imbued with a code of chivalry that had roots far back in time. There were accepted rules for treatment of civilians in sieges and during occupations;[25] there were equally accepted rules for treatment of officers and men who capitulated. Transgressions were publicly denounced, by interested parties naturally enough, but also by independent commentators. The burning of Altona by the Swedish general Stenbock, after the citizens had offered to pay the customary *Brandschatz* to have their town spared, was condemned as cruel though his purpose had been the legitimate destruction of enemy magazines in the town. Tsar Peter felt it necessary to defend himself for not keeping the capitulation of Perevolochna in terms other than the common-sense one ('I did not want brother Charles to have his officers back') and resorted to previous examples of the Swedes' having failed to honour their capitulations in full. Accepted codes also covered diplomatic relations, though compromise solutions to problems of precedence took some working out. It was the Dutch who, at Nijmegen, had a small house specially constructed with doors and tables, parchment and quills so arranged that the Spanish and French delegations could synchronize their movements through equally 'important' doors to sign the coveted side of their own copy of the peace treaty at precisely the same moment.[26] George I's arrest of the Swedish envoy Gyllenborg in 1717 gave rise to pamphlets which pointed to the dangers for European diplomacy of his breach of international law: George as Elector was at war with Sweden, but – in the legal sense – not George as King of Great Britain, and his much-publicized justification (Gyllenborg's correspondence with Jacobites) was judged insufficient. Correct behaviour would have entailed asking Charles XII to recall Gyllenborg.[27] While there were accepted codes which rendered warfare relatively humane, except in the case of 'irregular forces', i.e. guerrilla warfare, which could and were extended to cover the civil war in Poland, Hungary and Catalonia, it was equally accepted that war had to be harsh. Deserters were hanged (if caught) to prevent others from following their example; some breaches of discipline which threatened the cohesion on which the unit (whether military or naval) depended was punished by flogging. Civilians were often the innocent victims of war, particularly in north-eastern Europe where winter campaigns were the rule rather than the exception. In Poland and Lithuania Tsar Peter instigated in 1707 the 'scorched-earth' tactics which he later continued in his own country to lay a belt of totally wasted territory between Moscow and the advancing Swedish army. Swedish officers, needing food for their companies, suffered pangs of conscience over the methods they were driven to use to make Polish and Lithuanian civilians reveal hidden stores: capturing a young boy and pretending to be willing to kill him unless the desired information was given by the mother was felt as dishonourable behaviour.[28] They knew that the Russians had not felt bound by the same codes in the Swedish Baltic provinces where thousands of civilians had been uprooted from their homes and sold as slaves; but they held this to be barbarian and possibly the work of Cossacks who were thought of as 'irregular forces' even when part of a regular army.

The high incidence of war, though on the whole civilized war, in our period led rulers and statesmen to ponder how to prevent or limit war on a practical level. Experience had shown that the idea of the just and unjust war did not deter aggressors (even repentant ones like Louis[29]) – and that attackers such as those of the anti-Swedish coalition of 1700 regarded themselves as justified in breaking old treaties which they considered to have been obtained by aggression. Moreover, though negotiations often began simultaneously with hostilities, wars still proved long and exhaustive. To the rulers and practical men the model plans for a united Europe, which would make war unnecessary, seemed utopian. And when the most famous French as that of Sully and Henry IV at the opening of the seventeenth century had been anti-Austrian.* One first fruit of practical statesmanship grew, however, from the unsuccessful attempt of

* The less biased, but still pro-French, *Projet pour la Paix Perpétuelle* of Saint-Pierre was published in time (1712) to influence the congress-idea of 1718–20.

William III and Louis XIV to solve the Spanish succession issue. Written into the Quadruple Alliance of 1718 were clauses, part of a Peace Plan for the South, to be complemented by one for the North, which obliged all contracting parties in future to submit their quarrels to a European congress before resorting to arms. Pufendorf had already in 1672 postulated an arbitration obligation according to the 'law of nature'. 'Positive international law' now went further due to a general realization that international problems were intractable, that right was not usually all on one side and that the airing of problems at inter-European congresses might be of some use.[30] The 1718 clauses have not been given the attention they deserve, mainly because the congresses which were called by virtue of them did not succeed in preventing outbreaks of war. But it should be noted that the Congress of Cambrai, 1724–6, and that of Soissons, 1728–30, served to ventilate Spanish-Austrian and French-German problems which the peace treaties of Utrecht, Rastadt and Baden had left unsolved, and that the solutions which were adopted – after relatively small-scale warfare – were achieved more easily for having been previously discussed. The clauses therefore mark a significant stage on the long and hard road of the European nations in attempting to learn how to live together.

Even more significant is the fact that Pufendorf's pronouncement of peace as the 'normal' state of mankind was gaining acceptance. Previous authorities had stipulated 'war' as the norm and historical experience had seemed proof enough. The optimism of the Early Enlightenment probably explains the growing conviction that eventually the 'normal' state of peace with its opportunities for improving society could be achieved. In any case that hope had by the end of our period become part of European civilization itself.

EPILOGUE

The optimism of the Early Enlightenment is easy to ridicule. With the wisdom of hindsight it is easy to see that it underestimated the strength of irrational forces in man and society; for even if due allowance is made for the scepticism of individual thinkers and administrators in the period, the over-all impression is one of a strong and optimistic and basically healthy belief in the power of human rationality to solve problems. Some allowance must also be made for the historian's predilection, conscious or subconscious, for picking on some traits rather than others with which to characterize a period in a brief essay. Reasons of space, rather than conscious desire to neglect trends which do not fit in with the Early Enlightenment theme, have deferred reference to some facts which are of all times rather than of a specific period of history but in the light of which all periods are illuminated. Changes in philosophical or scientific points of view, like changes in art forms, seem to be a means whereby civilization renews itself. In part they seem dictated by a need for fresh inspiration or fresh problems to tackle. This explains our own astonishment that an age existed which, for example, did not appreciate the Mannerist school of painting, or one which found the tortured Baroque statue of Prince Eugène attractive. The revulsion against one age tends to produce appreciation of another in the world of art though all European art possesses a unity of heritage based on a common mythology and even a fairly homogeneous folk-art. In the realm of thought, renewal tends to come partly through a re-examination of past structures of thought, but partly also by the picking up of 'minority' trends in a given age. In any one period there are trends that run counter to the dominating ones, that is, every age tends to pose awkward questions which are taken up not at the time, but at a later stage. A good example of this is Leibniz's critique of Locke's treatise on human knowledge. Locke had convinced him but for the one vital point: how was the mind, postulated as free from innate ideas but capable of forming ideas, itself created? This question, not much heeded at the time, became a central question for later ages; and the problem of religious belief, the 'supernatural' of the rationalists, has not proved amenable to rational analysis and the early nineteenth century saw a new growth in Christian belief. Each age makes attempts at structural analysis to answer eternal human problems, and those that satisfy or suit our own age either in respect of the individual in society (like the modern French school of psychological synthesis) or in the behaviour of societies towards each other (as in the recent deductions from ethology) may – in time – seem as unsatisfactory and outmoded as Leibniz's *La Monadologie* of 1714 which so influenced the philosophy of the Enlightenment. In the God-given pre-established harmony which he postulated between the microcosm of the individual and the macrocosm of society and the universe, he leaves our own age dissatisfied with its 'all is for the best in the best of all possible worlds' message; but a reading of it is still impressive in its command and subtlety.

His 'rational souls' have different perspectives of the whole, yet are contained within it in a relationship that remains individual and is deeply satisfying just because it goes beyond a quantitative mechanistic explanation. His belief that the *jus strictum* must eventually be replaced with the *jus aequitatis* may seem utopian; but we feel at home when we read of his 'republic of spirits', his condemnation of slavery and his definition of the right of the individual to intellectual and moral improvement.

It is salutary for us who live in a 'technological age' to learn of scientific or technological discoveries made in earlier times. Every schoolboy knows that Leonardo da Vinci had worked out the principle of submarine travel and for that reason the information does not shock us into recognition. But the find in 1967 in a Spanish library of a hitherto unknown da Vinci drawing, which proves that he utilized the ball-bearing principle centuries before technological need encouraged independent discovery and production, created, when reproduced in the world press, a minor sensation, adding support to the theory that 'there is nothing new under the sun except the history we do not know'. And if we read one of the writers of the period we have discussed, Joseph Glanvill, who published his *Vanity of Dogmatising* in 1661 as part of the battle between Ancients and Moderns (but who insisted on the importance of scepticism in science and on the need for dogmatic doubt), we may, according to temperament, experience exhilaration at his optimistic predictions or a shiver at the 'supernatural' accuracy of his prophecy or sceptical doubt whether we have benefited from the advance of the Moderns:

And I doubt not but posterity will find many things that are now but Rumours, verified into practical Realities. It may be some Ages hence, a voyage to the Southern unknown tracts, yea possibly to the Moon, will not be more strange than one to America. To them that come after us, it may be as ordinary to buy a pair of wings, to fly into remotest Regions, as now a pair of Boots to ride a journey. And to conferr at the distance of the Indies by sympathetic conveyances may be as usual to future times, as to us in a litterary correspondence. The restauration of grey hairs to Juvenility, and renewing the exhausted marrow, may at length be effected without a miracle: and the turning of the now comparatively desert world into a Paradise may not improbably be expected from late Agriculture.

211

NOTES TO THE TEXT

CHAPTER ONE

1 Axel Lassen, 'The population of Denmark in 1660', *The Scandinavian Economic History Review* (Copenhagen) 1965, pp. 1–30.

2 P. Goubert, *Beauvais et le Beauvaisis de 1600 à 1730* (Paris 1960, 2 parts).

3 J. A. Faber, 'The Cattle-Plague in the Netherlands during the Eighteenth Century', *Mededelingen van de Landbouwhogeschool te Wageningen, Nederland*, 1962.

4 The Swiss civil wars (for which see *infra* p. 226) gave new impetus to emigration; for Swiss emigration in general see H. Moller, 'Population and Society during the Old Regime', *Population Movements in Modern European History* (New York 1964); for the emigration into France see R. Bonnaud-Delamare, *L'immigration helvétique dans les principautés de Murbach et de Lure après la guerre de Trente Ans, 1649–1719* (Paris 1966).

5 J. Orcibal, *Louis XIV et les Protestants* (Paris 1951), pp. 91 ff.; 'Missionaires Catholiques à l'intérieur de la France pendant le XVIIᵉ siècle', no. 41 of *XVIIᵉ Siècle*; (Amiens) 1958, with introduction by J.-E. d'Angers; cp. Ruth Kleinman and 'The Unquiet Truce: an Exploration of Catholic Feeling against the Huguenots in France 1646–1664', *French Historical Studies*, 1965, pp. 170 ff.

6 H. Lüthy, *La Banque Protestante en France de la Révocation de l'Edit de Nantes à la Révolution*, vol. 1: *Dispersion et Regroupement 1685–1730* (Paris 1959), pp. 93 ff.

7 W. C. Scoville, *The Persecution of the Huguenots and the French Economic Development* (Berkeley and Los Angeles 1960). Scoville's findings have been slightly modified by Carlo M. Cippola, *Clocks and Culture* (London 1967), pp. 72–5, who shows that the French watchmaking industry suffered a (relatively short) decline. The importance of Huguenot financial expertise has been emphasized by Alice C. Carter, 'The Huguenot Contribution to the Early Years of the Funded Debt 1694–1714', *Proceedings of the Huguenot Society of London*, 1955, and by P. G. M. Dickson, *The Financial Revolution* (London, 1967), pp. 259 ff.

8 See P. Deyon, 'La production manufacturière en France au XVIIᵉ siècle et ses problèmes', *XVIIᵉ Siècle* (Amiens) 1966, pp. 58 ff.

9 C. K. S. Sprinchorn, 'Madagaskar och dess sjöröfvare i Karl XII:s historia', *Karolinska Förbundets Årsbok* (Stockholm) 1921, pp. 241–79.

10 R. de Schryver, *Jan van Brouchoven, Graaf van Bergeyck, 1644–1725* (Brussels 1965), pp. 155 ff.

11 National Archives, Edinburgh, Abercairny MSS (G.D. 24/1), vol. 471, letter of John Drummond's brother to his father (the Laird of Blair Drummond), Leyden, 19 June O.S. 1697.

12 Huntingdon Library, San Marino, Stowe MSS, Brydges Papers, vol. 6, John Drummond to James Brydges, 30 May 1710.

13 Ruth Clark, *Sir William Trumbull in Paris, 1685–86* (Cambridge 1938), *passim*.

14 H. Kamen, 'The Destruction of the Spanish Silver Fleet at Vigo in 1702', *Bulletin of the Institute of Historical Research*, 1966, pp. 165–73.

15 Armin Reese, *Die Rolle der Historie beim Aufstieg des Welfenhauses* (Hildesheim 1967), p. 9.

16 Torcy's letters from the mission have been published, ed. by Jean Marchand in *La Mission extraordinaire du Marquis de Torcy en Danemark-Norvège et son voyage en Suède 1685* (Paris 1951).

17 *Aus den Erinnerungen des Hans Kaspar von Bothmer*, ed. Karl Freiherr von Bothmer and G. Schnath (Hildesheim and Leipzig 1936), p. 23 (mission of 1683–84).

18 *Le Bon Sens du curé Meslier suivi de son Testament* (Paris 1834); cp. Maurice Dommanget, *Le Curé Meslier, athée, communiste et révolutionnaire sous Louis XIV* (Paris 1965).

19 J. C. de Folard, *Nouvelles Descouvertes sur la Guerre* (Paris 1726), p. 83, and the same author's *Histoire de Polybe... avec un commentaire ou un corps de science militaire*, vol. III (Paris 1727), p. 61.

20 Public Record Office, State Papers Foreign Poland (88) vol. 16, Robinson's letter to Hedges from Danzig of 15 Jan. 1703/4: the cost for the three years was £450 and the circumstances surrounding the arrangement will be discussed, *inter alia*, in my forthcoming study *Presents and Pensions*.

21 *Die Memoiren des Kammerherrn Friedrich Ernst von Fabrice*, ed. R. Grieser (Hildesheim 1956), p. 26.

22 I owe this information to a paper read by J. Stoye at the Anglo-American historical conference in London, 1965: 'Count Luigi Marsigli, F. R. S. and the advancement of science.'

23 *Philosophical Transactions* (of the Royal Society), XXIX, for the years 1714, 1715, 1716 (London 1727), pp. 72–82.

24 *Arvet från Newton och Linné. Vetenskapelige förbindelser mellan Sverige och England i gångna tider* (Uppsala 1962), p. 22; cp. *Philosophical Transactions* (of the Royal Society), I (London 1665–66), pp. 350 ff., and Thomas Birch, *The History of the Royal Society of London*, vol. III (London 1757), pp. 5 ff.

25 Carl Magnus Posse's letter to Nils Posse of 27 Nov. 1707, printed in *Historisk Tidskrift* (Stockholm) 1882, p. 166. Cp. the comment by A. de la Motraye, *Travels through Europe, Asia and parts of Africa*, vol. II (London 1723), p. 49.

1 Z. S. P. Pach, *Die ungarische Agrarenentwicklung im 16–17 Jahrhundert. Abbiegung von Westeuropäischen Entwicklungsgang* (Budapest 1964), pp. 39 ff.

2 J. S. Faber, 'Het probleem van de dalende graanaanvoer uit de Ostzeelanden in de tweede helft van de zeventiende eeuw', *Agrarisch Geschiedenis Bijdragen* (Wageningen) 1963, pp. 3–28; English version in *Acta Historiae Neerlandica*, VI (Leiden), 1965.

3 E. Le Roy Laduire, *Les paysans de Languedoc*, vol. I (Paris 1966).

4 P. Goubert, *Louis XIV et vingt millions de Français* (Paris 1966), pp. 28 ff. for France and G. Olander, *Studier över det inre tillståndet i Sverige, under senare delen av Karl XII:s regering* (Gothenburg 1946), pp. 62–100 for Skaraborgs *län* in Sweden.

5 Comment from Stockholm, 9 May 1694, by the Danish diplomat Bolle Luxdorph on Nicodemus Tessin: dispatch printed in *Handlingar rörande Sveriges historia ur utrikes arkiver*, ed. A. Fryxell, vol. III (Stockholm 1839), p. 384.

6 R. Miller, 'Die Hofreisen Kaiser Leopolds I', *Mitteilungen des Instituts für Österreichische Geschichtsforschung* (Vienna) 1967, pp. 66 ff.

7 See e.g. Charles Wilson, *England's Apprenticeship, 1603–1763* (London 1965), pp. 44 and 278.

8 P. W. Bamford, *Forests and French Sea Power 1660–1789* (Toronto 1956), pp. 95 ff.; M. Devèze, *La grande réformation des forêts sous Colbert 1661–1683* (Nancy 1962), *passim*.

9 Blathwayt (on William III's order) to Nottingham, Grammen 29 Aug./8 Sept. 1692: *Report on the Manuscripts of the late Alan George Finch*, vol. IV (H.M.C. 71, London 1965), pp. 30–431; much correspondence (*ibid.*, pp. 367–441) on this topic between Blathwayt, Nottingham and Admiral Russell.

10 S. Tvette, 'Framgangen for norsk skipstart etter, 1690', *Sjöfartshistorisk Årbok* (Bergen) 1965, pp. 58–90.

11 British Museum: Harley Loan Papers 29/45 x (70, 1–2), part of an unsigned letter or report, endorsed as from Drummond of 22 Sept. 1704. (The 4 is illegible, but from later letters the date can be deduced, as also the fact that it was most probably written during a visit Drummond paid to London.) I gratefully acknowledge permission to quote from the Harley Loan Papers.

12 W. Mediger, *Mecklenburg, Russland und England-Hannover 1706–1721* (Hildesheim 1967), vol. I, pp. 95–96.

13 G. Lindeberg, *Svensk ekonomisk politik under den Görtzska perioden* (Stockholm 1941), pp. 358 ff. and the same author's *Krigsfinansiering och Krigshushållning i Karl XII:s Sverige* (Uppsala 1946), pp. 44–50; cp. Ragnhild Hatton, *Diplomatic Relations between Great Britain and the Dutch Republic 1714–1721* (London 1950), pp. 148, 153 ff.

14 See A. Loit, 'Sverige och Ostersjöhandelen under 1600-talet. Översikt över nyare litteratur', *Historisk Tidskrift* (Stockholm) 1964, pp. 320 ff. and authorities there cited for the controversy over what weight to give to the smugglers' trade.

15 Ralph Davis, 'English Foreign Trade 1660–1700', *The Economic History Review*, 1954, and the same author's *A Commercial Revolution* (Historical Association Pamphlet no. 64), 1967.

16 Edward Barlow's journal was brought to my attention by Dr Frances Armytage. The original, richly illustrated by the author, is in the Greenwich Maritime Museum. It has been transcribed by Basil Lubbock and published in a limited edition as *Barlow's Journal*, 2 vols. (London 1934). The quotation here is from vol. I, p. 15 of that edition.

17 Colin Simpson, 'How the Golden Armada went down', *The Sunday Times Weekly Review*, 11 Dec. 1966 and *The Sunday Times Magazine*, 18 Dec. 1966, illustrated article on 'Real Eight Inc.'

18 C. M. Cippola, *Clocks and Culture* (London 1967), pp. 90 ff. and authorities there cited.

19 I owe this information to Professor Charles Boxer; cp. his article, 'The Vergulde Draeck', *History Today*, 1968, pp. 173 ff.

20 The best study is by P. G. M. Dickson, *The Financial Revolution* (London 1967); for the French side see J. Saint-Germain, *Les financiers sous Louis XIV* (Paris 1950) and J. Bouvier and H. Germain-Martin, *Finance et financiers de l'Ancien Régime* (Paris 1964).

21 B. E. de Muinck, *Een Regentenhuishouding omstreeks 1700* (The Hague 1965) covers the career of Cornelis de Jonge van Ellemeet in detail; the same author's article, 'Private Life and Public Money', in *Progress* (The Unilever Quarterly) 1966, pp. 125–31 covers some aspects of his study while his 'A regent's family budget about the year 1700', *Acta Historiae Neerlandica*, (Leiden) 1967 summarizes the conclusions of the larger work.

22 There is much material on this in the Brydges Papers (Stowe MSS), Huntington Library, San Marino; some of Cadogan's letters form the basis for G. Davies, 'The Seamy Side of Marlborough's Wars', *Huntington Library Quarterly*, XV (1951–52), pp. 21–44. For diplomats also being drawn into the net see Brydges Papers, vol. 5, Cardonell's letter of 8 May 1709 for arrangements made with Horatio Walpole at The Hague to send information under the cover of the Under-Secretary Tilson: 'I have assured him you will be very secret.'

23 See L. Rothkrug, *Opposition to Louis XIV, The Political and Social Origins of the French Enlightenment* (Princeton 1965), p. 331.

24 Georges Snyders, *La Pédagogie en France aux XVIIe et XVIIIe siècles* (Paris 1965), p. 31.

25 *Ibid.*, pp. 57–58, citing a conversation reported by Saint-Évremond.

26 Fabrice's *Memoiren*, cited above note 21 to chapter I, were – alas – translated from their original French into German by the editor R. Grieser; those by Axel von Löwen, found in a loft in Stralsund in the 1920s, have been printed in their original French (but with a German introduction and notes in Swedish) in *Karolinska Förbundets Årsbok* (Stockholm) 1929, pp. 17–100, edd. F. Adler and S. Bonnesen.

27 See e.g. the memoirs of J. Hultman: *Historiska Handlingar*, ed. G. Floderus, vol. I (Stockholm 1834).

28 C. G. Stewart, 'A history of the medical use of tobacco 1692–1860', *Medical History* (London) 1967, pp. 228 ff.

29 For Temple's observations see *The Life, Works, and Correspondence of Sir William Temple*, ed. T. P. Courtenay, vol. I (London 1936), pp. 38, 47, 59; for Fabrice see his *Memoiren*, ed. R. Grieser (Hildesheim 1956), p. 27.

30 Cited in Alan Benjamin Bathurst, *Letters of Two Queens* (London 1925), p. 247.

31 Gist of a letter (to her brother Robin) in *Letters of Sarah Byng Osborn 1721–1773*, ed. M. McClelland (Stanford and London 1930), p. 8. Cp. the comments on male dress in England and France in the 1700s in Ludvig Holberg's autobiography (translated from Latin into English and published in London 1827 under the name Lewis Holberg).

32 For Charles XI's grief see A. Åberg, *Karl XI* (Stockholm 1958), p. 173; for that of King Pedro see A. D. Francis, *The Methuens and Portugal* (Cambridge 1966), p. 233; for that of Marlborough see David Green, *Sarah Duchess of Marlborough* (London 1967), pp. 89–90; for that of Prince Eugène see N. Henderson, *Prince Eugen of Savoy* (London 1964), pp. 196–8; cp. M. Braubach, *Prinz Eugen*, vol. V (Munich 1965), p. 327, for the grievous sudden loss of a great nephew in 1712.

33 C. H. Collins and M. I. Baker, *The Life and Circumstances of James Brydges, First Duke of Chandos, Patron of the Liberal Arts* (Oxford 1949), pp. 28–29, quoting from Brydges's 'Journal of my daily Actions'; cp. *ibid.*, pp. 23–30.

34 Leslie G. Matthews, *The Royal Apothecaries* (London 1967), p. 120.

35 A. Lewenhaupt, *Karolinen Edvard Gyldenstolpe* (Stockholm 1941), p. 150.

36 Sarah, Duchess of Marlborough, to James Craggs, cited by David Green, *Sarah Duchess of Marlborough* (London 1967), pp. 201–2.

37 For this sport see Bonnesen, 'Gåsgalgane i Ystad', *Karolinska Förbundets Årsbok* (Stockholm) 1931; the eyewitness account printed *ibid.*, 1952, pp. 121–8; and J. H. Plumb, *The First Four Georges* (London 1956), p. 15.

38 Huntington Library, San Marino, Stowe MSS, Brydges Papers, vol. 6, Senserf's letter to Brydges of 5 Nov. 1709.

39 L. Bernard, 'French Society and Popular Uprisings under Louis XIV', *French Historical Studies*, 1964, pp. 454–74; G. Lemarchand, 'Crises économiques et atmosphère sociale en milieu urbain sous Louis XIV', *Revue d'Histoire Moderne et Contemporaine* (Paris) 1967, pp. 244–65; I. I. Smirnov *et al.*, *Krest'janskie voyny v Rossii XVII–XVIII vv* (Moscow 1966); B. Kentrschynskyj, 'Peter och upproret vid Don 1707–8', *Karolinska Förbundets Årsbok* (Stockholm) 1963; E. P. Pod-japol'skaya, *Vosstanie Bulavina 1707–1709* (Moscow 1962); for unrest in England see M. Beloff, *Public Order and Popular Disturbances 1660–1714* (Oxford 1938).

40 S. Stolpe, *Christina of Sweden* (London 1966), pp. 41 ff. has a brief but good section on seventeenth-century theories of the female psyche as compared with that of the male; a fuller treatment in his two-volume Swedish biography of 1960–61.

CHAPTER THREE

1 I owe this information to a seminar paper read by Professor Francis Carsten at the School of Slavonic Studies in the spring of 1968.

2 For excellent surveys of work recently completed, or in progress, on these topics, see the double number (nos. 70–71) of *XVIIe Siècle* (Amiens) 1966, with the title *Aspects de l'économie française au XVIIe siècle*.

3 See Louis XIV's *Mémoires* in Grouvelle ed. of *Œuvres* (Paris 1806) vol. I, p. 29; in English transl. of J. Longnon, *A King's Lesson in Statecraft: Louis XIV's Letters to His Heirs* (London 1924), p. 53.

4 U. Sjödell, 'Kring de Bondeska Anekdoterna', *Scandia* (Lund) 1965, pp. 141–72; and K. Agren, 'Gods och ämbete. Sten Bielkes inkomster inför riksdagen 1680', *ibid.* pp. 227–45.

5 R. Wittram, *Peter I. Czar und Kaiser* (Göttingen 1964) and the same author's *Peter der Grosse* (Berlin 1954) – the Russian phrase being *svet razuma*.

6 H. Kamen, 'Melchior de Macanaz and the Foundations of Bourbon Power in Spain', *The English Historical Review*, 1965, pp. 699–716; R. de Schryver, 'Inflatie van Ambtenaren in de Spaanse Nederlanden. De Raad van de Financiën aan het eind van het seventiende eeuw', *Bijdragen voor de Geschiedenis der Nederlanden* (The Hague and Antwerp), vol. XVII (1962–63).

7 G. Otruba, 'Die Bedeutung englischer Subsidien und Antizipationen für die Finanzen Österreichs 1701 bis 1748', *Vierteljahrschrift für Sozial und Wirtschaftsgeschichte* (Leipzig) 1964, pp. 192–234.

8 E. H. Kossmann, 'Typologie der monarchieën van het Ancien Régime', in *Der Monarchie* (Amsterdam 1966).

9 British Museum, Harley Loan MSS 29/45 x (70, 2a–b), Drummond's letter (or report) of 22 Sept. 1704.

10 Q. Skinner, 'The Ideological Context of Hobbes's Political Thought', *The Historical Journal* (Cambridge) 1966, pp. 286 ff., cp. W. F. Church, 'The Decline of the French Jurists as Political Theorists 1660–1789', *French Historical Studies*, 1967.

11 D. C. Coleman, 'Eli Heckscher and the Idea of Mercantilism', *The Scandinavian Economic History Review* (Copenhagen) 1957, pp. 3–25, reprinted in 'Critical Issues in History', *The Early Modern Era 1648–1770*, ed. John C. Rule (Boston 1966), pp. 457–65.

12 Ragnhild Hatton, 'Opposition to Louis XIV ?', *Government and Opposition* (London) 1966, pp. 567–71.

13 E. F. Heckscher, *Mercantilism*, vol. II, chapters 1 and 2 (any edition, the best is the revised edition translated into English in 1955).

14 The Porchnev-Mousnier discussion (and its repercussions post-1954) and later research (such as that of A. D. Lublinskaya) can most easily be followed by English readers in J. M. H. Salmon, 'Venality of Office and Popular Sedition in Seventeenth-Century France. A Review of a Controversy', *Past and Present* (Cambridge) 1967, pp. 21–43; the E. H. Kossmann review-article 'Een blik op het Franse absolutisme', in Dutch, is less accessible but important: *Tijdschrift voor Geschiedenis*, 1965.

15 G. N. Clark, *The Dutch Alliance and the War against French Trade 1689–1697* (Oxford 1923), pp. 148 ff.; cp. J. S. Bromley, 'Le Commerce de la France de l'Ouest et la Guerre Maritime', *Annales du Midi* (Bordeaux) 1953, pp. 49–66.

16 E. Asher, *The Resistance to the Maritime Classes* (Berkeley and Los Angeles 1960), *passim*.

17 G. Olander, *Studier över det inre tillståndet i Sverige under senare delen av Karl XII's regering* (Gothenburg 1946), *passim*.

18 H. Pleijel, *Svenska Kyrkans Historia*, vol. V (Uppsala 1935), pp. 239–42.

19 On France's need for recruits see P. Bamford, 'Slaves for the galleys of France 1665–1708', *Merchants and Scholars. Essays in the history of exploration and trade collected in memory of James Ford Bell*, ed. J. Parker (Minnesota 1965); for Swedish prisoners of war in the Venetian galleys see E. Holmberg, 'Vår flottas fallne och fångna karoliner', *Karolinska Förbundets Årsbok* (Stockholm) 1915, pp. 38–39.

20 D. D. Aldridge, 'The Victualling of the British Naval Expeditions to the Baltic Sea between 1715 and 1727', *The Scandinavian Economic History Review* (Copenhagen) 1964, pp. 1–24. Cp. the many instances of bad food (not always condemned) in Barlow's *Journal*, vols. I and II, for both naval and merchant ships.

21 J. S. Bromley, 'The French Privateering War 1702–1713' in *Historical Essays 1600–1750 presented to David Ogg*, edd. H. E Bell and R. C. Ollard (London 1963), pp. 203–31; A. de Wismes, *Jean Bart et la guerre de course* (Paris 1965), *passim*.

22 William III to Shrewsbury, July 1696, cited by D. H. Somerville, *The King of Hearts. Charles Talbot, Duke of Shrewsbury* (London 1962), p. 115.

23 Charles Wilson, *England's Apprenticeship, 1603–1763* (London 1965), pp. 216 ff. and p. 335.

CHAPTER FOUR

1 H. Hantsch, *Reichsvizekanzler Friedrich Karl Graf von Schönborn* (Augsburg 1929), p. 268.

2 F. L. Ford, *Strasbourg in Transition 1648–1789* (Cambridge, Mass. 1958), pp. 29 ff.

3 R. M. Hatton, 'Louis and His Fellow-Monarchs' in *Louis XIV. The Craft of Kingship*, ed. John C. Rule (Columbus, Ohio 1969).

4 M. Braubach, *Prinz Eugen von Savoyen*, vol. III (Munich 1964), pp. 300–1 and, more fully, the same author's *Versailles und Wien von Ludwig XIV bis Kaunitz* (Bonn 1952) chapter 1; P. Sörensson, 'Keijsaren, Sverige och de nordiska allierade från Karl XII's hemkomst från Turkiet till alliansen i Wien 1719', *Karolinska Förbundets Årsbok* (Stockholm) 1926 and 1928, goes into more detail.

5 K. Koehler, *Die orientalische Politik Ludwigs XIV* (Leipzig 1907), *passim*; J. Stoye. *The Siege of Vienna* (London 1964), pp. 228 ff; very fully two as yet unpublished doctoral dissertations: F. Place (Minnesota 1963) *French Policy and the Turkish War 1679–1688* and S. Shapiro (Los Angeles 1966) *The Relations between Louis XIV and Leopold of Austria from the Treaty of Nymwegen to the Truce of Ratisbon.*

6 See e.g. R. M. Hatton, 'Sir James Jefferyes in the Army of William III, Queen Anne and George I', *Journal of the Society for Army Historical Research* (London) 1966, pp. 105 ff., for one who had 'lost much blood' fighting Turks and Tartars while in the service of Charles XI of Sweden.

7 A. Wandruszka, *Österreich und Italien im 18 Jahrhundert* (Vienna 1963), p. 16.

8 Cited, from 1709, by E. W. Dahlgren, *Les Relations commerciales et maritimes entre la France et les côtes de l'Océan Pacifique* (Paris 1909), p. 561: 'Le principal objet de la guerre présente est celui du commerce des Indes et des richesses qu'elle produisent.'

9 Charles Wilson, *England's Apprenticeship, 1603–1673* (London 1965), pp. 282–4.

10 Charles Wilson, *Profit and Power: A study of England and the Dutch Wars* (London 1957), p. 149.

11 P. Geyl, *The Netherlands in the Seventeenth Century, Part 2: 1648–1715* (London 1964), pp. 59–60.

12 A. D. Francis, *The Methuens and Portugal* (Cambridge 1966), pp. 84–85, has a good analysis of William III's attitude to the French in Italy.

13 M. A. Thomson, 'Louis XIV and the origins of the War of the Spanish Succession', reprinted from the *Transactions of the Royal Historical Society* (London 1954) in *Louis XIV and William III*, edd. Ragnhild Hatton and J. S. Bromley (Liverpool 1968), pp. 140–61.

14 R. M. Hatton, 'Louis and his Fellow-Monarchs', *loc. cit.*, does so.

15 William III to Heinsius: *Letters of William III and of Louis XIV and Their Ministers 1697–1700*, ed. P. Grimblot, vol. II (London 1848), p. 443. S. B. Baxter, *William III* (London 1966), pp. 372–3 assumes – erroneously – that William was the originator of this exchange and had inserted a secret clause for this purpose into the Second Partition treaty: see R. M. Hatton, 'European History, 1660–1713/21', *Annual Bulletin of Historical Literature*, No. LII (Historical Association, London 1968), p. 35.

16 H. von Srbik, *Wien und Versailles 1692–1700* (Munich 1944), pp. 124–36.

17 Heinsius to William III, 25 Jan. 1701: *Archives ou correspondence inédite de la Maison d'Orange-Nassau*, ed. F.J.L. Krämer, vol. III (Leiden 1909), p. 387.

18 See J. Stork-Penning, *Het Grote Werk, Vreedesonderhandelingen gedurende de Spaanse Successieoorlog 1705–1710* (Groningen 1958), *passim*, for the Dutch policy; the same author's 'Het gedrag van de Staten 1711', *Bijdragen voor de Geschiedenis der Nederlanden* (The Hague) XVIII (1963–64) pp. 193–229, with a summary of conclusions in English, 'The Ordeal of the States', in *Acta Historiae Neerlandica*, II (Leiden) 1967, pp. 107–41.

19 British Museum: Add. MSS. 20985, folios 56 ff., Drummond to Buys, London, 21 Jan. 1712, passing on (as requested by St John and Oxford) these sentiments.

20 M. Martin, in his unpublished doctoral thesis (London University 1962), 'Diplomatic Relations between Great Britain and Spain 1711–1714', has given the best analysis of the peace negotiations between London and Madrid and has, *inter alia*, unearthed a British promise to favour the recovery of the Tuscan ports for Spain.

21 R. de Schryver, 'Het eerste Staatse Barrière in de Zuidelijke Nederlanden 1697–1701', *Bijdragen voor de Geschiedenis der Nederlanden*, XVIII (1963–64), pp. 65–90, is the first historian to treat of this Dutch-Spanish convention; hitherto it has been assumed that the 'barrier' as such formed part of the 1697 Ryswick peace; cp. W. Hahlweg, 'Untersuchungen zur Barrierepolitik Wilhelms III. von Oranien und der Generalstaaten im 17. und 18. Jahrhundert', *Westfälische Forschungen*, XIV (1961), pp. 42–81.

22 For the Gibraltar issue within the context of this peace plan see Ragnhild Hatton, *Diplomatic Relations between Great Britain and the Dutch Republic 1714–1721* (London 1950), pp. 159 ff. and 213; see also S. Conn, *Gibraltar in British Diplomacy* (New Haven 1942), pp. 31 ff.

23 G. Quazza has, aptly, entitled his contribution to *Storia d'Italia*, ed. N. Valeri (2nd ed. Turin 1965), pp. 779–936, 'L'Italia e l'Europa durante la guerra di successione, 1700–1748'.

24 P. Torntoft, 'William III and Denmark-Norway, 1697–1700', *The English Historical Review*, 1966, pp. 1–25.

25 I tend (*vide* my *Charles XII of Sweden* (London 1968), pp. 100–9) to regard the historical controversy whether Tsar Peter or Augustus was the 'real' architect of the anti-Swedish alliance as somewhat fruitless: both were anxious to profit from the death of Charles XI, as was Frederick IV of Denmark-Norway; both had, however, alternative plans for expansion while Frederick IV's whole attention was directed towards the formation of the anti-Swedish coalition of which he was the cornerstone in the formative years 1698 to 1700.

26 F. Genzel, in his unpublished Bonn dissertation of 1951, *Studien zur Geschichte des Nordischen Krieges 1714–1720 unter besonderer Berücksichtigung der Personalunion zwischen Grossbritannien und Hannover*, and W. Mediger, *Mecklenburg, Russland und England-Hannover 1706–1721* (Hildesheim 1967), pp. 296 ff., have established beyond doubt the Hanoverian influence on British policy; for the effect on Sweden of British naval presence see my *Charles XII of Sweden*, pp. 404 ff.

CHAPTER FIVE

1 P. Geyl, *The Netherlands in the Seventeenth Century*, Part 2: *1648–1715* (London, New York 1964), p. 100, gives the correct version.

2 *Les Grandes Heures de l'Amitié Franco-Suèdoise* (Paris 1964, exhibition catalogue published by the Archives de France), p. 85, entries 241 and 242; cp. the anonymous pamphlet published in 1660 (Strassburg given as place of printing): *La Place des Victoires . . . Beschreibung der Ruhm-sücht und hochmütige Ehrenseule welche Ludovici XVI*, etc.

3 Public Record Office: Foreign Office series 95, vol. 556, D'Avaux to Louis XIV, Stockholm, 15 Feb. 1696.

4 Aubrey de la Motraye, *Travels through Europe, Asia and parts of Africa*, vol. II (London 1723), pp. 133–4.

5 By Germain Bazin, Conservateur-en-Chef of the Louvre, in his *A Concise History of Art* (3rd ed., revised, London 1964), p. 336.

6 For his career see the finely illustrated study by R. Josephson, *Nikodemus Tessin d.y. Tiden-Mannen-Verket* (Stockholm, 2 vols. 1930 and 1931).

7 Charles Wilson, *England's Apprenticeship, 1603–1673* (London 1965), pp. 177–8 and authorities there cited.

8 Watson Ross, 'Queen Christina's pictures', *History Today* (London) 1964, pp. 828–34; cp. the catalogue of the exhibition of 1966, *Christina of Sweden – a personality of European Civilization* (Eleventh Exhibition of the Concert of Europe. Nationalmusei Utställningskatalog 305, Stockholm 1966), pp. 420 ff.

9 David Green, *Sarah Duchess of Marlborough* (London 1967), p. 242 citing from the Blenheim archives a letter from Frances Tyrconnel: 'If I durst show youer pictors,

I wish I had youer one in litle by some sure hand, just as you are, which I heare is mighty well for a grandmother.'

10 R. M. Hatton, *Charles XII of Sweden* (London 1968), pp. 5–6, 340*, with references and illustrations.

11 A. Blunt, *Nicolas Poussin* (2 vols., London 1968), has brilliantly analyzed the intellectual content of Poussin's paintings; J. Huizinga, *Dutch Civilisation in the 17th Century and other essays* (London 1968), pp. 84–85, has stressed the 'elegiacal world, peaceful and calm' of Vermeer's compositions.

12 L. B. Simpson, *Many Mexicos* (4th revised ed., Berkeley and Los Angeles 1966), p. 142–3.

13 Barlow mentions this in his *Journal*: see Frances Armytage, *Adventure to the East* (London 1966), p. 27.

14 By Aaron Copland, in his *What to Listen for in Music* (New York, Mentor ed. 1953 onwards), p. 75.

15 Percy M. Young, *A History of British Music* (London 1967), pp. 255 ff.

16 Armin Reese, *Die Rolle der Historie beim Aufstieg des Welfenhauses* (Hildesheim 1967), p. 3 ff.

CHAPTER SIX

1 Evidence for this in Löwen's *Mémoires*, Fabrice's *Memoiren* and Motraye's *Travels*, vol. II; cp. R. M. Hatton, *Charles XII of Sweden* (London 1968), p. 13.

2 In the play *Jeppe paa Bierget* (a good recent ed. by F. J. Billeskov Jansen, Copenhagen 1961), translated into English as *The Transformed Peasant* by Reginald Spink (London 1957, in The Drama Library series on Ludvig Holberg).

3 E. M. Wilson, 'The Four Elements in the Imagery of Calderón', *The Modern Language Review* (Cambridge) 1936, pp. 34–37 and Spanish authorities there cited.

4 Gerald Brenan, *The Literature of the Spanish People* (London 1951), p. 185.

5 For a case-study of such pirating see R. M. Hatton, 'John Robinson and the *Account of Sueden*', *Bulletin of the Institute of Historical Research* (London) 1955.

6 P. J. W. von Malssen, *Louis XIV d'après les pamphlets répandus en Hollande* (Amsterdam 1936); F. Kleyser, *Die Flugschriften gegen Ludwig XIV zur Zeit der pfalzischen Krieges* (Berlin 1935); P. Fransen, *Leibniz und die Friedenschlüsse von Utrecht und Rastatt-Baden* (Purmerend 1933).

7 H. D. Schmidt. 'The establishment of "Europe" as a political expression', *The Historical Journal* (Cambridge) 1966, pp. 172 ff.

8 See e.g. H. G. Wright, 'Some English writers and Charles XII', *Studia Neophilologia* (Uppsala) xv (1942–3).

9 Barlow's *Journal* (transcribed by B. Lubbock), vol. I, p. 60.

10 *Agneta Horns Lefverne*, ed. Sigrid Leijonhufvud (Stockholm 1908); for commentaries on the autobiography of this grand-daughter of Axel Oxenstierna see references in E. N. Tigerstedt, *Svensk Litteraturhistoria* (Stockholm 1948), p. 523.

11 Löwen's *Mémoires* in *Karolinska Förbundets Årsbok* (Stockholm) 1929, p. 24.

12 Cited by R. S. Crane, *The Idea of the Humanities and other Essays Critical and Historical* (Chicago and London 1967), p. 76.

13 Armin Reese, *Die Rolle der Historie beim Aufstieg des Welfenhauses* (Hildesheim 1967), pp. 189 ff.

14 Holberg's memoirs, most easily accessible in the English translation from their original Latin (London 1827), p. 42: 'The strongest and the swiftest of foot generally succeeded in obtaining the prize.'

15 Cited by H. Woodbridge, *Sir William Temple: The Man and His Work* (Oxford 1940), p. 64.

16 C. M. Cippola, *Clocks and Culture* (London 1967), p. 69.

17 For 'Monsieur Papins Digestoire' used in the preparation of the feast see *The Diary of John Evelyn*, ed. E. S. de Beer, vol. IV: *Kalendarium, 1673–1689* (London 1955) pp. 278–9, entry for 1682.

CHAPTER SEVEN

1 The edition of 1627 which indicates the author only by initials was followed by a much enlarged edition of 1635 which gives the author's name in full. The British Museum possesses copies of both editions.

2 H. Butterfield, *Origins of Modern Science* (London 1950), p. 165.

3 P. Gay, *The Party of Humanity. Essays in the French Enlightenment* (New York 1964), pp. 185 ff., argues this forcefully.

4 James Lowde, *A Discourse Concerning the Nature of Man* (London 1694), p. 24 for the first quotation; the summary is from R. B. Crane's fine essay on 'The Emergence of the Man of Feeling', in *The Idea of the Humanities* (Chicago and London 1967), p. 198.

5 *Ibid.*, p. 198, citing from George Stanhope's foreword to his translation (3rd ed. London 1700) of *Epictetus His Morals*.

6 H. von Srbik, *Wien und Versailles 1692–1700* (Munich 1944), pp. 220, 268 ff.

7 S. B. Kanter, 'Archbishop Fénelon's Political Activity: The Focal Point of Power in Dynasticism', *French Historical Studies*, 1965, p. 331.

8 Friedrich Heer, *The Intellectual History of Europe* (translated from the Vienna edition of 1953 by J. Steinberg, London 1966), p. 389.

9 *Ibid.*, p. 388.

10 R. M. Hatton, *Charles XII of Sweden* (London 1968), pp. 430–1 and authorities there cited.

11 Cited from *Pensées*, section II, p. 151, by Georges Snyders, *La Pédagogie en France aux XVIIᵉ et XVIIIᵉ Siècles* (Paris 1965), p. 53.

12 *Ibid.*, p. 97, cited from P. Buffier's *Géographie universelle*. The whole verse goes as follows:

La Hollande ou plutôt les Provinces Unies
Comptent Utrecht pour une entre leurs sept parties;
Amsterdam, Rotterdam et La Haye en Hollande,
Nidelbourg se distingue aux îles de Zélande.
Dans la Gueldre Nimègue et comté de Zutphen;
En Over-Issel, Deventer; en Frise, Leuvarden;
Groningue en est encore. L'Ecluse et Sas de Gand
En Flandre; puis Maestricht; Bolduc dans le Brabant.

13 R. S. Crane, *The Idea of the Humanities and other Essays* (Chicago and London 1967), pp. 68–69, on A. Cowley's 1661 'Proposition for the advancement of experimental philosophy'.

14 The discussion round the 'Merton' thesis (after Robert K. Merton who in 1938 published *Science, Technology and Society in the Seventeenth Century*) can most easily be studied in the reprinted articles by Robert K. Merton, Theodore K. Rabb, and A. Rupert Hall in *The Early Modern Era 1648–1770* ('Critical Issues in History', Boston 1966), ed. John C. Rule, pp. 408–29.

15 For such signatures see Alice Carter, 'The Huguenot Contribution to the Early Years of the Funded Debt 1694–1714', *Proceedings of the Huguenot Society of London* (1955), p. 23.

16 J. Bossuet, *Discours sur l'Histoire universelle*, vol. III, chapter iv.

17 See my 'Louis XIV and His Fellow-Monarchs' in *Louis XIV. The Craft of Kingship*, ed. John C. Rule (Columbus, Ohio 1969).

18 K. W. Swart, *The Sale of Offices in the Seventeenth Century* (The Hague 1949), pp. 51 ff.

19 See my 'Gratifications and Foreign Policy', *William III and Louis XIV. Essays by and for Mark A. Thomson*, edd. Ragnhild Hatton and J. S. Bromley (Liverpool 1968).

20 H. H. Rowen, 'A second thought on Locke's First Treatise', *Journal of the History of Ideas*, 1956, and the introduction by Peter Laslett to John Locke, *Two Treaties of Government* (Cambridge 1961); cp. the important review-article by Michael Oakeshott in *The Historical Journal* (Cambridge) 1962, pp. 97–100.

21 Public Record Office: Foreign Entry Books (104) vol. 154, Harley to Robinson of 22 March/1 April 1706/7 and 11/22 April 1707, the latter enclosing a letter from the Attorney-General, Sir Edward Northey; see Robinson's letter to Harley from Leipzig 8/18 March 1706/7 for the background to the story.

22 P. Schönströms memoirs, ed. C. Hallendorff, *En karolins berättelse* (Stockholm 1915), p. 48.

23 For Locke's shares in slave trading companies see F. Heer, *The Intellectual History of Europe* (London 1966), pp. 370–1. The best treatment of Louis XIV's (initially successful) efforts to have the *Asiento* transferred to a French company (against compensation paid to the Portuguese Cacho Company for the unexpired period of its contract) see A. D. Francis, *The Methuens and Portugal* (Cambridge 1966), pp. 18 ff.

24 This has been brilliantly analyzed by G. Mattingley, *Renaissance Diplomacy* (London 1955), pp. 195 ff.

25 Fritz Redlich, *De praeda militari. Looting and Booty 1500–1815* (Wiesbaden 1956), pp. 44 ff.

26 P. Höynck, *Frankreich und seine Gegner auf dem Nymwegener Friedenskongress* (Bonn 1960), pp. 150–1.

27 Ragnhild Hatton, *Diplomatic Relations between Great Britain and the Dutch Republic 1714–1731* (London 1950), pp. 147 ff.; cp. J. J. Murray, 'The Görtz-Gyllenborg Arrests – A Problem in Diplomatic Immunity', *Journal of Modern History*, 1956, pp. 325 ff.

28 Edvard Gyldenstolpe's letter to his father of 17 April 1708, printed in A. Lewenhaupt, *Karolinen Edvard Gyldenstolpe* (Stockholm 1941), pp. 192–3.

29 See my 'Louis XIV and His Fellow-Monarchs' in *Louis XIV. The Craft of Kingship*, ed. John C. Rule (Columbus, Ohio 1969) for the argument and evidence of 'repentence' before the famous death-bed regret at having loved war too much.

30 Ragnhild Hatton, *War and Peace, 1680–1720* (Inaugural Lecture), London 1969, pp. 16–22.

GENEALOGY OF THE SPANISH SUCCESSION

(showing children who survived infancy)

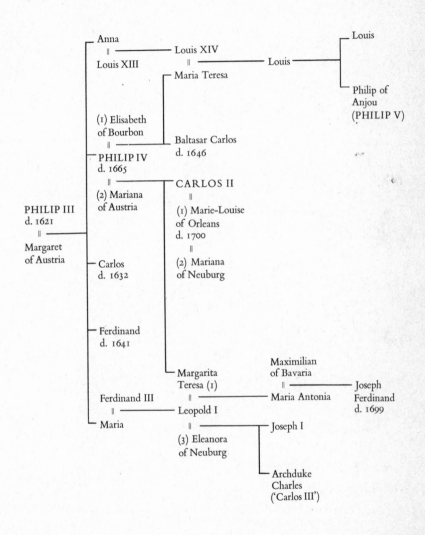

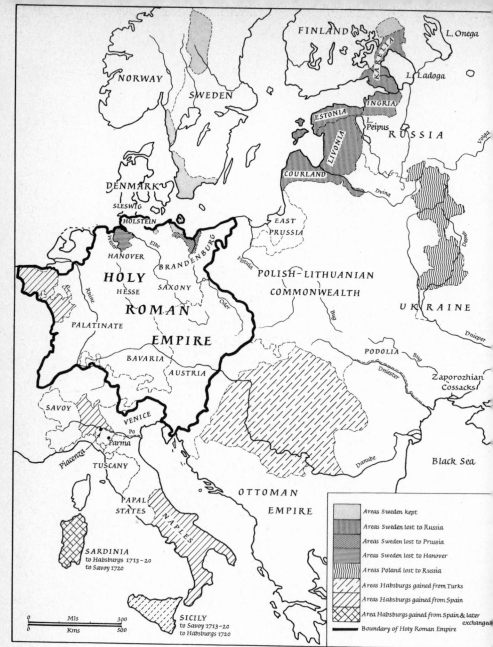

NORWAY

SWEDEN

FINLAND

L. Onega

L. Ladoga

INGRIA

ESTONIA

L. Peipus

RUSSIA

Volga

DENMARK

SLESWIG

HOLSTEIN

LIVONIA

COURLAND

Dvina

Don

EAST
PRUSSIA

Weser

Elbe

HANOVER

BRANDENBURG

HOLY

HESSE

SAXONY

Vistula

POLISH-LITHUANIAN

COMMONWEALTH

UKRAINE

ROMAN

Rhine

PALATINATE

Oder

Dnieper

EMPIRE

BAVARIA

AUSTRIA

PODOLIA

Bug

Dniester

Zaporozhian
Cossacks

SAVOY

VENICE

Po

Parma

TUSCANY

Piacenza

PAPAL
STATES

SARDINIA
to Habsburgs 1713–20
to Savoy 1720

NAPLES

OTTOMAN

EMPIRE

Danube

Bug

Black Sea

Areas Sweden kept

Areas Sweden lost to Russia

Areas Sweden lost to Prussia

Areas Sweden lost to Hanover

Areas Poland lost to Russia

Areas Habsburgs gained from Turks

Areas Habsburgs gained from Spain

Area Habsburgs gained from Spain & later
exchanged

Boundary of Holy Roman Empire

SICILY
to Savoy 1713–20
to Habsburgs 1720

0   Mls   300
0   Kms   500

1 Europe east of the Rhine, 1648–1721

220

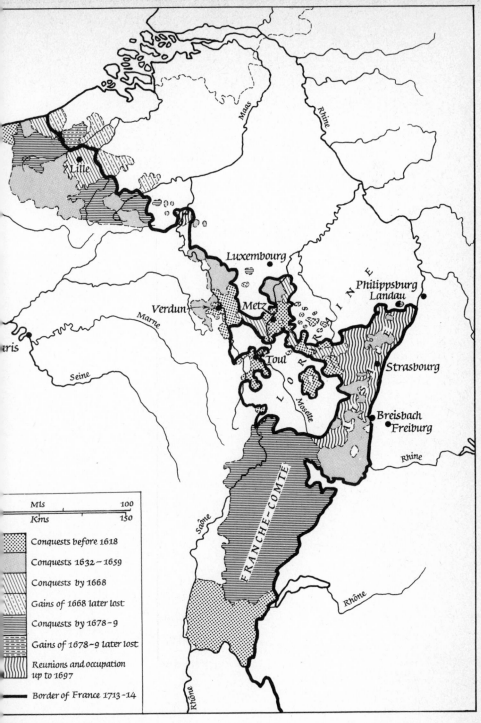

Lille

Luxembourg

Verdun

Metz

Philippsburg
Landau

Toul

Strasbourg

Breisbach
Freiburg

Paris

FRANCHE–COMTÉ

L O R R A I N E

Maas

Rhine

Marne

Seine

Saône

Moselle

Rhône

Rhine

Rhône

he French frontier, 1618–1714

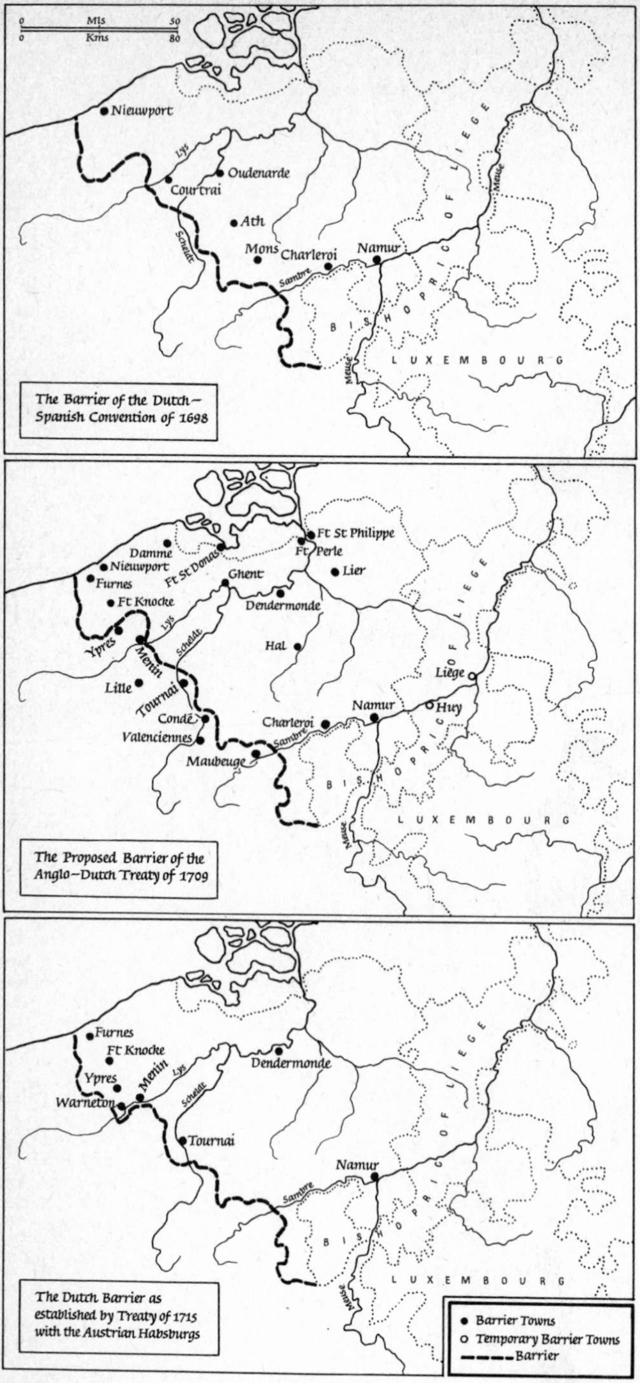

Map 1: The Barrier of the Dutch–Spanish Convention of 1698

Mls 0 — 50
Kms 0 — 80

Nieuwport
Oudenarde
Courtrai
Ath
Mons Charleroi Namur
BISHOPRIC OF LIEGE
Lys
Schelde
Sambre
Meuse
Maese
LUXEMBOURG

The Barrier of the Dutch–Spanish Convention of 1698

Map 2: The Proposed Barrier of the Anglo–Dutch Treaty of 1709

Damme
Nieuwport
Furnes
Ft Knocke
Ft St Donas
Ft St Philippe
Ft Perle
Ghent
Lier
Dendermonde
Ypres
Menin
Lys
Schelde
Litle
Tournai
Condé
Valenciennes
Maubeuge
Hal
Charleroi
Namur
Huy
Liège
BISHOPRIC OF LIEGE
Sambre
Maese
LUXEMBOURG

The Proposed Barrier of the Anglo–Dutch Treaty of 1709

Map 3: The Dutch Barrier as established by Treaty of 1715

Furnes
Ft Knocke
Ypres
Warneton
Menin
Lys
Dendermonde
Schelde
Tournai
Namur
BISHOPRIC OF LIEGE
Sambre
Maese
LUXEMBOURG

The Dutch Barrier as established by Treaty of 1715 with the Austrian Habsburgs

● Barrier Towns
○ Temporary Barrier Towns
▬ ▬ ▬ Barrier

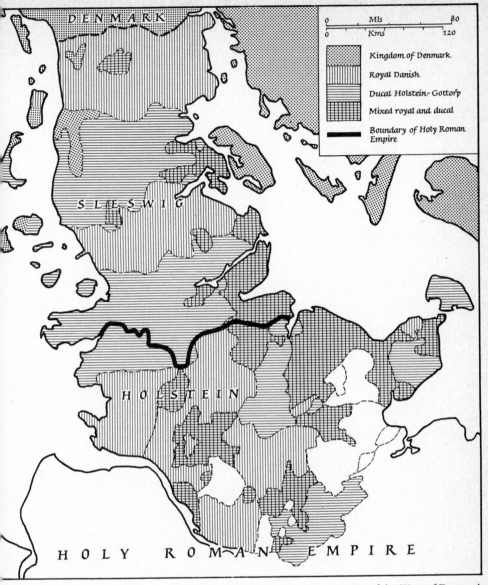

4 The Duchies of Sleswig and Holstein, showing territories of the King of Denmark and the Duke of Holstein-Gottorp

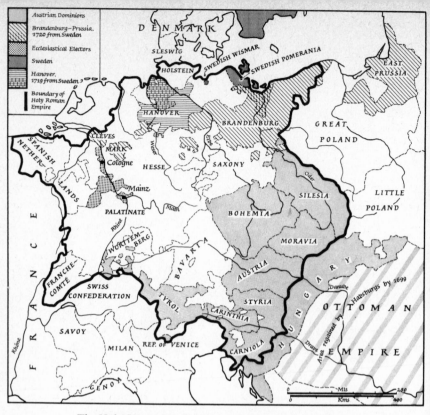

5 The Holy Roman Empire of the German Nation, 1648–1720

6 Overseas possessions of European powers, 1648–1713

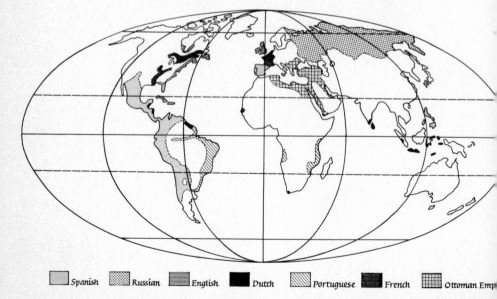

I The elected office of Emperor of the Holy Roman Empire of the German Nation (traditionally first in diplomatic table of ranks)

Ferdinand III 1637–57
Interregnum 1657–58
Leopold I 1658–1705
Joseph I 1705–11
Charles VI 1711–40

II The elected office of Pope, head of the Catholic Church and temporal ruler of Papal States

Innocent X 1644–55
Alexander VII 1655–67
Clement IX 1667–69
Clement X 1670–76
Innocent XI 1676–89
Alexander VIII 1689–91
Innocent XII 1691–1700
Clement XI 1700–21
Innocent XIII 1721–24

II Hereditary monarchs in alphabetical order according to states

DENMARK-NORWAY ('The Twin Kingdoms')
Frederick III 1648–70
Christian V 1670–99
Frederick IV 1699–1730

ENGLAND, Great Britain after the Union with Scotland in 1707
Charles II 1660–85
James II 1685–88 (brother of Charles II)
William III and Mary 1689–94/1702
Anne 1702–14
George I 1714–27

FRANCE ('His Most Christian Majesty' in diplomatic usage)
Louis XIV 1643–1715
Louis XV 1715–74 (Regent during his minority 1715–23 Philippe, Duc d'Orléans)

PORTUGAL
John IV 1640–56
Alfonso VI 1656–67 (exiled 1667, died 1683. Regents after 1667: first his mother, Queen Maria Luisa, then his brother Pedro from 1671)
Pedro II 1683–1706
John V 1706–50

RUSSIA (usually called Muscovy till the end of the seventeenth century)
Aleksey 1645–76
Fyodor III 1676–82
Ivan V and Peter 1682–89 (their sister Sophia as Regent till Ivan, who survived till 1696, overthrown 1689)
Peter I 1689–1725

SPAIN ('His Most Catholic Majesty' in diplomatic parlance)
Philip IV 1621–65
Carlos II 1665–1700 (till 1676 his mother, Maria Ana of Austria, Regent)
Philip V 1700–46 (Archduke Charles of Austria recognized as 'Carlos III' 1703–13 by Maritime Powers and did not relinquish title 'King of Spain' till 1720)

SWEDEN
Charles X 1654–60
Charles XI 1660–97 (regency technically till 1672, in effect till 1675)
Charles XII 1697–1718
Ulrika Eleonora 1718–20
Frederick I 1720–51

IV The Holy Roman Empire of the German Nation

(a) Important hereditary rulers below monarch's rank.

BAVARIA, Elector of
Maximilian I 1623–51
Ferdinand Maria 1651–79
Maximilian (or Max) Emanuel 1679–1726

BRANDENBURG, Elector of, after 1701 also King of Prussia, ruling also East Prussia (sovereignty achieved in 1660), and the duchies of Cleves and Mark.
Frederick William, 'The Great Elector', 1640–88
Frederick III 1688–1713, from 1701 King Frederick I (literally King in Prussia, König in Preussen)
Frederick William I 1713–40

HANOVER, Duke, after 1692 Elector of Electorate created in 1692 from territories of the Lüneburg dukes, Ernst August of Brunswick-Lüneburg-Calemberg and Georg Wilhelm of Brunswick-Lüneburg-Celle, though the actual transference of Celle to Hanover did not take place till the death of Georg Wilhelm in 1704).
John Frederick 1641–79
Ernst August 1679–98 (Elector from 1692)
Georg Ludwig, Elector 1698–1727

HESSE-CASSEL, Landgrave of
William VI 1637–63 (regency till 1650)
Charles 1663–1730 (till 1670 his mother, Hedwig Sophia, Regent)

RHINE DUCHIES, Duke of JÜLICH AND BERG
Wilhelm Wolfgang 1614–53
Philip Wilhelm 1653–90
Johann Wilhelm 1690–1716
For the Rhine Duchies of CLEVES AND MARK see
Brandenburg.

SAXONY, Elector of
John George I 1611–56
John George II 1656–80
John George III 1680–91
John George IV 1691–94
Frederick Augustus I 1694–1733 (known after 1697 as
Augustus II, King of Poland)

WÜRTTEMBERG, Duke of
Eberhard III 1628–74
Wilhelm Ludwig 1674–77
Eberhard Ludwig 1677–1733 (regency for first sixteen
years of reign)

(b) The Electoral, ecclesiastical and temporal rulers (appointed by Chapter and Pope) in the Empire.
Cologne, Archbishop, Elector of
Mainz, Archbishop, Elector of
Trier, Archbishop, Elector of

(c) THE UNITS OF THE EMPIRE. The Empire had an
Imperial Diet consisting of 3 'Colleges', that of the
Electors (8 in 1648, 9 by 1692) who elected the Emperor;
that of the Princes (37 ecclesiastic and 63 temporal votes,
some of which were composite ones), and that of the 51
Free Imperial Cities. The Empire was divided into 10
Circles (*Kreisen*): the Austrian, Bavarian, Burgundian,
Franconian, Rhenish (2 Circles), Lower and Upper
Saxony, Swabian and Westphalian.

V Hereditary rulers in the Italian peninsula

MILAN (THE MILANESE) formed part of the Spanish
empire till the war of the Spanish Succession when it
was occupied, after struggles 1701–04, by Austrian and
Savoyard troops. It was ceded to Charles VI of the
Austrian Habsburg branch in 1713–14.

NAPLES AND SICILY (THE TWO SICILIES) formed
part of the Spanish empire till 1707 when Austrians
occupied them; Naples was ceded to Austria by Treaty
of Utrecht, Sicily to Savoy. In 1720 Austria exchanged
Sicily for Sardinia; and in 1735 ceded Naples and Sicily
to the Spanish Bourbons as *secondo geniture*.

SAVOY, Duke of, between 1713 and 1720 King of Sicily,
after 1720 King of Sardinia.
Charles Emmanuel II 1638–75 (with regency till 1663 of
mother)
Victor Amadeus II 1675–1730 (with his mother, Jeanne de
Nemours, as Regent till 1680)

Tuscany, Mantua, Parma, Piacenza and other Italian
duchies played a minor role in European affairs in this
period.

Elected heads of Commonwealths and Republics

COMMONWEALTH IN ENGLAND 1649–60

*Cromwell, leader of army after 1649; Lord Protector of the
Commonwealth of England, Scotland and Ireland 1653–58*
Cromwell, Richard, Lord Protector 1658–59

POLISH-LITHUANIAN COMMONWEALTH, the
RZECZPOSPOLITA POLSKA (Republic of Poland, or
Poland in contemporary parlance)

John III Kazimierz, King 1648–68
Michael Wiśniowecki, King 1669–73
John III Sobieski, King 1674–96
Interregnum 1696–97 during contested election of
Augustus of Saxony and the Prince of Conti
Augustus II 1697–1704, King★ and again 1709–33
Stanislaus Leszczyński, King from 1704 (effective only till
1709, though he kept his title of King till his death
in 1766)

DUTCH REPUBLIC (United Provinces, States General,
Their High Mightinesses in diplomatic parlance)

William II, Stadhouder 1647–50
First stadhouderless period *1650–72*
Grand Pensionary *(Raadpensionaris), Johan de Witt
1650–72*
William III, Stadhouder 1672–1702
Second stadhouderless period *1702–47*
Grand Pensionary, *Antonie Heinsius 1702–20*
Grand Pensionary, *Isaac van Hoornbeck 1720–27*

GENOESE REPUBLIC was in a difficult position between
Spain and France; for its bombardment by Louis XIV
in 1683 see Chronology of War and Peace.

REPUBLIC OF VENICE was preoccupied with wars
against Turkey; see Chronology of War and Peace,
1645–69, 1664 and 1684.

SWISS CONFEDERATION. From 1663 the federal structure
more or less collapsed, there being no meeting of the
federal Diet till 1776; after the civil war of 1656 religious
issues were left in the control of the individual canton.

★ He did not accept the election of Stanislaus (1704) till the
Treaty of Altranstädt (1706).

226

CHRONOLOGY OF WAR AND PEACE, CIVIL AND INTERNATIONAL

1640–59 Revolt of the Catalans. Most rights and privileges were retained in the settlement of 1660, but these were lost during the War of the Spanish Succession when the Catalans embraced the cause of 'Carlos III'.

1640–68 Revolt of Portugal against Spain with French and English support. Invasion of Spain 1644 and important victories 1659, 1663 and 1665. Spain recognized Portuguese independence in 1668.

1645–69 The Candian War between Venice and the Ottoman empire. France helped Venice, but in the end Candia (Crete), besieged 1658–69, was obliged to give in and it was ceded at the peace of 1670, though Venice retained some fortified posts on the island.

1648 (Jan.) Separate peace between Spain and Dutch Republic whereby the independence of the latter was recognized, as was the closure of the Scheldt river; cession of some land in Limburg, Brabant and Flanders to the Dutch.

1648 *Peace of Westphalia* (after negotiations at Osnabrück and Münster 1645–48). Frontiers of Empire redrawn to exclude the Dutch Republic and the Swiss cantons; the *Landeshoheit** and *Bündnisfreiheit†* of the German princes and Imperial Free Cities was recognized; the Augsburg settlement was extended to embrace Calvinists as well as Lutherans; the Edict of Restitution was repealed and 1 January 1624 was set as the date which entitled Catholics to keep land resumed; Sweden and France received *satisfactio* (compensation) for their help to the Protestant cause (the former in Pomerania, Wismar, Bremen-Verden, with seat and voice in Diet; the latter in Alsace, without such seat and voice, and in the sovereignty granted in respect of Metz, Toul and Verdun). Brandenburg, Bavaria and Saxony benefited territorially.

1648–51 Civil war in England, Ireland and Scotland: Stuart cause lost to Cromwell and Puritans.

1648–52 The Fronde (anti-Mazarin, anti-absolutist also) in France.

1648–59 War between France and Spain, Cromwell's England participating on the French side after 1656. *Peace of Pyrenees:* Spain lost to France frontier fortresses in Flanders and Artois and gave back Roussillon and Cerdagne (given to Spain in 1494 in an attempt to buy Ferdinand the Catholic's neutrality in the Italian wars); Spain ceded Dunkirk and Jamaica to England; Spain's ally, the Duke of Lorraine, was restored to most of his duchy though the French kept Bar, Clermont and some other places and were permitted a 'military route' of passage for their troops.

* See above p. 67.
† i.e. freedom to enter into alliances.

1652–54 First Anglo-Dutch War (Denmark-Norway ally of Dutch Republic). *Peace of Westminster:* the Dutch accepted the English Navigation Act of 1651; the Province of Holland agreed to exclude all members of the House of Orange from the post of *stadhouder.*

1653 Blake's expedition to and bombardment of Tuscany and Papal States (retaliation for injuries suffered by English merchants).

1654–67 Struggle for the Ukraine between Russia and Polish-Lithuanian Commonwealth, sparked off by Bogdan Khmelnitsky putting himself under Russian protection. *Peace of Andrusovo* by which Russia gained eastern Ukraine and the Smolensk area; the hope of regaining these territories (referred to as the *avulsa imperii*) remained potent in Polish-Lithuanian policies.

1655–60 The Northern War in which Charles X of Sweden invaded Poland (having failed to get Polish co-operation in a venture against Russia) allied to Brandenburg. Russia, Denmark (1657) and the Empire declared war on Sweden, and Brandenburg – in return for the Poles' relinquishing sovereignty over East Prussia – changed sides. During the war Charles X (abandoning Poland) invaded Denmark from the south. The hard frost of 1658 made possible a bold crossing of the Belt; Copenhagen was threatened and by the *Peace of Roskilde 1658* Denmark-Norway felt obliged to cede to Sweden the island of Bornholm and Halland, Blekinge and Scania (Danish districts on the Scandinavian peninsula) and Båhus, Herjedal and Jæmteland (Norwegian provinces) as well as Trondhjem district and town. A clause in the treaty promised a joint Scandinavian policy of an anti-Dutch nature. War restarted with Denmark when Charles's suspicions were aroused as to Danish intentions in respect of this clause, but strong Dutch support for Denmark counteracted the second Swedish invasion and on Charles X's death in 1660 peace was made. (The Swedes had already in late 1659 reluctantly granted Dutch subjects equality with Swedish subjects in respect of customs and dues levied on trade). In the peace with Denmark-Norway, at *Copenhagen 1660*, Bornholm and Trondhjem were restored though the other Roskilde gains were kept, and sovereign rights, including *jus armorum*, were granted to the Duke of Holstein-Gottorp in respect of his lands in Sleswig and Holstein (see map 4). In that with Poland, Brandenburg and the Empire, *Oliva 1660*, the Polish Vasas abandoned their claims to the Swedish throne and accepted the loss of Livonia to Sweden, while confirmation was given to Brandenburg of a Swedish guarantee for East Prussia. In that with Russia, at *Kardis 1661*, the *status quo* was re-established.

1657–61 War between the Dutch Republic and Portugal over Brazil: the Dutch abandoned their hold of Brazil (established in the 1630s) on being involved with war with England in 1654; by 1661 they had to acknowledge Portuguese sovereignty over the whole of Brazil.

1660 Restoration of the Stuarts in England.

1661–64 War between the Austrian Habsburgs and the Ottoman empire. After the battle of St Gotthard (to which many states, including France, sent contingents) 1664, won by Montecuccoli the Austrian general, followed the *Truce of Vasvar* for twenty years: the Sultan lost no territory but recognized the election of the Prince of Transylvania by the local Estates.

1664 Holy League of Pope, Emperor, Poland and Venice against Turks.

1664–71 Hungarian nobility's war (with Turkish help) against the Habsburgs.

1665–67 Second Anglo-Dutch War. Hostilities opened in 1664 with English seizure of New Amsterdam in North America and of Dutch trading-stations in Africa. France and Denmark were allied to the Republic and gave some help. *Treaty of Breda:* The Dutch ceded New Netherlands in North America (including New Amsterdam), received in return Surinam and important concessions in the Navigation Act. England ceded to France Acadia; France to England, Antigua, Montserrat and St Kitts.

1667 Denmark annexed Oldenburg and Delmenhorst on extinction of ruling house.

1667–68 *War of Devolution* in which Louis XIV claimed as his wife's inheritance part of the Spanish Netherlands, she being a daughter of an earlier marriage of Philip IV than Carlos II (king since 1665): it was argued that local laws of inheritance demanded a division of the father's estate at the time of his death. *Treaty of Aix-la-Chapelle* (under Anglo-Dutch-Swedish mediation): France retained twelve fortified places in Flanders, among them Lille, Charleroi and Tournai.

1668 Spain recognized Portuguese independence (having refused Louis XIV's 1664 offer to help crush the rebellion against compensation in land).

1668 Secret partition treaty between Louis XIV and Leopold as to the Spanish inheritance: Louis XIV to receive the Spanish Netherlands, Franche-Comté, Naples and Sicily, Navarre, the Philippines and the African harbours of Spain; Leopold to have Spain and its American empire, Milan, Minorca and the Balearic islands (Leopold denounced treaty in 1673).

1670 French occupation of Lorraine.

1671–72 Revolt of Stenka Razin of 1667 against Moscow develops into 'Peasant War'.

1672–76 War between Poland and Turkey for control of the Ukraine unleashed by Cossack revolt, led by Doroshenko, against the Poles. *Treaty of Zuravna:* Poland lost most of Podolia and Polish Ukraine.

1672–78 General war occasioned by Louis XIV's invasion of the Dutch Republic. Louis's main ally, Charles II of England, was obliged by public opinion, as expressed in Parliament, to make peace with the Dutch in 1674; and the Republic found allies in the same year, namely Spain, Leopold of Austria, and Brandenburg. In 1675 Sweden was drawn in on the French side in respect of Brandenburg, and Denmark-Norway then staged an attack ('The Scanian War') to recover the provinces lost in 1658 and 1660 and to break the Holstein-Gottorp alliance with Sweden. *Peace of Nijmegen 1678:* the Dutch Republic (as the attacked party) received *satisfactio* from Louis XIV in the form of important commercial concessions, but Spain (which had declared war on France) lost Franche-Comté, Artois and sixteen fortified places in Flanders, among them Ypres, Cambrai and St Omer; also Haiti in the West Indies. *Peace of Saint-Germain-en-Laye 1679* between Sweden and Brandenburg, mediated by Louis XIV, in which Brandenburg received a strip of Swedish Pomerania (see map 1). In the *Peace of Fontainebleau 1679* Louis XIV mediated peace between Sweden and the Dutch Republic and Sweden and Denmark: the *status quo* was in both cases restored, but the Swedes felt bitter that the commercial advantages granted to the Dutch in 1659 were not repealed.

1674–78 Messina revolt against Spain; initial support by France withdrawn because of the peace negotiations above.

1677–81 First war between Russia and the Ottoman empire on account of border trouble, the two states having come into close contact following the Ottoman gains at the *Peace of Zuravna*. By the *Peace of Radzin* the Sultan lost most of Turkish Ukraine and had to grant trading rights on the Black Sea to the Cossacks.

1680 Bohemian revolt against Leopold I.

1681 Louis XIV achieves the 'voluntary' inclusion of Strassburg with France (the town keeping autonomy in religious and local affairs) and buys Casale (the key to north Italy) from the Duke of Mantua.

1682–99 War between Ottoman empire and Austrian Habsburgs in alliance with Poland from 1683 and with contingents from princes of the Empire. Siege of Vienna 1683. From 1684 a *Holy League War*, inspired and partly financed by the Pope in which Venice, Poland and, from 1686, Russia, also participated. Greater Hungary was conquered from the Turks by the Imperial generals Charles of Lorraine, Louis of Baden and Prince Eugène: Ofen (Budapest), under Turkish rule since 1541, was freed. During the war the rising of the Hungarian nobility, which had started in 1681 with Turkish help and contributed to the outbreak of the war, was crushed.

228

Treaty of Karlowitz: the Habsburgs (for twenty-five years) secured all Hungary (except the Banat of Temesvar, Transylvania, Croatia, Slavonia); Venice gained the Morea and the greater part of Dalmatia; Poland had Podolia restored to her. Russia in 1700 signed a truce with the Turks which brought Azov into Russian hands.

1683 Spain declared war on France, after treaties with the Dutch Republic and Sweden, to stem Louis XIV's reunion policy and safeguard the Spanish Netherlands and Luxemburg. Genoa, as an active ally of Spain, was bombarded by Louis XIV and the fortress of Luxemburg was taken.

1684 *Truce of Regensburg (Ratisbon),* for twenty years whereby Louis XIV obtained recognition from the Emperor, the Empire and Spain of the extension of his frontiers implied in the work of the *Chambres des Réunions* (1680–83), his occupation of Strassburg, the occupation of Lorraine, of Luxemburg and of Trier. In return France promised to present no further claims. The Dutch Republic agreed the terms of the truce.

1685 *Palatinate Succession* issue to the fore: Louis XIV's requests for papal mediation in respect of his sister-in-law's claims ignored. The Empire argued that the devolution of the Palatinate to the Neuburg branch took place according to arrangements settled in 1648; Louis XIV feared Leopold's influence in the Palatinate in view of the close ties of Vienna with the Neuburgs.

1688 William III's invasion of England. James II's flight to France and establishment of Jacobite court in exile at Saint-Germain. James having been deemed to abdicate his throne by flight, William and Mary became joint King and Queen of England (1689). James's attempt (1689–90) to keep Ireland, with French help, failed. Revolt in his favour in Scotland was crushed.

1689–97 *Nine Years War* (also called War of the League of Augsburg after League of 1686). Louis sponsored the claim of the Prince of Fürstenberg, Bishop of Strasbourg, to be Archbishop-Elector of Cologne and made certain claims, on behalf of his sister-in-law, to allodial land in the Palatinate where the direct male line had died out with Charles, Elector Palatine, in 1685. The French occupied and (later) devastated the Palatinate in October 1688, acts which provoked the Grand Alliance of May 1689 and brought a general war in which France was ranged against Bavaria, Brandenburg, the Palatinate and Saxony in the Empire, Leopold I, Carlos II, the Dutch Republic, England and Savoy. The Scandinavian states, uneasy at the union of the Maritime Powers under Willem III (*stadhouder*) and William III (king) remained neutral; and Savoy left the anti-French coalition in 1696 to adopt a neutral position. *Peace of Ryswick:* Conquests were mutually restored between France and the Maritime Powers; William III was recognized as King of England and Anne as his successor by Louis XIV; Louis restored to Spain most of the places he had 'reunited' since Nijmegen (though eight-two remained French); Louis similarly restored places he had 'reunited' from the

Emperor and the Empire, and in return received confirmation of his possession of Strasbourg and of the French interpretation of sovereignty over Alsace; Lorraine was restored, with the exception of Saarlouis, to Duke Charles's son Leopold Joseph; free navigation was agreed for the Rhine. The Cologne and Palatinate issues were submitted to arbitration: decision in both cases went against Louis XIV

1697 Frederick Augustus I, Elector of Saxony, maintained his title as Augustus II, King of Poland, after a contested election (other candidate Prince of Conti) and was duly crowned.

1698 Secret war league of Danish king and Augustus against Sweden; Tsar Peter told of this at his meeting with Augustus at Rawa.

1698 *First Partition Treaty* (France and the Maritime Powers). Joseph Ferdinand, Electoral Prince of Bavaria, to inherit the major part of Spain and its empire in Europe and overseas; the Archduke Charles of Austria to receive the Duchy of Milan; the Dauphin to have Naples and Sicily, the Tuscan ports and the province of Guipúzcoa in Spain. The Electoral Prince's father, Maximilian of Bavaria, to succeed him in Spain if he died without heirs. Invitations to others to accede and especially to Leopold.

1698 Last of several Streltsy revolts in Moscow: crushed on Tsar Peter's return from European tour and regiments disbanded 1705.

1698 *The Barrier Convention* between Spain and the Dutch Republic (foreshadowed during the Ryswick negotiations) whereby Dutch troops were to garrison, jointly with the Spaniards, certain towns (see map 3) to provide a 'barrier' against French aggression.

1700 *Second Partition Treaty* (necessitated by the death in 1699 of the Electoral Prince). The Archduke Charles to receive the whole of Spain, its empire overseas and the Spanish Netherlands; the French Dauphin to receive the Duchy of Milan (which by a secret clause was to be offered to the Duke of Lorraine in exchange for Lorraine, and – if he refused – to the Duke of Savoy in return for Savoy and Nice) as well as Naples and Sicily, the Tuscan ports and Guipúzcoa in Spain. Invitations to other rulers, and most urgently to Leopold I, to accede.

1700 (Oct.) Will of Carlos II, leaving Spain and its entire empire in Europe and overseas to Philip, Duke of Anjou (grandson of Louis XIV).

1701 Frederick III, Elector of Brandenburg, assumed, with permission of Emperor Leopold I, the title of *König in Preussen.*

1700–21 *Great Northern War.* Attack by a coalition consisting of Frederick IV of Denmark-Norway, Augustus of Saxony and Tsar Peter of Russia on Sweden. The war brought civil war to the Polish-Lithuanian Commonwealth where one party embraced Augustus's cause, another (the 'patriot' group) that of Charles XII of

Sweden in order to reconquer the territories lost to Russia in 1667, while a third remained neutral: effective co-operation with Charles XII was limited to the period when Stanislaus Leszczyński held a measure of real power (1704–09). During the war the Ottoman empire issued four separate declarations of war on Russia which had some connection with the Great Northern War, but neither the Turks nor the Tartars became formal allies of Charles XII between 1709 and 1714 in the way Mazepa, hetman of the Ukraine, and Hordiyenko, hetman of the Zaporozhian Cossacks, had done in 1709 and remained so after Poltava. That Russian victory brought Frederick IV of Denmark-Norway and Augustus of Saxony (militarily inactive since the late summer of 1700 and 1706 respectively) back into the war; and in 1714–15 Frederick William I, King of Prussia, and Georg Ludwig, Elector of Hanover (and as George I, King of Great Britain), joined Sweden's enemies. *Peace of Stockholm 1719:* Hanover obtained the duchies of Bremen and Verden; Great Britain obtained commercial advantages in return for a promise of naval help against Russia. *Peace of Stockholm 1720:* Prussia received Swedish Pomerania (including Stettin and the islands of Wollin and Usedom) up to the Peene river. *Peace of Frederiksborg 1720:* Denmark-Norway obtained cancellation of Sweden's freedom from Sound dues and Frederick IV received a promise that the Holstein-Gottorp alliance would become inoperative. *Peace of Nystad 1721:* Russia obtained Sweden's Baltic provinces of Ingria, Estonia and Livonia; had most of Karelia restored to her (see map 1).

1705–08 During this war the Astrakhan and Don Cossack risings took place in Russia; during the War of the Spanish Succession (for which see below) the Camisard revolt took place in France 1702–10

1702–13/1714 *War of the Spanish Succession.* Louis's allies were Philip V of Spain, Maximilian of Bavaria, the Prince-Bishop Elector of Trier and the Prince-Archbishop of Cologne. The Allies of the anti-French coalition were joined by Savoy and Portugal in 1703 and a widening of the war aims followed: to the specifically English demand for a recognition of the Protestant Succession by France and the removal of James Edward Stuart (recognized by Louis XIV in 1701 as James III) was added the claim of the whole of the Spanish possessions for the Archduke Charles, provided a safe 'barrier' was granted to the Dutch – for this purpose an Anglo-Dutch condominium of the Southern Netherlands was established in 1706 after victories in that theatre of war. *1705* The population of Upper Bavaria, occupied by Austrian troops after Allied victory of 1704, rebelled in vain: the Sendlinger *Mordweihnacht* (murder-Christmas).

1703–11 Hungarian and Transylvanian independence movement led by Prince Francis II Rákóczi became entwined in the War of the Spanish Succession since Louis XIV encouraged the Prince in order to weaken the Habsburgs. By the *Peace of Szatmar 1711* Rákóczi's

followers made a compromise settlement with Charles VI: the Hungarian constitution was to be respected, grievances were to be redressed and in return they accorded the house of Habsburg hereditary right of government. Rákóczi himself fled to Turkey. Negotiations between the belligerents in the War of the Spanish Succession were a feature from the early years of the war. They were most actively pursued in the years 1706–10, but Allied unity did not break till the change of government in Great Britain in 1710. This led to a separate Anglo-French agreement, to the withdrawal of British troops (and money) from the Allied war effort and eventually to the *Peace of Utrecht 1713* for western Europe: the Protestant Succession was confirmed; James Edward Stuart left France; the permanent separation of France and Spain was arranged; the fortifications of the harbour of Dunkirk (from which privateers had operated) were destroyed; France restored or ceded to Britain Newfoundland, the Hudson Bay territory, Acadia (Nova Scotia) and St Kitts. France in return was permitted to incorporate the principality of Orange and had Lille restored to her, while the partition of Spain which was now effected (Philip V to retain the Spanish empire overseas intact as well as the whole of Spain on the Iberian peninsula, though sacrificing Spain's European territories in the Southern Netherlands and Italy) was a considerable gain for Louis who avoided Habsburg encirclement on the eastern frontier (where the peace upheld the French interpretation of 1648 and the treaties of Nijmegen and Ryswick). Spain ceded to Britain Gibraltar and Minorca and permitted the *Asiento* to become hers for thirty years, and in return received a guarantee for Philip's territories as arranged under the partition outlined above and a promise of diplomatic support for acquisition of the Tuscan ports (see above, p. 216, for this promise neglected by historians of the peace till Dr M. Martin's thesis of 1962). The Republic received a 'barrier' much smaller than that stipulated by the Anglo-Dutch treaty in 1709; Frederick William I of Prussia had his royal title recognized and obtained Upper (Spanish) Guelders and Neuchâtel; Victor Amadeus II, on giving up all claims to the Spanish crown as long as the Bourbon line survived, received Sicily and a royal title thereto and, on evacuating territory occupied in the Duchy of Milan, obtained frontier rectifications in Upper Italy; the frontier with France was at the same time modified in accordance with the flow of the rivers of the region; Portugal secured frontier rectifications at Spain's expense in South America. Reserved for the Emperor: the Southern Netherlands on achieving agreement with the Dutch over the 'barrier', the Duchy of Milan, Naples and Sardinia; reserved for the Empire: reaffirmation of the Peace of Ryswick. The *Peace of Rastadt 1714* (March): After an unsuccessful campaign, 1713–14, Charles VI made peace with Louis on the terms outlined in the Peace of Utrecht, entered into immediate possession of the Italian former Spanish possessions and took over the Southern (now Austrian) Netherlands after the Barrier Treaty of 1715 agreed with the Maritime Powers. The terms for the Empire had been agreed at

Rastadt and were signed at the *Peace of Baden* (also in Switzerland) *1714* (Sept.): the Electors of Bavaria and Cologne were reinstated in their lands and dignities; the Peace of Ryswick was confirmed though Landau was left in French hands since the campaign had on the whole gone in Louis' favour.

1710–11 War between Turkey and Russia. After a disastrous campaign Tsar Peter by the *Peace of Prut 1711* (July) had to hand back Azov, to raze fortified places near Azov and to promise non-interference in Polish affairs that Charles XII might return safely to his Swedish dominions. It took a further war (declared Dec. 1711, ended by *Peace of Constantinople 1712* (April) to obtain the execution of the first two clauses; and the third was never fulfilled (in spite of a third and fourth declaration of war on 29 Oct. 1712 and 30 April 1713 respectively) nor were those clauses of the *Peace of Adrianople 1713* (June) which attempted to safeguard the integrity and independence of Poland, of the Cossacks south of the Dnieper and of the Zaporozhian Cossack state.

1714–18 War between Turkey and the Republic of Venice in which the Emperor Charles VI intervened in 1716. *Peace of Passarowitz 1718:* The Republic Venice lost its fortified places in Crete and had to return the Moreà; Charles VI gained the Banat of Temesvar, northern Serbia and Little Wallachia. The Austrian acquisition of Belgrade was particularly important.

1715 *Barrier Treaty* between Austria and the Dutch Republics regulated the Dutch Barrier (see map 3) and fixed the Austrian Netherlands income to be reserved for payment of the Dutch garrisons. Further Barrier convention, for security of payment, Dec. *1718.*

1715–16 Civil war in Polish-Lithuanian Commonwealth, basically directed against the centralizing attempts of Augustus II. Tsar Peter intervened and dictated a *Peace of Danzig 1716* which circumscribed Augustus' power, as well as limiting the armed forces of the Commonwealth to make sure of the preponderance of Russian influence.

1715–16 Stuart rebellion in Great Britain in favour of 'James III' crushed.

1717–20 *Aftermath of the War of the Spanish Succession.* No peace had been made in 1713/14 between Charles VI (who still claimed to be Carlos III of Spain) and Philip V (who still resented the loss of the Italian territories of Spain to the Habsburgs). The Spanish navy was increased and Sardinia (1717) and Sicily (1718) were invaded. Great Britain, France and the Emperor retaliated to keep the 1713/14 settlement: the British fleet landed an Austrian army on Sicily, a French army invaded the Basque provinces and Catalonia in a *petite guerre démonstrative. Peace of Madrid/The Hague 1720:* Philip sacrificed Sardinia, Sicily, Naples and the Duchy of Milan in return for Charles V's relinquishing his claims to Spain and his title of King of Spain and for a promise of the succession to Parma, Piacenza and Tuscany for Charles, the elder son of his marriage with Elizabeth Farnese. The Emperor was gratified by the exchange (with Victor Amadeus) of Sardinia for Sicily. Dubois, the French negotiator, achieved a 'Family Compact' with Spain (a double dynastic marriage union being part of it) without sacrificing the English alliance.

EUROPE AND OVERSEAS:
Chronology of Discovery, Expansion, Retraction and Changes in Territorial Ownership

1645–54 *Brazil.* The Portuguese ended Dutch occupation (established in the 1620s and 1630s); by treaty of 1661 Portugal's sovereignty was acknowledged.

1648 The Russian explorer Deschnev discovers easternmost point in Asia (on the Bering Straits).

1650 Ali, Bey of Tunis, declares himself independent of the Sultan.

1650–51 Russian fort at Albazin in the Amur founded by the Russian explorer Khabarov who reached Manchuria and went on to occupy Siberia.

1652 *Cape Town* founded by the Dutch (Jan van Riebeck) as fort and hospital.

1655 *New Sweden* conquered by the Dutch West India Company (Peter Stuyvesant) and incorporated with New Netherlands.

1656 Russian embassy to China, Chinese embassy to Moscow in 1670.
Jamaica captured from Spain by expedition dispatched by Cromwell. Dutch occupied *Ceylon* (hitherto Portuguese-held).

1657, 1658 Dutch occupied Portugese ports of Tuticorin and Negapatam on Indian coast.

1650s to 1690s *West Indies.* Buccaneering and privateering activities, endemic in the area, form the background to new acquisitions and changes in sovereignty; Surinam was ceded by England to the Dutch in 1667 (*Peace of Breda*) and western Española (renamed *Haiti*) by Spain to France in 1697 (*Peace of Ryswick*); France acquired Martinique, St Croix, St Lucia and Tortuga; Denmark acquired St Thomas.

1660 Dutch Boers settle Cape Colony in South Africa.

1661 The Jesuits Dorville and Grüber reach Tibet's capital.

1662 *Tangier* and *Bombay* ceded by Portugal to England by virtue of Catherine's dowry.

1664 England conquers New Amsterdam in North America from the Dutch and (with Danish help) the Dutch (formerly Swedish) Carolusborg on the African Guinea coast.

1665 French bombardment of pirates of Algiers and Tunis.

1666 Dutch in Celebes.

1666–67 Anglo-French war: conflict as a result of Louis XIV's entry into the Anglo-Dutch war of 1665. *Treaties of Breda*: France ceded to England Antigua, Montserrat, St Kitts and received in return Acadia; Anglo-Dutch settlement at Breda (after war 1665–67): Cape Coast Castle in Africa and New Netherlands in North America to England, Surinam and the East Indies Pulo-Run to the Republic, and England accepted in principle that (a) flag covered the ship, and (b) that contraband was confined to the implements of war.

1668 French in the Surat (India).

1670 English get permission to trade in China.

1669–77 La Salle's explorations of Missouri region.

1672 French driven out of Madagascar.

1674 French crown colony in Pondichéry (India).

1675–76 *'King Philip's War'* between settlers and Indians in New England.

1676 Bacon's rebellion in Virginia to force frontier defence against Indians on the English government.

1677 Dutch annex Java. *Senegal* forts of the Dutch conquered by France.

1679–99 *Mississippi Valley and rivermouth*. Exploration by La Salle, Foliette, Marquette, Hennequin and d'Iberville and establishment of the French colony of *Louisiana* named after Louis XIV.

1680s to 1713 Anglo-French rivalry in North America, north of the Great Lakes, for Acadia, Hudson's Bay, Newfoundland.

1680–83 *South and Central America*. Conflict between Portugal and Spain over the left bank of the Rio de la Plata leading to clashes over demarcation lines in general: these persisted throughout the colonial period.

1680–1696 *New Mexico*. Revolt of the natives drove the Spaniards out in 1680; the area was reconquered by 1696.

1681 French bombardment of Tripoli.

1682 onwards *Penn's treaties* with the Indians which kept Pennsylvania (founded 1681) free from Indian wars.

1683–1720 *Guinea coast*. Brandenburg-Prussia's colonizing activities in Africa. Fort of Grossfriedrichsburg built 1683, sold in 1717 to the Dutch.

1683 onwards German immigration, through Pennsylvania, south and westward into North America, reaching a peak after 1710.

1683–87 *Algiers*: French expeditions against the piratical beys: Christian slaves recaptured and coastal towns bombarded in an effort to limit privateering preying on French commerce; 1687 promise not to molest French ships obtained.

1685 *China* opens ports to all traders, but in practice the Portuguese managed to keep competitors down by judicious use of local bribes.

1685 *Siam* French try (unsuccessfully) to introduce Christian religion; some influence achieved and a Siam embassy sent to Louis XIV.

1685–89 Russian conflict with China. By the *Treaty of Nerchinsk* (1689) Russia withdrew from territory occupied in the Amur region and abandoned Fort Albazin.

1686 *Madagascar* annexed by Louis XIV.

1689–97 *'King William's War'*: the Anglo-French counterpart overseas to the Nine Years War in Europe; mutual conquests were restored at *Peace of Ryswick*.

1697 The Cossack Atlassov discovers and occupies the peninsula of Kamchatka.

1697–1715 *Senegal* conquests completed by France.

1698 *East coast of Africa*. Portuguese expelled from their posts by Arabs from Oman, though Mozambique was retained.

1699 Louis XIV's emissary Poncet travelled overland from Cairo to Ethiopia.

1702 Detroit founded by Cadillac as a centre for Illinois trade of the French.

1702–13 *'Queen Anne's War'*, the Anglo-French counterpart to the War of the Spanish Succession in Europe. Acadia conquered by the English 1710, but the Montreal campaign of 1711 failed. At *Peace of Utrecht*, Acadia (renamed Nova Scotia), Newfoundland, Hudson's Bay territory were ceded by France to Great Britain.

1705 Hussein ibn Ali declares Tunis independent of the Ottoman Sultan.

1705 Papal attempt to stop ancestor worship in China leads to expulsion of many missionaries.

1708 *Oran*. The Spaniards expelled.

1708–09 *'War of the Emboabas'* in which the Portuguese increased their hold on central Brazil.

1710–11 *'War of the Mascates'* in which the Portuguese of Recife prevailed over the native Brazilians of Polinda (in Pernambuco).

1711–12 *'Tuscarora War'* in North Carolina, ending in defeat and resettlement of the Indians.

1714 Spotswood's expedition to the Shenandoah Valley.

1714–18 *Bengal* Denmark successfully maintains Fort Danmarksnagore.

1715 Castiglione (Italian Jesuit) settles in China; through him European influence, especially noticeable in paintings and decorations.

1718 New Orleans founded by French settlers.

1718–20 *Texas* The War of the Quadruple Alliance in Europe led to hostilities between Spanish and French troops in Florida and Texas (where local rivalry had led to clashes even when France and Spain were allies during the War of the Spanish Succession). Spanish possession of Texas was confirmed, and the area was settled and administered on a more permanent footing between 1720 and 1722.

1719 Tsar Peter's embassy to Peking.

1720 *Greenland* The Norwegian missionary Hans Egede establishes Godthåb colony on west coast in name of Frederick IV of Denmark-Norway.

TRADING COMPANIES, TREATIES
and other arrangements bearing on trade in Europe and overseas

(Pre-1648 trading companies: English East India 1600; Dutch East India (the *Vereenigde Oost-Indische Compagnie*) 1602; Dutch West India 1621).

1649 Portuguese Brazilian Trading Company (till 1663 when transformed into a royal council).
Dutch ships (by the treaty with Denmark known as *Redemtionstraktaten*) obtained freedom from Sound dues against a fixed yearly tribute.

1651 English Navigation Act to reserve trade with Asia, Africa and America for English ships (or those of her colonies) modified by the Navigation Act of *1660* and related Acts of 1662, 1663, 1664, and 1673 (the Navigation Laws).

1650s and 1660s Swedish measures to stimulate exports of worked metal goods.

1654 English treaty with Portugal which gave commercial entry to Portugal and the Portuguese colonies.

1656 Dutch mission (Pieter van Goyer and Jacob van Kayser) to China secured tributary status for merchants which was improved by the Pieter van Hoorn mission of *1667*

1656–63 Dutch hold on spice trade in Moluccas, Ceylon and the Malabar coast complete; trade agreements with Asian rulers established and the Dutch position in Japan maintained on the island of Deshima off Nagasaki.

1660 China gives France permission to trade.

1661 Dutch treaty with Portugal which gained the Republic commercial access to Portugal and the Portuguese colonies.

1663 French commercial treaties with Denmark-Norway and Sweden to promote trade in the Baltic.

Catherine of Braganza's dowry brings Charles II of England Tangier and Bombay (the latter sold more or less immediately to the East India Company).

1664 Dutch commercial treaty with Siam, though the monopoly position expected did not materialize owing to French opposition.

1664 French East India Company (*Compagnie des Indes Orientales*).

1665 French North Africa Company.

1667 French commercial tariff directed at Dutch and English trade (very aggressive compared to the mildly protective tariff of 1664).

1669 French Company of the North (*Compagnie du Nord*), privileges revoked 1689.

1670 French Levant Company (*Compagnie du Levant*).

1670 English Hudson's Bay Company.

1670 Portuguese embassy (Manuel de Saldanha) to China gained confirmation of the Macao privileges; they were again reaffirmed 1678–9 (mission of Bento Pereyra de Faria).

1670–71 French preferential duties on sugar increased (aimed at Dutch refineries).

1671–72 Dutch retaliatory tariff on French wines and brandies.

1672 (English) Royal African Company.

1673 French Senegal Company.

1678–85 English retaliatory measures against French imports.

1682 French Hudson's Bay Company (*Compagnie de la Baie d'Hudson*).

1682 Brandenburg Africa Company founded (after a 1679 expedition to Gold Coast financed by a Dutch company), but it did not prosper and was sold in 1717 to the Dutch West India Company.

1684 England cedes Tangier to Bey of Morocco.

1685 Huguenots plant vines in Cape Colony.

1689–1717 English embargoes or prohibitive duties on French imports.

1680s onwards Spanish attempts to protect native industries (silk and woollen).

1689 After the *Treaty of Nerchinsk* with China, the Russians aimed at peaceful commercial expansion, and by *1720–21* succeeded in establishing a trading agency and an Eastern Orthodox church in Peking (L.V. Ismailow mission).

1689 English trade in Canton – first factory 1715.

1690 Fort William trading post at Calcutta established by English merchant Job Charnock.

1691 Dano-Swedish treaty of armed neutrality to defend trade, renewed 1693.

1695 Scots company attempted unsuccessfully to establish a colony in the Isthmus of Darien.

1698 New East India Company which competed with the 'Old'.

1703 Methuen treaty between England and Portugal.

1709 Amalgamation of New and Old East India Company into one 'United Company of Merchants of England trading to the East Indies', a combination which scored successes in Canton and in *1714* secured a privileged trading position (by an embassy to the Mughal court) in India.

1710 South Sea Company formed in Britain.

1715 Japan drastically reduced the amount of copper available for export due to their own need of the metal; Dutch trade hit.

1718 John Law's Mississippi Company formed in France.

1720 Japan permits study of European books with the exception of those on religion; many Japanese learn Dutch and adopt European ideas in technology and commerce.

SELECT BIBLIOGRAPHY

I have listed below, after initial sections on Works of Synthesis, National Histories, and The Expansion of Europe, some books and articles (arranged alphabetically for each of my seven chapters according to author) which I have enjoyed or found useful, concentrating, other things being equal, on recent works to bring these to the reader's notice. I have included books and articles in the less well-known European languages only where they seemed essential and have made a point of mentioning synopses in English even where I have used the original. All sections are far too short, but luckily there is no shortage of bibliographical aids to reading in the period (for official documents and private memoirs and letters of all kinds as well as for secondary material) and I have listed some of the less familiar of these aids as well as other helps to study, e.g. atlases. I have attempted to pick some books and articles for their historiographical importance or for their useful bibliographies and in a penultimate section I have drawn attention to reprints of articles, collections of essays and excerpts of documents in English, French and German. I have concluded my list with a selection of biographical studies since, in recent years, this branch of history has born respectable fruit.

(a) WORKS OF SYNTHESIS

ENGLISH AND AMERICAN
The New Cambridge Modern History, vol. v: *The Ascendancy of France, 1648–1688* (1961), ed. F.L. Carsten; vol. vii: *The Old Regime, 1713–1763* (1957), ed. J. Lindsay.

'The Rise of Modern Europe' series, ed. W. Langer: C.J. Friedrich, *The Age of the Baroque, 1610–1660* (1952); F.L. Nussbaum, *The Triumph of Science and Reason, 1660–1685* (1953); J.B. Wolf, *The Emergence of the Great Powers, 1685–1715* (1951) – all available in paperback.

FRENCH
'Clio series', vol. vii: E. Préclin, V.-L. Tapié, *Le XVIIe Siècle* (Paris 1952). A 'Nouvelle Clio' series is now in progress, but no volume covering Europe in the age of Louis XIV has as yet been announced. Note, however, the appearance in 1969 of P. Jeannin, *L'Europe du Nord-Ouest et du Nord aux XVIIe et XVIIIe Siècles*.

'Peuples et Civilisations' series, vol. x: P. Sagnac and A. de Saint-Léger, *La prépondérance française: Louis XIV, 1661–1715* (3rd ed. Paris 1949).

'Histoire des relations internationales' series, vol. iii, part 2: G. Zeller, *Les temps modernes: De Louis XIV à 1789* (Paris 1955).

'Histoire Genérale des Civilisations' series, vol. iv: R. Mousnier, *Les XVIe et XVIIe Siècles: Les progrés de la civilisation européenne et le déclin de l'Orient, 1492–1715* (Paris 1961).

GERMAN

'Propyläen Weltgeschichte', vol. VII: *Von der Reformation zur Revolution* (Berlin, Frankfurt, Vienna 1964), edd. Golo Mann and A. Nitschke – a most successful volume with excellent treatment both of politics and culture.

W. Hubatsch, *Das Zeitalter des Absolutismus, 1600–1789* (Brunswick 1962) is briefer but three-quarters of the book is devoted to the period before 1721 and it has a fine bibliography.

LESS TEXTBOOK-LIKE TREATMENT

P. Hazard, *La Crise de la conscience européenne, 1680–1715* (Paris 1935), translated under the title *The European Mind: The Critical Years, 1680–1715* (London and New Haven 1952 and 1953).

P. Chaunu, *La civilisation de l'Europe classique* (Grenoble-Paris 1966), stimulating treatment of the period 1630 to 1760, though the first part (on political development) is less successful than parts II and III (on economic and intellectual trends).

G.N. Clark, *War and Society in the Seventeenth Century* (Cambridge 1958).

J.U. Nef, *War and Human Progress* (New York 1950, London 1951).

L. Dehio, *Gleichgewicht oder Hegemonie* (Krefeld 1948, with English translation, *The Precarious Balance*, 1963). The English works of synthesis by D. Ogg and G.N. Clark, with the titles respectively of *Europe in the Seventeenth Century* (6th revised ed. 1952) and *The Seventeenth Century* (2nd revised ed. 1947), are still eminently worth reading.

b) NATIONAL HISTORIES (in alphabetical order)

BALTIC STATES

M. Hellman, *Grundzüge der Geschichte Litauens und des litauischen Volkes* (Darmstadt 1966).

R. Wittram, *Baltische Geschichte* (Munich 1954).

DENMARK-NORWAY (The Twin Kingdoms)

L. Krabbe, *Histoire du Danemark* (Copenhagen, Paris 1950).

P. Lauring, *A History of Denmark in Pictures* (Copenhagen 1963).

'Schultz Danmarkshistorie', collective work ed. by Aage Friis, vol. III (Copenhagen 1942).

DUTCH REPUBLIC (United Provinces)

The collective work 'Algemene Geschiedenis der Nederlanden', edd. J.A. Van Houtte and J. Presser, covers both Northern and Southern (Spanish, Austrian after 1713) Netherlands. The relevant vol. VII: *Op Gescheiden Wegen, 1648–1748* (Utrecht, Antwerp 1954), is not detailed enough and should be supplemented with the following:

C. Boxer, *The Dutch Seaborne Empire 1600–1800* (London and New York 1965).

S.J. Fockema Andreae, *De Nederlandse Staat onder de Republiek* (The Hague 1961).

P. Geyl, *The Netherlands in the Seventeenth Century*, Part 2: *1648–1715* (London 1964).

T.P. van der Kooy, *Hollands stapelmarkt en haar verval* (Amsterdam 1931).

G.J. Renier, *The Dutch Nation* (London 1944).

Charles Wilson's books on Anglo-Dutch relations (*Anglo-Dutch Commerce and Finance in the Eighteenth Century* of 1941, and *Profit and Power. A Study of England and the Dutch Wars* of 1957) are indispensable.

ENGLAND (Great Britain after the Union with Scotland in 1707)

D. Ogg, *England in the Reigns of James II and William III* (Oxford 1955).

M.A. Thomson, *A constitutional history of England, 1642–1801* (London 1938).

G.M. Trevelyan, *England under Queen Anne* (3 vols. London 1930–34).

C. Wilson, *England's Apprenticeship 1603–1763* (London 1965) – a fine piece of synthesis of the author's own research and the researches of other specialists in social and economic history.

For Ireland see J.C. Beckett, *The Making of Modern Ireland 1603–1923* (London and New York 1966); for England's relationship to Europe see R.J. Jones, *Britain and Europe in the Seventeenth Century* (London 1967) and D.B. Horn, *Great Britain and Europe in the Eighteenth Century* (Oxford 1967).

FRANCE

The collective work *La France au temps de Louis XIV* (Paris 1966) can be recommended; beautifully and lavishly illustrated, chapters by historians of the first class – Georges Mongrédien, Jean Meuvret, Roland Mousnier, R.-A. Weigert, Robert Mandrou, Antoine Adam and V.-L. Tapié. Equally important, though written for the specialist, are those volumes in the periodical *XVIIe Siècle* devoted to important themes (e.g. to religion in 1955, to the theatre in 1958, to the administration in 1959, to Louis XIV's foreign policy in 1960, to philosophy in 1962, to law in 1963, to poetry in 1965). The 1966 double number (70–71) concerned with *Aspects de l'économie française* has articles summarizing new research by J. Meuvret, J. Jacquand, P. Deyon, J.-Y. Tira, J. Delumeau and R. Pillorget. The consistent high quality of this periodical is such that any university teacher (to say nothing of a university library) neglects it at his peril or at least at the peril of his pupils. Of individual works should be noted:

L. André, *Louis XIV et l'Europe* (Paris 1950).

E. Esmonin, *Études sur la France des XVIIe et XVIIIe Siècles* (Paris 1964).

P. Goubert, *Louis XIV et vingt millions de Français* (Paris 1966) – brief and stimulating.

R. Mandrou, *La France aux XVIIe et XVIIIe Siècles* (in 'Nouvelle Clio' series, Paris 1967) – distinguished synthesis of demographic and economic research; good bibliography.

C.G. Picavet, *La Diplomatie française au temps de Louis XIV, 1661–1715* (Paris 1930) – important for method and organization.

235

P. Sagnac, *La societé et la monarchie absolue, 1661–1715* (vol. I of 'La formation de la société française moderne', Paris 1945).

I. Streitberger, *Der Königliche Prätor von Strassburg 1685–1789: freie Stadt im absoluten Staat* (Wiesbaden 1961) – important as a case study for the relationship between France and the territories Louis XIV acquired.

G. Zeller, *L'Organisation défensive des frontières du Nord et de l'Est au XVIIᵉ Siècle* (Nancy 1928) and the same author's essays collected under the title *Aspects de\la politique française sous l'Ancien Régime* (Paris 1964).

HABSBURG DOMINIONS (Austria in common parlance; including Hungary, in hereditary dynastic union after 1687).

H. Hantsch, *Geschichte Österreichs*, vol. I (4th revised ed. Vienna 1959).

O. Redlich, *Weltmacht des Barocks. Österreich in der Zeit Kaiser Leopold I, 1658–1705* (4th ed. Vienna 1961 of the 1921 work) – though never significantly revised, still useful.

G. Stadtmüller, *Geschichte der habsburgischen Macht* (Stuttgart 1966) – brief, full of facts.

J.H. Stoye, *The Siege of Vienna, 1683* (London 1964) and the same author's 'Emperor Charles VI: The early years of the reign', *Transactions of the Royal Historical Society*, 1962.

H. Sturmberger, 'Vom Weissen Berg zur Pragmatischen Sanktion', *Österreich in Geschichte und Literatur* (Vienna 1961) – important for constitutional developments.

A. Wandruszka, *Das Haus Habsburg* (Stuttgart 1956), translated as *The House of Habsburg* (London 1964).

E. Zöllner, *Geschichte Österreichs* (Munich 1961).

For Hungary see J. Bérenger, 'La Hongrie des Habsbourgs au xviiᵉ siècle. Republique nobiliaire ou monarchie limitée?', *Revue Historique*, 1967. The standard Hungarian history is the one ed. by S. Domanovszky, *Magyar müvelödestörtenet*, with good illustrations and excerpts from contemporary European sources on Hungary, e.g. travel descriptions; it will in its main text be inaccessible to most of us (I have no Magyar myself); the best brief history in English is by C.A. Macartney, *A Short History of Hungary* (Edinburgh 1961).

HOLY ROMAN EMPIRE OF THE GERMAN NATION (as a unit, or treating of several states):

I. Bog, *Der Reichsmerkantilismus* (Stuttgart 1959).

F.L. Carsten, *Princes and Parliaments in Germany* (Oxford 1959) and the same author's 'Die Ursachen des Niederganges der deutsche Landstände', *Historische Zeitschrift*, 1961.

B. Gebhardt, *Handbuch der deutschen Geschichte*, vol. 2 (Stuttgart, new ed. of 1955).

H. Holborn, *A History of Modern Germany*, vol. II: *1648–1840* (London 1964). Particularly useful because it includes those Habsburg territories which were part of the Empire – most 'German' histories tend to leave Austria out.

Roger Wimes, 'The Imperial Circles. Princely Diplomacy and Imperial Reform 1681–1714', *Journal of Modern History*, 1967 (essential).

(Some individual states):

BAVARIA. M. Strich, *Das Kurhaus Bayern im Zeitalter Ludwigs XIV und die europäischen Mächte* (2 vols. Munich 1933).

BRANDENBURG-PRUSSIA. A. Berney, *König Friedrich I und das Haus Habsburg 1701–1707* (Munich 1927)

S.B. Fay, *The Rise of Brandenburg-Prussia to 1786* (ed. revised by Klaus Epstein, New York 1964).

E. Hassinger, *Brandenburg-Preussen, Schweden und Russland 1700–1713* (Munich 1953).

C. Hinrichs, *Preussen als historisches Problem* (Berlin 1964).

HANOVER. W. Mediger, *Mecklenburg, Russland und England-Hannover 1706–1721* (2 vols. Hildesheim 1967).

G. Schnath, *Geschichte Hannovers*, vol. I: *1674–1692* (Hildesheim 1938).

HOLSTEIN. O. Brandt, *Geschichte Schleswig-Holsteins. Ein Grundriss* (Kiel 1949).

LORRAINE. H. Mahuet, *La cour souveraine de Lorraine et Barrois 1641–1790* (Nancy 1960).

WÜRTTEMBERG. A. Fauchier-Magnan, *The Small German Courts in the Eighteenth Century* (London 1958, translated from the French edition of 1947) deals, after a brief introductory chapter, mainly with Württemberg.

ITALIAN STATES. General coverage is given in *Storia d'Italia*, ed. N. Valeri, the relevant volume being II (Turin 2nd ed. 1965) and in B. Croce, *Storia della eta barocca in Italia* (2nd ed. Bari 1946); see also R. Quazza, *La preponderanza spagneola* (Milan 1950) and G. Quazza's *Il problema italiano e l'equilibrio europeo 1720–1738* (Turin 1965).

For Naples see F. Nicolini, *L'Europa durante la guerra di successione de Spagna* (2 vols. 1938) which, in spite of its title, deals mainly with Naples, and H. Benedikt, *Das Königreich Neapel unter Kaiser Karl VI* (Graz-Köln 1959).

For Savoy see A. Baraudon, *La Maison de Savoie et la Triple Alliance, 1713–1722* (Paris 1896) and A. Tallone, 'Vittorio Amedeo II e la quadruplice alleanza', *Studi su Vittorio Amedeo II* (Turin) 1933.

For the Papacy see P. Sonnino, *Louis XIV's View of the Papacy 1661–67* (Berkeley and Los Angeles 1966) and P. Pierling, *La Russie et le Saint-Siège* (Paris 1896).

POLISH-LITHUANIAN COMMONWEALTH (the *Rzeczpospolita Polska*, The Republic of Poland, or Poland in contemporary parlance).

The standard work is the collective one *Historia Polska*, the relevant vol. I *Do roku 1764* (Warsaw 1955). For those, like myself, who have little Polish, the excellent maps can be utilized. Some of the work of J. Feldman and W. Konopzyński has been made accessible by summaries or translations into Swedish (in view of the importance of the relationship between Sweden and Poland in this period) – see *Karolinska Förbundets Årsbok*

for 1924 and 1936 – or has been published in French (see bibliography for chapter III).
Research by some of the present generation of Polish historians is available in English, French, and German; see e.g. J. Gierowski, 'From Radoskowice to Opatów – the history of the decomposition of the Stanislaw Leszczyński Camp', *Poland at the XIth International Congress of Historical Sciences* (Warsaw 1960); A. Maczak and A. Samsonowitz, 'La zone baltique: l'un des elements du marché européen', *Acta Poloniae Historica* (Warsaw) 1966, pp. 71–99; and the collective work *Um die polnische Krone. Sachsen und Polen während des Nordischen Krieges 1700–1721*, edd. J. Kalisch and J. Gierowski (Berlin 1962).
The following contributions on Poland's relations to Russia might also be noted: G. Kiss, 'Franz Rakoczi, Peter der Grosse und der Polnische Thron um 1707', *Jahrbücher für Geschichte Osteuropas*, 1965, and L.R. Lewitter, 'The Russo-Polish Treaty of 1686 and its antecedents', *The Polish Review*, 1964.

PORTUGAL

A.D. Francis, *The Methuens and Portugal 1691–1708* (Cambridge 1966) is most informative about Portugal in our period.

H.V. Livermore, *A New History of Portugal* (Cambridge 1966).

E. Prestage, *Chapters in Anglo-Portuguese relations* (Watford 1935).

RUSSIA (Muscovy in common parlance before the 1690s)

The standard present-day Russian history is the collective work ed. by M.V. Nechkina *et al.*, *Istoriya SSSR*. I: *s drevneyshikh vremen do 1861 g.* (Moscow 1964).

E. Amburger, 'Das neuzeitliche Narva als Wirtschaftsfactor zwischen Russland und Estland', *Jahrbücher für Geschichte Osteuropas*, 1967.

C. Bickford O'Brien, *Russia under Two Tsars 1682–1689* (Berkeley and Los Angeles 1952).

S. Feygina, *Alandskiy Kongress* (Moscow 1959).

D. Gerhard, *England und der Aufstieg Russlands* (Munich and Berlin 1933).

W. Mediger, *Moskaus Weg nach Europa* (Brunswick 1952).

A.L. Nikiforov, *Russko-angliyskie otnosheniya pri Petre I* (Moscow 1950 with a German translation of 1954).

Zinaïda Schakovsky (pseud. for Jacques Croisé), *Precursors of Peter the Great* (London 1964) translated from the French.

I.I. Smirnov *et al.*, *Krest'janskie voyny v Rossii XVII–XVIII vv* (Moscow 1966) deals with the 'peasant war' rebellions of Bolotnikov, Razin, Bulavin and Pugachev – non-Russian readers can gather something about the book from a review article in *Istoria SSSR* 1967 translated in *Soviet Studies in History*, 1967–68, no. 3.

I. Smolitz, *Geschichte der russischen Kirche 1700–1917* (Leiden 1964).

G. Stöke, *Russische Geschichte* (Stuttgart 1962).

E. Tarle, *Severnaya voyna is shvedskoye nashestvye na Rossiyi* (Moscow 1958).

Many general histories of Russia are available: H.T. Florinsky, N.A. Riasanovsky, J.D. Clarkson, B.H. Sumner in English; P. Milyoukov (ed., vol. I Paris 1932) in French; K. Stählin in German; S.F. Platonov and V.O. Klyuchevsky translated into English.

SPAIN (with Spanish Netherlands)

Prince Adalbert von Bayern, *Das Ende der Habsburger in Spanien* (2 vols. Munich 1929).

J.H. Elliott, *Imperial Spain 1469–1716* (London 1963) and the same author's article 'The decline of Spain', *Past and Present*, 1961.

H. Kamen, 'The decline of Castile: the last Crisis', *The Economic History Review*, 1964.

Gabriel de Maura, *Vida y Reinado de Carlos II* (3 vols. Madrid 1942).

A. Dominguez Ortiz, *La Sociedad Española en el siglo XVII* (Madrid 1963).

J.H. Parry, *The Spanish Seaborne Empire* (London and New York 1966).

J. Deleitoy Pinuela, *El declinas de la monarquia Española* (3rd ed. Madrid 1955).

J.P.M. Riba, 'Un Organismo-Piloto en la Monarquia de Felipe V: la Superintendencia de Cataluña', *Hispania. Revista Española de Historia* (Madrid 1966 and 1967).

P. Voltes Bou, *Barcelona durante el gobierno del Archiduque Carlos de Austria, 1705–1714* (Barcelona 1963).

SPANISH NETHERLANDS

S. Despretz-Van de Castelle, 'Het protectionisme in de Zuidelijke Nederlanden gedurende de tweede heelft der 17e eeuw', *Tijdschrift voor Geschiedenis* (The Hague and Antwerp), 1965.

L.P. Gachard, *Histoire de la Belgique au commencement du XVIIIe siècle* (The Hague and Brussels 1880).

E. Hubert, *Les Pays-Bas espagnols et la République des Provinces-Unies . . . 1648–1713* (Brussels 1907).

F. van Kalken, *La fin du régime espagnol aux Pays-Bas* (Brussels 1907).

C. Smit, *De Scheldekwestie* (Rotterdam 1966) – important in that it demonstrates a growth of trade, in spite of the closing of the Scheldt, by the Southern Netherlanders' skilful use of canals.

SWEDEN (with Finland)

I. Anderson, *History of Sweden* (London 1956, abbreviated version of the Swedish edition of 1944).

E.F. Heckscher, *An Economic History of Sweden* (Cambridge, Mass. 1954) – an expanded translation of *Svenskt arbete och liv* of 1941; the author's two-volume *Sveriges Ekonomiska Historia* remains indispensable for specialists.

S.P. Oakley, *The Story of Sweden* (London 1966).

M. Roberts, *Essays in Swedish History* (London 1967) – particularly important for the essay on Charles XI.

J. Rosén, *Sveriges Historia*, I (Stockholm 1961) – the standard university textbook with excellent bibliography).

The collective work dealing with foreign policy, *Svenska Utrikespolitikens Historia*, is indispensable: relevant volumes by G. Landberg and J. Rosén.

237

TURKEY (Ottoman empire, the Porte in diplomatic parlance) though not part of the system of European states had many European subjects and its relations with Europe were significant. The most satisfactory history is still that by J. Hammer Purgstall, *Geschichte des Osmanischen Reiches* (Pest 1827–35) vols. V–VII. Worth consulting are B.H. Sumner, *Peter the Great and the Ottoman Empire* (Oxford 1949); D. Vaughan, *Europe and the Turk 1350–1700* (Liverpool 1954, new ed. in preparation); J. Odenthal, *Österreichische Türkenkrieg 1710–1718* (Cologne 1938) and the pioneer work of Georg Wagner, *Das Türkenjahr 1664* (2 vols. Eisenstadt 1964). Of general interest for the troubled frontiers of eastern Europe are B. Kentrschynskyj, 'Rebelldiplomati och vasallaktivism i ÖstEuropa vid 1600 talets mitt', *Karolinska Förbundets Årsbok* (Stockholm) 1965, and G.E. Rottenberg, *The Austrian Military Border in Croatia 1522–1747* (Urbana 1960).

(c) THE EXPANSION OF EUROPE

J. Brønsted, ed. *Vore gamle Tropekolonier* (Copenhagen 1952) – finely produced and illustrated collective work on the Danish colonial empire.

K.G. Davies, *The Royal African Company* (London 1957).

M.M. Dunn, *William Penn. Politics and Conscience* (Princeton 1967).

W.J. Eccles, *Canada under Louis XIV, 1663–1701* (Oxford 1964).

M. Giraud, *Histoire de la Louisiane française*, vols. I–III (Paris 1952–65).

K. Glamann, *Dutch-Asiatic Trade 1620–1740* (The Hague 1958).

G.S. Graham, *Empire of the North Atlantic: The Maritime Struggle for North America* (Toronto 1950)

G.H. Guttridge, *The Colonial policy of William III in America and the West Indies* (Cambridge 1922, Cass reprint 1967).

F. Mauro, 'Towards an "Intercontinental Model". European overseas expansion between 1500 and 1800', *The Economic History Review*, 1961.

J.C. Roberts, *The Story of Tobacco in America* (3rd ed. Chapel Hill 1967).

G. Williams, *The Expansion of Europe in the Eighteenth Century* (London 1966).

CHAPTER I

Ariès, P. *Centuries of Childhood; A Social History of Family Life* (London and New York 1962, translation of French ed. of 1960).

Dupaques, J. 'Sur la population française du XVIIe et au XVIIIe Siècle', *Revue Historique*, 1968.

Glass, D.V. and Eversley, D.E.C., edd. *Population in History: Essays in Historical Demography* (London 1964) – I am particularly indebted to Dr Hajnal's contribution and to a seminar-paper he gave to my seminar at the Institute of Historical Research.

Ilsoe, H. *Udlændingers reijser i Danmark indtil aar 1700* (Copenhagen 1963).

John, A.J. 'The course of agricultural change 1660–1700', *Studies in the Industrial Revolution, Essays presented to T.S. Ashton*, ed. L.S. Pressnell (London 1960).

Krüger, H.-J. *Die Judenschaft von Königsberg in Preussen 1700–1812* (Marburg 1966) – good case study of immigration after the 1671 edict permitting settlement.

LeRoy, Ladurie E. *Les Paysans de Languedoc* (2 vols. Paris 1965)

Lettwin, W. *The origins of scientific economics: English economic thought 1660–1776* (London 1963).

Laslett, P. *The World we have Lost* (London 1965).

Moller, H. ed. *Population Movements in Modern European History* (New York 1964), particularly the editor's contribution 'Population and Society during the Old Regime'.

Nadal, J. and Giralt, E. *La population catalane de 1553 à 1717* (Paris 1960, translated from Spanish study of 1953).

Roupnel, D. *La ville et la campagne au XVIIe siècle* (Paris 1922).

Slicher van Bath, B.H. 'Report on the study of historical demography in the Netherlands', *A.A.G. Bijdragen* (Wageningen 1964).

Schove, D.J. 'The Reduction of Annual Winds in North Western Europe A.D. 1635 to 1900', *Geografiska Annaler* (Stockholm) 1962.

Stoye, J.W. *English Travellers Abroad 1604–1667. Their Influence in English Society and Politics* (Oxford 1952).

Utterström, G. 'Climatic fluctuations and population problems in early modern history', *The Scandinavian Economic History Review*, 1955, and the same author's 'Population and agriculture in Sweden circa 1700–1830', *ibid.*, 1961.

Most of the information about travellers and students abroad has come from memoirs, letters (published and unpublished) and biographies too numerous to mention.

CHAPTER II

Arnheim, A. 'German Court Jews and Denmark during the Great Northern War', *The Scandinavian Economic History Review*, 1966.

Bamford, P.W. 'Entrepreneurship in Seventeenth Century France', *Exploration in Entrepreneurial History*, 1957

Blum, J. *Lord and Peasant in Russia from the Ninth to the Nineteenth Century* (Princeton 1961), supplemented by the important review article by A. Tikhinov and Z.K. Janel translated from *Voprosy Istorii* 1966 in *Soviet Studies in History*, vol. VI, no. 2 (New York 1967) pp. 40–43: this, based on Sakharov's research into Russian village life, stresses the similarity of development with the West in such matters as rents paid in money rather than kind etc.

Bloch, M. *French Rural History. An essay on its basic characteristics* (London 1966 from the French ed. of 1931 published Oslo and Antwerp).

Clark C. *Conditions of Economic Progress* (London 1951).

Deholte-Hoek, C.H.A. *Het gastmaal en de tafel in de loop der tijden* (Amsterdam 1965).

Erlanger, P. *The Age of Courts and Kings. Manners and Morals 1558–1715* (London 1966, expanded version of the French edition).

Forster, R. 'The Provincial Noble: a Reappraisal', *American Historical Review*, 1963 (about the French noble).

Goodwin, A. *The European Nobility in the Eighteenth Century* (London 1953).

Hansen, S. A. *'Adelsvældens Grundlag'* (Copenhagen 1965), to be read with the review by T. Dahlerup and J. Jørgensen in *The Scandinavian Economic History Review*, 1965, pp. 190–3.

Hole, Christina *English Sports and Pastimes* (London 1949).

Jutikkala, E. *Bonden i Finland genom tiderna* (Helsinki 1963).

Kellenbenz, H. *Der Merkantilismus in Europa und die soziale Mobilität* (Wiesbaden 1965).

Kossmann, E. H. *La Fronde* (Leiden 1954).

Lafue, P. *La vie quotidienne des cours allemandes au XVIIIᵉ siècle* (Paris 1963).

Levron, J. *La vie quotidienne à Versailles aux XVIIᵉ–XVIIIᵉ siècles* (Paris 1965).

Mandrou, R. *De la culture populaire aux XVIIᵉ et XVIIIᵉ siècles* (Stockholm and Paris 1964).

Merrien, J. *La vie quotidienne des marins au temps de roi soleil* (Paris 1964).

Millespierrès, F. *La vie quotidienne des médecins au temps de Molière* (Paris 1964).

Olsen, Gunnar. *Hovedgaard og bondegaard. Studier i stordriftens udvikling i Danmark i tiden 1525–1744* (Copenhagen 1957) – important for the development of manors.

Raeff, M. *Origins of the Russian Intelligentsia. The Eighteenth Century Nobility* (New York 1966) – to be read with M. Confino, 'Histoire et psychologie. A propos de noblesse russe au XVIIIᵉ Siècle', *Annales E.S.C.*, 1967.

Sakharov, A. N., *Russkaia derevnia XVII v. po materialam Patriarshej khoziaistva* (Moscow 1966) excerpts of which are translated in *Soviet Studies in History*, vol. VI, no. 2 (New York 1967) pp. 3–39.

Slicher van Bath, B. H. *The Agrarian History of Western Europe 500–1850* (London 1953 from Dutch ed.).

Soininen A. 'Burnbeating in Finland in the 16th and 17th centuries', *The Scandinavian Economic History Review*, 1960.

Wagner A., *Heralds of England* (London 1968).

Wilson C. 'The other face of Mercantilism', *Transactions of the Royal Historical Society*, 1959.

Woolf, S. J. *Studia sulla nobiltà Piemontese nell'epoca dell'assolutismo* (Turin 1963).

Zajaczako, A. 'Cadres structurels de la noblesse', *Annales E.S.C., 1963* (deals with Polish nobility).

CHAPTER III

Baxter, S. B. *The Development of the Treasury 1660–1702* (London and New York 1957).

Blomdal, R. *Förmyndarräfstens huvudskede. En studie i Stora kommissionens historia* (Stockholm 1963).

Böhme, K.-R. *Bremish-Verdische Staatsfinanzen 1645–1676; Die Schwedische Krone als Deutsche Landesherrin* (Stockholm 1967).

Castilla, A. 'Dans la monarchie espagnole du XVIIᵉ siècle: Les banquiers portugais et le circuit d'Amsterdam', *Annales E.S.C.*, 1964.

Dahlgren, S. *Karl X Gustav och reduktionen* (Uppsala 1964).

Davies, J. C. *The Decline of the Venetian Nobility as a Ruling Class* (Baltimore and Oxford 1962).

Dorn, W. 'The Prussian bureaucracy in the eighteenth century', *Political Science Quarterly*, 1931 and 1932.

Ducasse, A. *La guerre des Camisards. La résistance huguenote sous Louis XIV* (Paris 1962) – good bibliography.

Ellis, K. J. *The Post Office in the eighteenth century: a study in administration* (London 1958).

Grosperrin, B. *L'influence française et le sentiment national français en Franche-Comté 1647–1780* (Paris 1961).

Kafengauz, B. B. Essays in honour of, published under the title *Absoluytizm v Rosii XVII–XVIIIvv* (Moscow 1964) – note especially the contribution by N. M. Druzhinin.

Kaplan, F. I. 'Tatisceva and Kantemiri. Two eighteenth century exponents of a Russian bureaucratic style of thought', *Jahrbücher für Geschichte Osteuropas*, 1965.

Kellenbenz, H. *Sephardim an der unteren Elbe* (Wiesbaden 1958).

King, J. E. *Science and Rationalism in the Government of Louis XIV, 1661–83* (Baltimore 1949).

Klaveren, J. van 'Die historische Erscheinung der Korruption in ihrem Zusammenhang mit der Staats und Gesellschafts Struktur', *Vierteljahrschrift für Sozial und Wirtschaftsgeschichte*, 1957, and the same author's 'Fiskalismus-Merkantilismus-Korruption: Drei Aspekte der Finanz und Wirtschaftspolitik während des Ancien Regime', *ibid.*, 1960.

Konopczyński, W. *Le Liberum veto: étude sur le développement du principe majorité* (Paris 1930).

Livet, G. *L'Intendance d'Alsace sous Louis XIV, 1648–1715* (Strasbourg 1956).

Melles, J. J. *Ministers aan de Maas. Gechiedenis van de Rotterdamse pensionarissen met een inleiding over het stedelijk pensionaraat 1508–1705* (The Hague 1962).

Nordmann, C. J. 'Monnaies et finances suédoises au XVIIᵉ siècle', *Revue du Nord*, 1964.

Peters, J. 'Unter der schwedischen Krone', *Zeitschrift für Geschichtswissenschaft*, 1966.

Plumb, J. H. *The Search for Political Stability* (Oxford 1966).

Ravitch, N. *Sword and mitre. Government and episcopate in France and England in the age of autocracy* (The Hague 1966).

Robbins, Caroline 'Discordant Parties. A study of the acceptance of Party by Englishmen', *Political Science Quarterly*, 1958.

Roberts, C. 'The growth of ministerial responsibility to Parliament in later Stuart England', *Journal of Modern History*, 1956.

Roorda, D. J. *Partij en factie. De oproeren van 1672 in de Steden van Holland en Zeeland* (Utrecht 1961), with synopsis of findings in *Acta Historiae Neerlandica*, II (Leiden 1967).

Rosenberg, H. 'The composition of the new bureaucratic elite in Prussia', reprinted in *European Social Class* edd. B. and E. Barker (New York 1965).

Saint-Germain, J. *La Reynie et la police au Grand Siècle* (Paris 1962) – showing the responsibility for hygiene, town planning and economic improvement in general which also fell to the 'police'.

Schnee, J. H. *Die Hoffinanzen und der moderne Staat* (3 vols. Berlin 1953).

Shennan, J. H. *The French Parlements* (London 1968).

Simms, J. G. *The Williamite Confiscation in Ireland* (London n.d.).

Sooms, A. 'Die merkantilistische Wirtschaftspolitik Schwedens und die baltische Städte im 17 Jahrhundert', *Jahrbücher für Geschichte Osteuropas*, 1963.

Stern, Selma *The Court Jew* (Philadelphia 1950).

Straka, G. 'The Final Phase of Divine Right Theory in England 1688–1702', *The English Historical Review*, 1962.

Swart, K. W. *The Sale of Offices in the Seventeenth Century* (The Hague 1949) – new revised ed. in preparation.

XVIIe Siècle, double number 42–43 (Amiens 1959) with the title 'Serviteurs du Roi. Quelques aspects de la fonction publique dans la société française du XVIIe siècle'.

CHAPTER IV

Benedikt, H. *Kaiseradler über den Appeninen. Die Österreicher in Italien 1700 bis 1865* (Vienna-Munich 1964).

Bérenger, J. 'Une tentative de rapprochement entre la France et l'Empereur: la traité de partage secret de la Succession d'Espagne du 19 janvier 1668', *Revue d'Histoire Diplomatique*, 1965.

Bouvier, J. 'La Banque Protestante en France', *Annales E.S.C.*, 1963 – useful review article summarizing the Lüthy conclusions referred to in text.

Braubach, M. *Versailles und Wien von Ludwig XIV bis Kaunitz* (Bonn 1952), and the same author's 'Die Reichsbarriere', *Zeitschrift für Geschichte Oberrheins* (Karlsruhe), 1936.

Coombs, D. *The Conduct of the Dutch: British opinion and the Dutch alliance during the War of the Spanish Succession* (The Hague 1958).

Corvisier, A. *L'armée française de la fin du XVIIe siècle. Le Soldat.* (2 vols. Paris 1964–65).

Dahlgren, E. *Les Relations Commerciales et Maritimes entre la France et les Côtes de l'Océan Pacifique* (Paris 1909).

Davies, G. 'The control of British foreign policy by William III', *Essays on the Later Stuarts* (San Marino 1958).

Davis, R. *The Rise of the English Shipping Industry in the Seventeenth and Eighteenth Centuries* (London 1963).

Ehrman, J. *The Navy in the War of William III 1689–1697* (Cambridge 1958).

Fayard, J. 'Les tentatives de constitution d'un "tiers party" en Allemagne du Nord, 1690–1694', *Revue d'Histoire Diplomatique*, 1965 – on the shipwreck of Louis XIV's German policy.

Ford, F. *Strasbourg in Transition 1648–1789* (Cambridge, Mass. 1958).

Gembruch, W. 'Zwei Denkschriften zur Kolonial und Aussenpolitik Frankreichs aus den Jahren 1699 und 1700', *Historische Zeitschrift*, 1962.

Gibbs, G. C. 'Parliament and foreign policy in the age of Stanhope and Walpole', *The English Historical Review*, 1962.

Giraud, M. 'La Compagnie d'Occident (1717–1718)', *Revue Historique*, 1961.

Höynck, P. *Frankreich und seine Gegner auf dem Nymwegener Friedens-Kongress* (Bonn 1960).

Hubert, Norbert *Österreich und der Heilige Stuhl von Ende des Spanischen Erbfolgekrieges bis zum Tode Papst Klemens' XI, 1714–1721* (Vienna 1967).

Jones, G. H. *The mainstream of Jacobitism* (London 1954).

Jonge, J. C. *Geschiedenis van het nederlandse Zeewesen* (6 vols. Haarlem 1860).

Koehler, K. *Die orientalische Politik Ludwigs XIV* (Leipzig 1907).

Kurat, A. N. 'Der Prutfeldzug und der Prutfrieden von 1711', *Jahrbücher für Geschichte Osteuropas*, 1962.

Lapeure, H. 'De L'Atlantique au Pacifique. Les trafics maritimes de l'empire colonial espagnol', *Revue Historique*, 1962.

Lindeberg, G. *Krigsfinansiering och krigshushållning i Karl XII: s Sverige* (Stockholm 1946).

Mémain, R. *La marine de guerre sous Louis XIV* (Paris 1937).

Narotchnitzky, A. 'Russie et France: XVIIe Siècle à 1789', *Revue Historique*, 1967 (good bibliography).

O.Connor, J. T. O. Unpublished doctoral thesis, Minnesota 1965, 'William-Egon von Fürstenberg: French diplomacy in the Rhineland prior to the outbreak of the War of the League of Augsburg 1688'; part of which has been utilized – though the focus is more on Fürstenberg – in the author's article 'William-Egon von Fürstenberg, German agent in the service of Louis XIV', *French Historical Studies*, 1967.

Pagès, G. 'Notes sur la rôle d'argent dans la politique française en Allemagne', in his *Contributions à l'histoire de la politique française en Allemagne sous Louis XIV* (Paris 1905), and the same author's *Louis XIV et l'Allemagne 1661–1715* (Paris 1937).

Pfandl, L. *Karl II. Das Ende des spanischen Machtstellung in Europa* (Munich 1940).

Price, J. M. *Enterprise, Politics and Diplomacy. The Tobacco Adventure to Russia, 1676–1722* (Philadelphia 1961).

Rowen, H. H. *The ambassador prepares for war: the Dutch embassy of Arnauld de Pomponne 1669–1671* (The Hague 1957).

Scouller, R. E. *The armies of Queen Anne* (Oxford 1966).

Silberner, E. *La guerre dans la pensée économique de XVIe au XVIIe siècle* (Paris 1939).

Sperling, J. 'The international payments mechanism in the seventeenth and eighteenth centuries', *The Economic History Review*, 1962.

Srbik, H. von *Wien und Versailles, 1692–1700* (Munich 1944).

Stork-Penning, G. F. *Het Grote Werk* (Groningen 1958) and the same author's 'Het gedrag van de staten 1711', *Bijdragen voor de Geschiedenis der Nederlanden*, XVIII (1963–64): synopses of both in *Acta Historiae Neerlandica*, II, under the title 'The Ordeal of the States'.

Symcox, G. Unpublished U.C.L.A. doctoral thesis, 'Louis XIV and the War in Ireland – A Study in his Strategic thinking and Decision making' (1967).

Veenendaal, A. J. *Het Engels-Nederlands Condominium in de Zuidelijke Nederlanden tijdens de Spaanse Successieoorlog* (Utrecht 1945).

Vrankrijker, A. J. C. de *Die Grenzen van Nederland* (Amsterdam 1945).

Wandruszka, A. *Österreich und Italien im 18 Jahrhundert* (Vienna 1963).

Wijn, J. W. *Het staatse Leger*, vol. II in three parts, completed by 1964 (The Hague) – indispensable for the Dutch war effort.

CHAPTER V

Ainalow, D. *Geschichte der russischen Kunst* (Berlin 1932).

Badt, Kurt *Die Kunst des Nicolas Poussin* (2 vols. Cologne 1968).

Blunt, Sir Anthony *Art and Architecture in France 1500–1700* (Harmondsworth 1953); and the same author's *Nicolas Poussin* (2 vols. London 1968).

Brecy, R. *Louis XIV et l'Art français* (Paris 1948).

Bukofzer, M. F. *Music in the Baroque Era* (New York 1947).

Burke, G. L. *The Making of Dutch Towns* (New York 1960) – well illustrated.

Clark, Sir Kenneth *Landscape into Art* (London 1946); the same author's *The Nude, A study of ideal art* (London 1956 and paperback 1960).

Charpentier, P. (text to the splendidly illustrated) *Baroque Architecture. Italy and Central Europe* (London 1967).

Francastel, P. *La sculpture de Versailles. Essai sur les origines et l'évolution du gout français classique* (Paris 1930).

Griseri, A. *Le metamorfosi del Baroco* (Turin 1967).

Hart, F. *Love in Baroque Art* (New York 1964).

Hautecœur, L. *Louis XIV, Roi soleil* (Paris 1953) in series 'Ars et Historia' – important for symbolism.

Huizinga, J. *Dutch civilisation in the 17th century and other essays* (London 1968).

Isarlo, G. *Caravage et le Caravagisme européen* (Aix 1941).

Joly, Agnès, 'Le Roi-Soleil, histoire d'une image', *Revue de l'Histoire de Versailles*, 1937.

Kaufmann, E. *Architecture in the Age of Reason* (Cambridge, Mass. 1955).

Kjellberg, S. T. ed. *Slott och herresäten i Sverige. Ett konst och kulturhistorisk samlingsverk* (3 vols. Malmö 1966) – covering Scanian castles and manor-houses – richly illustrated.

Lough, J. *Paris theatre audiences in the Seventeenth and Eighteenth Centuries* (London 1957).

Lund, H. and Millech, D. *Danmarks bygningskunst fra oldtid til nutid* (Copenhagen 1963) – well-illustrated history of architecture with summaries of text in world languages.

Mackerness, E. D. *A Social History of English Music* (London 1964).

Magne, É. *Les Plaisirs et les fêtes en France au XVIIe Siècle* (Geneva 1944).

Malins, E. *English landscape and literature, 1660–1840* (Oxford 1966).

Mann, M. 'Ästhetik und Soziologie der Musik, 1600–1800', *Propyläen Weltgeschichte*, VII (1964).

Nolhac, P. de *Versailles et la Cour de France: l'Art de Versailles* (Paris 1930).

Pascal, G. *Largillière* (Paris 1928).

Pevsner, N. *Academies of art, past and present* (Cambridge 1940).

Pigler, A. *Barock Themen* (2 vols. Budapest 1956).

Piper, D. *The English Face* (London 1957).

Reyval, A. 'L'Eglise et le théâtre aux XVIIe Siècle', *XVIIe Siècle*, 1958.

Sitwell, S. *Southern Baroque Revisited* (London 1967).

Snyders, Georges 'L'évolution du gout musical en France aux XVIIe et XVIIIe siècles', *Revue des sciences humaines*, 1955.

Summerson, J. *Georgian London* (London 1945).

Tapié, V.-L. *Baroque et Classicisme* (Paris 1957), translated as *The Age of Grandeur* (London 1960) – finely illustrated.

Young, Percy M. *A History of British Music* (London 1967).

Wackernagel, M. *Renaissance, Barock und Rokoko*, vol. II (Berlin 1964).

Weigert, R. A. *L'Epoque Louis XIV* (Paris 1962), beautifully illustrated; and the same author's *Le Style Louis XIV* (Paris 1944).

Weisbach, W. *Der Barock als Kunst der Gegenreformation* (Berlin 1921).

Weise, G. *Spanische Plastik* (Reutlingen 1925).

Wittkower, R. *Bernini's bust of Louis XIV* (Oxford 1951), and the same author's *Art and Architecture in Italy 1600–1750* (Harmondsworth and Baltimore 1958).

CHAPTER VI

Adam, A. *Histoire de la Littérature française au XVII siècle* (3 vols. Paris 1948–52).

Beer, E. S. de 'The English newspaper from 1695 to 1702', in *William III and Louis XIV*, edd. Ragnhild Hatton and J. S. Bromley (Liverpool 1968).

Beyer, H. *A History of Norwegian Literature* (New York 1952).

Brenan, Gerald *The Literature of the Spanish People* (Cambridge 1951).

Brown, H. *Scientific Organizations in Seventeenth Century France 1620–1680* (Baltimore 1934).

Čisevškij, Dmitrij *History of Russian Literature* (The Hague 1960).

Coreth, Anna *Österreichische Geschichtsschreibung in der Barockzeit 1690–1740* (Vienna 1950).

Crane, R. S. *The Idea of the Humanities and other Essays* (Chicago and London 1967).

Hatin, E. *Les gazettes de Hollande* (Paris 1865).

Handover, P. M. *A History of the London Gazette 1665–1965* (London 1965).

Hanson, L. *Government and the Press 1695–1763* (London 1963).

Howarth, W. D. *Life and Letters in France*, vol. 1: *The Seventeenth Century* (Edinburgh 1965).

Kann, R. *A Study in the Intellectual History of Austria in the Eighteenth Century* (London 1960).

Kridl, Manfred *A Survey of Polish Literature and Culture* (The Hague, 1956, revised ed. of the New York translation of 1945).

Meyer, R. *Die Flugschriften der Epoche Ludwigs XIV, 1661–1679* (Basel 1955).

Mouy, P. *Le développement de la physique cartésienne 1646–1712* (Paris 1934).

Pottinger, D. T. *The French Book Trade in the Ancien Régime* (Cambridge, Mass. 1957).

Robertson, J. G. *A History of German Literature* (London revised ed. 1959).

Tigerstedt, E. N. *Svensk Litteraturhistoria* (Stockholm 1948).

Woolf, A. *A History of Science, Technology and Philosophy in the Eighteenth Century* (London 1952).

CHAPTER VII

Atkinson, G. A. *Le sentiment de la nature et la retour à la vie simple 1690–1740* (Paris and Geneva 1960), and the same author's posthumous (ed. by A. C. Keller) *The Sentimental Revolution: French Writers of 1690–1740* (Seattle 1966).

Bisonette, G. 'Peter the Great and the Church as an Educational Institution', *Essays in Russian and Soviet History in honour of G. T. Robinson* (Leiden 1963).

Burckhardt, C. J. *Der Honnete Homme. Das Eliteproblem im 17 Jahrhundert* (Zurich 1941).

Chaunu, P. 'Jansénisme et frontière de catholicité: A propos du Jansénisme lorrain', *Revue Historique*, 1962.

Cherniavsky, M. 'The old believers and the new religion', *Slavic Review*, 1966.

Clark, G. N. *Science and Social Welfare in the Age of Newton* (Oxford 1937).

Coreth, Anna *Pietas Austriaca. Ursprung und Entwicklung barocker Frömmigkeit in Österreich* (Munich 1959).

Cragg, G. R. *The Church in the Age of Reason* (London 1960).

Daniel-Rops, H. *The Church in the Seventeenth Century* (London and New York 1963), translated from vol. v of *Histoire de l'Eglise* (Paris 1958).

Dodge, G. H. *The Political Theory of the Huguenots of the Dispersion* (New York 1947).

Focault, M. *Histoire de la folie à l'âge classique. Folie et déraison* (Paris 1961) – with English translation, *Madness and Civilization* (New York 1965).

Fransen, P. *Leibniz und die Friedenschlüsse von Utrecht and Rastatt-Baden* (Purmerend 1933).

Giraud, M. 'Crise de conscience et d'autorité à la fin du règne de Louis XIV', *Annales E.S.C.*, 1952.

Goslinga, W. J. *De Rechten van den Mensch en Burger* (The Hague 1953).

Guilick, E. V. *Europe's Classical Balance of Power: a case history of the theory and practice of one of the great concepts of European statecraft* (New York and London 1956).

Hahlweg, W. 'Barriere-Gleichgewicht-Sicherheit . . . 1646–1715', *Historische Zeitschrift*, 1959, pp. 54–89.

Hall, A. R. *The Scientific Revolution 1500–1800. The formation of the Modern Scientific Attitude* (revised ed. Boston 1956).

Heath, J. *Eighteenth Century Penal Theory* (Oxford 1963).

Heer, F. *The Intellectual History of Europe* (London 1966, translation of the Stuttgart ed. of 1933).

Höss, Irmgard 'Die konfessionelle Lage im Brandenburg-Preussen und Österreich im Zeitalter des Absolutismus', *Zeitschrift für Geschichte, Wissenschaft und Unterricht*, 1964.

Israels, E. M. Unpublished doctoral thesis U.C.L.A., 'The Historical Argument. The debate over the Reformation in France 1671–1691' (1966).

Jones, M. G. *The Charity School Movement. A Study of 18th century Puritanism in Action* (Cambridge 1938).

Kirkinen, H. *Les origines de la conception moderne de l'homme machine; Le problème de l'âme en France à la fin du règne du Louis XIV* (Helsinki 1960).

Lavalle, T. *Madame de Maintenon et la maison royale de Saint-Cyr 1686–1793* (Paris 1862).

Leonard, E. *Histoire générale du protestantisme* (Paris 1961).

Macpherson, C. B. *The political theory of possessive individualism: Hobbes to Locke* (Oxford 1962).

Milsom, S. F. C. 'Reason in the development of the Common Law', *The Law Quarterly Review*, 1965.

Notestein, W. *A History of Witchcraft in England 1558–1718* (Oxford 1911).

Owen, D. *English Philanthropy 1660–1900* (Oxford 1965).

Perkins, Merle *The moral and political philosophy of the Abbé de Saint-Pierre* (Geneva and Paris 1959).

Préclin, E. and Javy, A. *Les luttes politiques et doctrinaires au XVII⁰ et XVIII⁰ Siècles* (vol. 19 of *Histoire de l'Eglise*, edd. A. Fliche and V. Marin, Paris 1955).

Radzinowicz, L. *A History of English Criminal Law*, vol. 1 (Oxford and New York 1948).

Raumer, K. von *Ewiger Friede: Friedensrufe und Friedenspläne seit der Renaissance* (Freiburg 1953).

Servier, J. *Histoire de l'utopie* (Paris 1967).

Snyders, Georges *La Pédagogie en France au XVII⁰ et XVIII⁰ Siècles* (Paris 1965).

Taveneaux, R. ed. *Jansénisme et politique* (Paris 1965).

Vietsch, E. von *Das europäische Gleichgewicht* (Leipzig 1942).

Zeller, G. 'Le principe d'équilibre dans la politique internationale avant 1789', *Revue Historique*, 1956.

See, H. *Les Idées politiques en France au XVII⁰ Siècle* (Paris 1923).

BIBLIOGRAPHICAL AND OTHER AIDS TO STUDY

Advanced students will know where to find the large detailed bibliographies such as Davies and Pargellis and Medley for England; Bourgeois and André for France; Dahlmann-Waitz for Germany; Pirenne for Belgium; Bring for Sweden, etc., though the recent H. de Buck *Bibliografi der Geschiedenis van Nederland* (Leiden 1968) might be worth bringing to their notice. For less specialized work, however, shorter guides are most useful. Of these I would recommend the Historical Association bibliography on Modern European History by Alun Davies; the *Annual Bulletin of Historical Literature* published by the same Association (most entries are commented on); the lists printed in every number of the periodical *French Historical Studies* (Worcester, Mass.); the review-articles in the *Jahrbücher für Geschichte Osteuropas* which enable the student without eastern European languages and Swedish to keep in touch with research. Many countries that do not regard their languages as world ones have adopted the habit of giving summaries of their learned articles in historical periodicals in English, French or German (e.g. all the Scandinavian historical periodicals and some of the Spanish ones). Some have gone further than this: the *Excerpta Nordica* and *Acta Poloniae Historica* have for a considerable number of years given digests of theses and scholarly monographs; the Dutch *Acta Historiae Neerlandica* have now followed suit and two volumes (1966 and 1967) have so far appeared, much to our benefit. For the years before 1966 E. H. Kossmann's annual bibliographical articles in *Revue du Nord* are most helpful. *Studies in Soviet History* (published in New York in recent years) offers translations of reviews, summaries of research and sometimes excerpts from monographs.

HISTORICAL ATLASES. The best are German: the *Grosser Historischer Weltatlas* published by the Bayerische Schulbuch-Verlag (vol. III: *Neuzeit*, Munich 1957, is the relevant volume) and *Westermanns Grosser Atlas zur Weltgeschichte* (Berlin 1966). Atlases covering maps and culture are useful: e.g., for Russia and eastern Europe the sumptuous *Atlas historique et cultural de la Russie et du monde slave* (Paris 1961).

SELECTIONS
ESSAYS

Crisis in Europe, ed. T. Aston (London 1866), from articles in *Past and Present*; to be read with I. Schöffer 'Did Holland's Golden Age coincide with a period of crisis?' in *Acta Historiae Neerlandica*, 1 (Leiden 1966), translated from his 1964 Dutch article.

Britain and the Netherlands, edd. J. S. Bromley and E. H. Kossmann, I (London 1960) and II (Groningen 1964) – valuable essays from two Anglo-Dutch conferences of historians; a third will shortly appear.

Louis XIV. The Craft of Kingship, ed. John C. Rule (Ohio 1969) – papers read at a Columbus conference in 1964.

Men and Places by J. H. Plumb (London 1963) – collected essays, and, edited by the same historian, *Studies in Social History. A Tribute to G. M. Trevelyan* (Cambridge 1955).

Intellectual Origins of the English Revolution – Ford lectures by Christopher Hill (Oxford 1965).

Spiegel der Geschichte, edd. K. Repgen and S. Skalweit (Münster 1964) – this massive *Festschrift* in honour of Max Braubach is something of a lucky dip: prizes for our period are essays by M. Merks, S. Skalweit and R. Nürnberger. In the *Festgabe* for Kurt von Raumer, *Dauer und Wandel der Geschichte*, edd. R. Vierhaus and M. Botzenhait (Münster 1965), note contributions by D. Gerhard and G. Winne.

Utopie et Institutions du XVIIe Siècle. Le pragmatisme des Lumières, ed. P. Francastel (Paris 1963) – helps to put the Enlightenment into perspective.

William III and Louis XIV. Essays by and for Mark A. Thomson. 1688–1728, edd. Ragnhild Hatton and J. S. Bromley (Liverpool 1968) – the most convenient way of sampling Mark Thomson's fine scholarship with essays in his memory.

REPRINTED ARTICLES

In the series 'Critical Issues in History', *The Early Modern Era 1648–1770*, ed. John C. Rule (Boston 1966).

In the series 'Main Themes in European History', *Agrarian Conditions in Modern European History*, ed. C. K. Warner (New York 1966); *Diplomacy in Modern European History*, ed. L. W. Martin (New York 1966); *European Social Class; Stability and Change*, edd. B. Barker and Elinor G. Barker (New York 1965).

In the series 'Problems in European Civilization', *Peter the Great. Reformer or revolutionary?*, ed. M. Raeff (Boston 1963); *The Greatness of Louis XIV. Myth or Reality?*, ed. W. F. Church (Boston 1959).

In the series 'Problems and Perspectives in History', *Louis XIV*, ed. H. Judge (London 1966) – good bibliography.

Historical periodicals have recently started to reprint selections of articles: e.g. the *Economish-Historische Herdrukken* from the Dutch side; *The Eighteenth Century* from the *English Historical Review*.

SELECTED DOCUMENTS meant for the general reader and student but edited in a scholarly manner. The French are masters of this art; note the series 'Les grand textes historiques' in which the *Journeaux Camisards 1700–1715*, ed. Ph. Joutard (Paris 1965), has appeared. Other selections worth mentioning are *Louis XIV par lui-même*, ed. M. Déon (Paris 1964); *Les Coulisses de Versailles*, ed. G. Ziegler (Paris 1963), which has been translated as *The Court of Versailles in the reign of Louis XIV* (London 1966), and *Les Précieux et les Précieuses* ed., G. Mongrédien (Paris 1967). In German note a good selection in the series 'Lesewerk zur Geschichte', *Absolutismus und Aufklärung 1648–1789*, ed. Erich Stahleder (Eibenhausen

243

1964). In English in the series 'Sources in Western Civilization' there is a particularly successful volume: *The Seventeenth Century 1600–1715*, ed. Andrew Lossky (New York 1967); and in the new series 'Documents of Modern History' the brief but impressive first volume *Sweden as a Great Power 1611–1697*, edited and translated by Michael Roberts (London 1968), should be noted.

MEMOIR-LITERATURE, LETTERS AND DIARIES Selections have mainly been published from the French, though sometimes translated into English, as in the case of *The Age of Magnificence*. *Memoirs of the Court of Louis XIV by the Duc de Saint-Simon*, selected by S. de Gramont (New York, Capricorn Books 1964), and the J. Longnon selection of 1923 (published in London) from Louis XIV's *Mémoires* translated under the title *A King's Lesson in Statecraft: Louis XIV's Letters to his Heirs* (London 1924). It should be noted that Longnon produced a fuller edition in French in 1927, and that a new edition of Louis' *Mémoires et divers écrits* appeared in Paris in 1961, edited by B. Champigneulle.

The two older editions of Louis' *Œuvres*, the one by P. Grouvelle of 1806 and the one by C. Dreyss of 1860, are still worth consulting but should, for the *Mémoires* part, be used with the important article by P. Sonnino, 'The dating and authorship of Louis XIV's Mémoires', *French Historical Studies*, 1964. A new edition of the *Mémoires*, translated and edited by Sonnino, is in preparation in the U.S.A. A new edition of the *Œuvres* of Saint-Simon is in progress in France, under the editorship of R. Dupuis *et al.*, vol. 1 having been published in 1964; the standard ed. in 41 vols. is by A. de Boislisle (Paris 1923–28). Scholarly editions of the letters, papers and memoirs of figures of our period have appeared in considerable quantity in recent years (or are in progress): among such riches we have to mention a few samples, e.g. Esmond de Beer's 1955 edition of John Evelyn's letters and diaries (*Kalendarium*) and M. Goudeket's 1964 edition of the letters (in French) of Charlotte Elisabeth, Duchess of Orléans, also known as Liselotte von der Pfalz.

SOME BIOGRAPHIES WHICH ILLUMINATE ASPECTS OF THE FIELD SURVEYED

RULERS (in alphabetical order)

CARLOS II of Spain: J. Langdon-Davies, *Carlos, the King Who Would Not Die* (London 1962); J. Nada, *Carlos The Bewitched, the last Spanish Habsburg 1661–1700* (London 1962).

CHARLES XII of Sweden: R. M. Hatton, *Charles XII of Sweden* (London 1968, New York 1969).

CHRISTINA of Sweden: S. Stolpe, *Christina of Sweden* (London and New York 1966).

GEORGE I of Great Britain: pen-portrait in J. H. Plumb, *The First Four Georges* (London 1956) – a

biography is needed as are studies of the Austrian Habsburgs Leopold I, Joseph I, Charles VI.

JOHN III of Poland-Lithuania: O. Forst de Battaglia, *Ian Sobieski. König von Polen 1629–1696* (Zurich 1946).

LOUIS XIV of France: *Louis XIV* by J. B. Wolf (New York and London 1968); *Louis XIV*, by P. Erlanger (Paris 1965); *La vie privée de Louis XIV*, by G. Mongrédien (Paris 1938).

PETER OF RUSSIA: *Peter der Grosse* by R. Wittram (Berlin 1954), and the same author's splendid 2-volume work *Peter I. Czar und Kaiser* (Göttingen 1964); *Peter I: materialy dlya biografii* by N. M. Bogoslovsky (5 vols. Leningrad 1940–8) goes to 1700 only; I. Grey, *Peter the Great. Emperor of all Russia* (New York 1960, London 1962) is somewhat superficial; while the welcome reprint in preparation of the classic E. Schuyler two-volume work from 1884, *Peter the Great, Emperor of Russia*, will lack contact with modern research. B. H. Summer, *Peter the Great and the emergence of Russia* (London 1950) is brief but good.

WILLIAM III of Great Britain. The best treatment is by Johanna K. Oudendijk, *Willem III. Stadhouder van Holland, Koning van Engeland* (Amsterdam 1954); S. B. Baxter, *William III* (New York and London 1966) and Nesca A. Robb, *William of Orange, A Personal Portrait* (2 vols. New York and London 1962 and 1966) tend to complement each other, the former being the more scholarly with a fine command of administrative and military achievement, the latter giving a more subtle interpretation of the personality.

SUBJECTS (in alphabetical order of author or of authors if more than one biography is given)

GENERAL: M. Braubach, *Eugen von Savoyen* (5 vols. Munich 1963–66)
N. Henderson, *Prince Eugen of Savoy* (London 1964).

NOBLEMAN: O. Brunner, *Adeliges Landleben und europäischer Geist. Leben und Werk Wolf Helmhards von Hohberg 1612–1688* (Salzburg 1949).

SOLDIER-DIPLOMAT: I. Burton, *The Captain General* (London 1968), – covers the Duke of Marlborough's career 1702–11.

BANKER: D. C. Coleman, *Sir John Banks, Baronet and Businessman* (Oxford 1963).

KING'S BROTHER: P. Erlanger, *Monsieur, frère du Louis XIV* (Paris 1964).

KING'S GARDENER: Helen M. Fox, *Andre Le Nôtre, Gardener architect to Kings* (London n.d.).

POLITICIAN-DIPLOMAT: M. A. Franken, *Conraad van Beuningens politieke et diplomatieke aktiviteiten in de jaren 1667–1684* (Groningen 1966).

PAINTER: W. Friedländer, *Claude Lorrain* (Berlin 1921).

DRAMATIST: L. Goldmann, *Jean Racine, dramaturgue* (Paris 1956).

EDUCATIONALIST: Agnès La Gorce, *Le vrai visage de Fénelon* (Paris 1955).

FEMME FATALE: Jean Goudal, *Ninon de Lanclos, Une grande courtisane au siècle de Louis XIV* (Paris 1937).

ECONOMIST-ADMINISTRATOR: C. Grau, *Der Wirtschaftsorganisator, Staatsmann und Wissenschafter Vasilij Tatiščev 1686–1750* (Berlin 1963).

QUEEN'S GARDENER: D. Green, *Gardener to Queen Anne. Henry Wise 1653–1738 and the formal garden* (New York and Oxford 1956).

ROYAL CONFESSOR: G. Guitton, *Le Père de la Chaize, confesseur de Louis XIV* (2 vols. Paris 1959).

CAMERALIST: H. Hassinger, *Johann Joachim Becher 1635–1682* (Vienna 1951).

AMBITIOUS PRINCE: W. Holst, *Fredrik I* (Stockholm 1953) – biography of Prince Frederick of Hesse who became King of Sweden in 1720.

CIVIL SERVANT: Gertrude A. Jacobsen, *William Blaythwayt, a late seventeenth century administrator* (New Haven and London 1932).

INDEPENDENCE LEADER: B. Kentrschynskyj, *Mazepa* (Stockholm 1962).

MINISTER: J.P. Kenyon, *Robert Spencer, Earl of Sunderland* (London 1958).

JURIST: L. Krieger, *The Politics of Discretion: Pufendorf and the acceptance of Natural Law* (Chicago 1965).

ENTREPRENEUR-ADMINISTRATOR: J. Jørgensen, *Henrik Müller. En studie over enevældens etablering I Danmark* (Copenhagen 1966).

THINKER: Elisabeth Labrousse, *Pierre Bayle* (2 vols. The Hague 1963 and 1964).

ROYAL BASTARD: W.H. Lewis, *The Sunset of the Splendid Century* (New York 1955) – a biography of the Duc de Maine.

MYSTERY MAN: C. de Massini, *L'homme au masque de fer* (Paris 1964). G. Mongrédien, *Le Masque de Fer* (Paris 1952).

FINANCIAL WIZARD: B.E. de Muinck, *Een Regentenhishouding omstreeks 1700: Cornelis de Jonge van Ellemeet* (The Hague 1966, with English synopsis in *Acta Historiae Neerlandica*, I, Leiden 1966).

PROFESSOR-OFFICIAL: S. Olsson, *Olof Hermelin. En karolinsk kulturpersonlighet och statsman* (Stockholm 1953).

JACOBITE EXILE: Sir Charles Petrie, *The Marshal Duke of Berwick* (London 1953).

MINISTER-STATESMAN: J.H. Plumb, *Sir Robert Walpole:* (2 vols. so far, London 1956 and 1961 – the third in preparation).

ECONOMIST: Hazel Roberts, *Boisguilbert, Economist of the reign of Louis XIV* (New York 1935).

FINANCIER: J. Saint-Germain, *Samuel Bernard, banquier des rois* (Paris 1960).

INDEPENDENT ADMINISTRATOR: R. de Schryver, *Jan van Brouchoven, Graaf van Bergeyck 1644–1725* (Brussels 1965) – important for the Southern Netherlands.

ARCHITECT: H. Sedlmayr, *Johann Bernard Fischer von Erlach* (Vienna 1956).

SCULPTOR: R. Wittkower, *Gian Lorenzo Bernini, the sculptor of the Roman Baroque* (London 1955).

COMPOSER: F.B. Zimmerman, *Henry Purcell 1659–1695. His life and Times* (London 1967)

LIST OF ILLUSTRATIONS

248

105 Gobelins tapestry. Musée de Versailles. Photo Giraudon

106 Louis XIV and family; painting by J. Nocret, 1670. Musée de Versailles. Photo Bulloz

107 Plaque from Versailles; one of many used to decorate walls and furniture. Bibliothèque Nationale, Paris, Cabinet des Médailles

108 Caricature of Louis XIV; from the series *Les héros de la ligue ou la procession monacale conduite par Louis XIV pour la conversion des Protestants*. Published chez Père Peters, Paris, 1691. Bibliothèque Nationale, Paris, Department des Imprimés

109 Carlos II; painting by J. Carreno de Miranda, *c.* 1685. Kunsthistorisches Museum, Vienna

110 Archduke Charles of Austria; engraving by P. van Gunst (1659–1724) after F. Stampart (1675–1750): British Museum, Prints and Drawings, Folder 'Portraits of Austrian Emperors'

111 Louis XIV accepting the will of Carlos II; from an almanach of 1701. Bibliothèque Nationale, Paris, Cabinet des Estampes

112 The Duke of Marlborough; painting by G. Kneller, *c.* 1706. National Portrait Gallery, London

113 Peter the Great; engraving on copper by A. Zubov (1699–1741). British Museum, Prints and Drawings, Folder 'Russian Imperial Portraits'

114 Frederick IV of Denmark; engraving by P. van Gunst (1659–1724) after L. Weyant (*fl.* 1691–1765). British Museum, Prints and Drawings, Folder 'Denmark Royal Portraits'

115 Medal by John Croker to commemorate the arrival of George I in Britain. British Museum, Coin Room, English coins 1714 Tray

116 Augustus of Saxony-Poland and Frederick William I of Prussia; painting by L. Silvestre, 1730. Photo Deutsche Fotothek, Dresden

117 Verse sent by Ralph Palmer in a letter to his nephew Ralph Verney, 12 June 1704. From the Verney Letters at Claydon House

118 Fireworks at Vienna in 1683; anonymous engraving. British Museum, Prints and Drawings, Foreign History Folder 1686

119 Coronation of James II in 1685; detail of engraving by F. Sandford, 1685. Victoria and Albert Museum, London, Prints and Drawings

120 Town Hall, The Hague; from a collection of engravings by R. de Hooghe published under the title *Relation du Voyage de Sa Majesté Britannique en Hollande* (The Hague 1692), p. 33

121 Medal commemorating the Treaty of Aix-la-Chapelle by C. Adolphi, 1667. Photograph Royal Coin Cabinet, The Hague

122 St Peter's, Rome; from J. Barbault, *Les Plus Beaux Edifices de Rome Moderne* (Rome 1763), plate 1

123 The Karlskirche, Vienna; engraving after S. Kleiner by H. Sperling. From S. Kleiner, *Vera et accurata delineatio omnium templorum et coenobiorum quae tam in Caesarea urbe ac sede Vienna Austriae*, vol. 1 (Augsburg 1724), plate 32

124 Zwinger Palace, Dresden; engraving by Anna Maria Werner. (1688–1753). Kupferstichkabinett, Dresden. Photo Deutsche Fotothek, Dresden

125 Bernini's third project for the Louvre; engraving by J. Marot (1619–79). Photo Courtauld Institute of Art

126 Place des Victoires, Paris; anonymous engraving, published by N. Langlois. Bibliothèque Nationale, Paris, Cabinet des Estampes

127 Apotheosis of Prince Eugène; wood sculpture by B. Permoser. Österreichisches Barockmuseum, Vienna

128 Louis XIV; bronze sculpture by F. Girardon. Nelson Gallery – Atkins Museum (Nelson Fund), Kansas City, Missouri

129 Charles II; marble bust by H. Pellé. Victoria and Albert Museum, London

130 Robert Walpole; bust by J.M. Rysbrack. National Portrait Gallery, London

131 Robert de Cotte (1656–1735); bronze bust by A. Coysevox. The Frick Collection, New York

132 J. Vanbrugh's original elevation for the Grand Bridge at Blenheim. *Nouveaux Théâtres de la Grande Bretagne*, vol. III (1715), plate 22

133 Wren's design for London after the Great Fire of 1666. All Souls Wren Drawings, I, no. 7. Reproduced by permission of the Warden and Fellows of All Souls College

134 Foundation medal of St Petersburg, 1703. British Museum, Coin Room, Russia 1703 Tray

135 St Bride's Church built by C. Wren 1671, steeple 1701–03; engraving by T. Bowles after J. Donowell, 1753. British Museum, Map Room, K 23 10a

136 *View of Delft*; painting by J. Vermeer, 1658. Mauritshuis, The Hague

137 *The Toilet of Venus*; painting by D.R. de S. Velázquez, *c.* 1651. Courtesy the Trustees of the National Gallery, London

138 Charles Le Brun; painting by Largillière, 1686. Louvre, Paris. Photo Giraudon

139 Louis XIV; painting by Rigaud, 1701. Louvre, Paris

140 Augustus the Strong; painting by Largillière. Nelson Gallery – Atkins Museum (Nelson Fund), Kansas City, Missouri. There is a famous study of the hands in the Louvre

141 Charles XII of Sweden; detail of painting by D. Swartz, 1707. Gripsholm Castle. Photo Nationalmuseum, Stockholm.

142 John Maitland, Duke of Lauderdale (1616–82); painting by B. Gennarf, c. 1674. By kind permission of Lord Tollemache

143 Johan Gyllenstierna af Björksund (1635–80); painting by a pupil of D. Ehrenstrahl, c. 1675. In the collection at Björksund. Photo Nationalmuseum, Stockholm

144 *Adoration of the Shepherds*; painting by F. de Zurburan (1598–1664). Musée de Grenoble

145 Glorification of the Protestant Succession; detail of ceiling of the Painted Hall, Greenwich, painted by J. Thornhill, c. 1710. Photo Ministry of Public Buildings and Works

146 *Las Meninas*; painting by D. R. de S. Velázquez, c. 1656. Prado, Madrid

147 *Assemblée dans un parc*; detail of painting by J. A. Watteau (1684–1721). Louvre, Paris. Photo Giraudon

148 *A Cock and other birds*. Painting by M. Hondecoeter (1636–95). Reproduced by permission of the Trustees of the Wallace Collection

149 *The Music Lesson*; painting by J. Vermeer, c. 1655. Copyright reserved.

150 The Grande Galerie at Versailles; engraving by S. Leclerc (1637–1714). Bibliothèque Nationale, Paris, Cabinet des Estampes

151 Detail of font in the Palace Chapel, Stockholm, by J. F. Cousinet. Photo Nationalmuseum, Stockholm

152 Covered goblet, engraved in Dresden between 1707 and 1714. Courtesy the Trustees of the British Museum

153 Spanish bodice ornament; early eighteenth century. Victoria and Albert Museum, London

154 Bridal crown. Vestlandske Kunstindustrimuseum, Bergen

155 *A tea party in the time of George I*; anonymous painting. Victoria and Albert Museum, London

156 Lacquered cabinet, Japanned in the Chinese style, c. 1670. Victoria and Albert Museum, London

157 Chi'en Lung meat dish. By kind permission of Mrs Helen Glatz

158 *Michel de La Barre and other musicians*; painting ascribed to R. Tournières and dated c. 1710 from the costume. Courtesy the Trustees of the National Gallery, London. Earlier identification as Lully is now discarded, as the music displayed is of 1707

159 *Boy playing the flute*; painting by Judith Leyster (1610–60). Nationalmuseum, Stockholm

160 J. S. Bach (1685–1750) as a young man; anonymous painting. Erfurt Museum

161 G. F. Handel (1685–1759); painting by J. Thornhill, after 1710. Reproduced by permission of the Syndics of the Fitzwilliam Museum, Cambridge

162 A. Vivaldi (1678–1741); anonymous presumed portrait. Conservatorio Musicale, Bologna

163 F. Couperin (1668–1733); engraving by J. C. Flipart, 1735

164 Setting for A. Cesti's *Il Pomo d'Oro*; engraving by M. Küsel after L. Burnacini, 1668. Victoria and Albert Museum, London, Prints and Drawings

165 Charles II in exile; detail from painting by C. Janssen, 1650. Copyright reserved

166 Frontispiece to *Bérénice* in *Œuvres de Racine* (Paris 1676), p. 1

167 J. Racine; engraving after G. Edelinck (1640–1707). From E. Bourgeois, *Le Grand Siècle* (Paris 1896), facing p. 400

168 J. B. Molière; painting by P. Mignard (1612–1695). Musée Conde, Chantilly. Photo Giraudon

169 Setting for a play by Calderón; attributed to F. Ricci, c. 1680. Biblioteca Nacional, Madrid

170 French and Italian actors; anonymous painting, c. 1670. Comédie Française, Paris. Photo Giraudon

171 *The Inspiration of the Epic Poet*; painting by N. Poussin. Louvre, Paris. Dated 1628–29 by A. Blunt, *The Paintings of Nicolas Poussin: A Critical Catalogue* (London 1966), no. 124

172 Madame Marie-Madeleine de la Fayette (1634–93); engraving by L. Elle (1612–89). Photo Courtauld Institute of Art

173 Marie de Rabutin-Chantal, Marquise de Sévigné (1626–96); painting by P. Mignard (1612–95). Uffizi, Florence. Photo Mansell-Alinari

174 'The Coffehous Mob'; engraving from E. Ward, *Vulgus Britannicus or the British Hudibras* (London 1710), facing p. 117

175 Frontispiece to 1693 edition of J. Bunyan, *The Pilgrim's Progress* (London)

176 Page from Edward Barlow, 'The Journal of his life at Sea, 1659–1703'. National Maritime Museum, Greenwich

177 Title-page of J. Ogilby, *Britannia*, vol. 1 (London 1675)

178 Queen Christina with Descartes; painting by P. Dumesnil (d. 1710). Musée de Versailles

179 Pierre Bayle; frontispiece by J. Smith to P. Bayle, *The Dictionary, Historical and Critical of Mr. Bayle* (English translation, London 1734, of original of 1697, enlarged 1702)

180 The comet of 1680–81; anonymous Italian engraving. Bibliothèque Nationale, Paris, Cabinet des Estampes

INDEX

Page numbers in italics refer to illustrations

The German ö, the Swedish ä, ö and å, the Danish and Norwegian ø, the Polish ł have been listed, for convenience, as if they were a, o, a, o and l respectively. The Danish and Norwegian æ has been put at the end of the alphabet. Topics clearly indicated in chapter heading and subheadings are not included; neither are titles of books and paintings.

259